RUSSIAN
IN THE
1740s

RUSSIAN IN THE 1740s

Thomas Rosén

Boston
2022

Library of Congress Control Number: 2021952344

ISBN 9781644694145 (hardback)
ISBN 9781644697979 (paperback)
ISBN 9781644694169 (ePub)
ISBN 9781644698303 (Open Access)

Book design by PHi Business Solutions
Cover design by Ivan Grave

Published by Academic Studies Press
1577 Beacon Street
Brookline, MA 02456, USA

press@academicstudiespress.com
www.academicstudiespress.com

For Lina, Julius, and Alma

Contents

Author's Notes

Notes on Transliteration

The present investigation contains many examples from printed and handwritten eighteenth-century documents. All examples from eighteenth-century sources will be presented in their original orthography, as far as this is technically possible.

In the transliteration of handwritten documents, a slash "/" indicates a line break; a double slash "//" indicates a page break. Square brackets "[ ]" contain comments and conjectures by the editor. Brackets containing dots "[...]" indicate an illegible passage with the number of dots indicating the assumed number of illegible characters. Curly brackets {...} indicate parentheses in the original text.

Superscript characters are brought down into the line and *italicized*, thus identifying them as superscripts in the original: ⟨военную⟩ → ⟨военную⟩.

Texts will be separated into words. Thus, cases where additional words, such as conjunctions, prepositions, or negations are attached to the following word, this will be broken up: ⟨исакричал⟩ → ⟨и сакричал⟩, ⟨ѿ8чрежденнагѡ⟩ → ⟨ѿ 8чрежденнагѡ⟩. The principles applied in this investigation are thus in accordance with the established scholarly tradition.[1]

In the Bibliography, the spelling of all pre-1918 titles has been modernized.

Transliterations of Cyrillic are made according to the Library of Congress System (without diacritics).

Spelling of Names

Names are treated according to the Library of Congress System standard. However, if a historical person has a well-established name in English, that form will be used. Thus, Peter the Great will be named by this traditional epithet, not as Pëtr Alekseevich. His daughter will be called Elizabeth, not "Elizabet, Elisabet" or "Elizaveta Petrovna." For persons of German, Irish and other,

---

1 Cf. A. I. Sumkina and S. I. Kotkov, *Pamiatniki moskovskoi delovoi pis'mennosti XVIII veka* (Moscow: Nauka, 1981).

non-Russian origins, for example, von Bühren (Biron), Lacy (Lassi), and others, the original forms and Russian alternatives of their names will be presented.

The Old Style Calendar

In Russia prior to 1700, years were counted "from the Creation of the World." This was changed by Peter the Great to conform with the rest of Europe.[2] However, the Russian Empire retained the Julian calendar, which is now referred to as the Old Style (O.S.), throughout the period covered by the present investigation and until 1917.

In the 1700s, the Julian calendar was eleven days behind the Gregorian one. Thus, January 1, 1740 Old Style (O.S.) was January 12, 1740 New Style (N.S.). In this book, dates found in eighteenth-century documents are all in the Old Style, thus reflecting the Julian calendar.

Translation of Quotations

Quotations originally written in languages other than English have been translated into English. All translations are made by the author, unless indicated otherwise. Translations of longer excerpts are found in the footnotes, in parentheses.

---

2   *Britannica Academic*, s.v. "Peter I," accessed May 8, 2021, https://academic-eb-com.ezproxy. ub.gu.se/levels/collegiate/article/Peter-I/108537.

Acknowledgements

This book was long in the making. The idea for it came to me ten years ago at the Uppsala branch of the Swedish national archives, when I stumbled across some letters in Russian from the 1740s while looking for something else. At that point, having been trained as a philologist, I was vaguely familiar with seventeenth-century Russian, but this was something else. As I actively started assembling documents from the 1740s, I became fascinated by them and the language of their (often anonymous) authors. Since then, the writing of this book has been the educational journey of my life.

Many people have contributed to making this book possible. I want thank Irina Lysén for commenting on drafts of the investigation, and Kathleen Anderson de Miranda for reviewing my English. Furthermore, I owe my thanks to many colleagues at the universities of Uppsala and Gothenburg who have, through the years, patiently listened to me by coffee machines and in corridors. Sometimes my tale has been one of woe and despair, sometimes one of bubbling enthusiasm.

At Academic Studies Press, I am indebted to my editor, Ekaterina Yanduganova, for her encouragement and advice. I am also indebted to the anonymous reviewers who read an earlier version of this book, and whose comments have improved the investigation in significant ways. Any remaining errors or inconsistencies are entirely my own.

Finally, I am forever grateful to my wife, Lina, for her love, unwavering patience and willingness to support a project that many times, I am sure, must have seemed like a pushy and obnoxious acquaintance, constantly demanding her husband's attention.

Thomas Rosén
Gothenburg, November 2021

CHAPTER 1

Introduction

———

Having won the Great Northern War against Sweden (1700–1721), the Russian Empire emerged as one of the great powers of Europe during the second quarter of the eighteenth century. Although the empire was highly diverse ethnically and linguistically, the scope of this study concerns a single language during a single decade: Russian in the 1740s.

Today, speakers of Russian are universally literate, and an overwhelming majority have access to information at the touch of a screen or a button. In the 1740s, the situation was entirely different. The vast majority of Russian speakers did not know how to read or write. In all probability, a majority of the population had seen writing and knew of its existence from an early age, but few were given the opportunity to learn such skills. The educational system catered to a small fraction of the population. For the majority, Russia was an oral society. People communicated in native dialects as they always had, and changes in people's language were likely slow and gradual, with pronunciations or grammatical forms competing for generations. As K. Anipa concludes, "[a]t any given time, a language overwhelmingly represents continuity."[1]

The empire's new status as a great power and the proximity of its new capital, St. Petersburg, to Western Europe, inevitably brought the Russian language into close contact with other languages and idioms. For example, the Danish theologian Peder von Haven spent several years in Russia at the beginning of the 1740s and picked up the following example of codeswitching that he found remarkable:

---

1 K. Anipa, "The Use of Literary Sources in Historical Sociolinguistic Research," in *The Handbook of Historical Sociolinguistics*, ed. J. M. Hernández-Campoy and J. C. Conde-Silvestre (Oxford: Wiley-Blackwell, 2012), 173.

> Monsieur, Paschalusta, wil ju nicht en Schalken Vodka trinken,
> Isvollet, Badusca. Hvilket skal hede så meget: Monsieur, kjære,
> vil De ikke drikke et glass brendevin, værsågod eller behager De,
> lille fader.[2]

Strangely enough, however, the traditional image of the Russian language during the eighteenth century is one where the element of continuity is lacking entirely. Everything is focused on sudden change and renewal: "[i]n the Middle ages, the Russian language was dozing. It was aroused by the reign of Peter the Great."[3] The reign of the Great Reformer allegedly witnessed a "cultural revolution."[4] Even Viktor Zhivov, one of the world's foremost authorities on eighteenth-century Russian, assessed the period's linguistic situation with the following words: "[t]he eighteenth century witnessed a radical transformation of the Russian linguistic situation that encompassed all levels of the Russian language and all of the spheres in which it functioned."[5]

Looking at existing research, one quickly encounters voices that disagree with Zhivov. Was there, in fact, a "revolution" or was there gradual change? If there was a gradual change, what was changing, and whom did the changes affect?

Zhivov's argument has been opposed by the hypothesis that Russian language experienced a succession of "synchronies" rather than a "revolution." Synchrony, in the words of another prominent linguist, Vitalii Kostomarov, "... represents a virtual period in which the diachrony is hidden or reveals itself by means of variation, irritating 'errors' and other witnesses of linguistic dynamic."[6]

---

2 Alf Grannes, *Vsjakaja vsjatjina: Om folk og språk i "Sovjetunionen", Russland og Bulgaria* (Bergen: Universitetet i Bergen, Russisk institutt, 1992), 3 (Monsieur, pozhaluista, wil ju nicht en Schalken Vodka trinken, izvol'te, batiushka. Which amounts to: Monsieur, my dear, will you not drink a glass of vodka, please little father).

3 V. G. Kostomarov, *Iazyk tekushchego momenta: poniatie pravil'nosti* (s. l.: Zlatoust, 2014), 152.

4 James Cracraft, *The Petrine Revolution in Russian Culture* (Cambridge, MA, and London: The Belknap Press of Harvard University Press, 2004).

5 Victor Zhivov, *Language and Culture in Eighteenth-Century Russia* (Boston: Academic Studies Press, 2009), 1.

6 Iuliia Goriacheva, "Vitalii Kostomarov: 'Sekret prost: dlia togo, chtoby poliubit' russkii iazyk, nado poliubit' Rossiiu," *Novyi russkii mir*, January 14, 2020, accessed February 17, 2021, https://russkiymir.ru/publications/267504/; V. G. Kostomarov, *Stilistika, liubov' moei zhizni* (St. Petersburg: Zlatoust, Moscow: IRIa, 2019), 179.

1.1 Aim and Purpose of the Investigation

This investigation examines the functions of language in society. It is thus a sociolinguistic investigation, "[а] задача социолингвистического исследования состоит как раз в том, чтобы получить представление о реальной языковой жизни людей."[7] In the words of sociolinguist J. V. Neustupný, "[l]anguage is reactive to other socioeconomic phenomena and is thus continuously adapting to changes in other spheres."[8] Finding out about "people's real linguistic life" therefore includes studying developments in society in conjunction with the linguistic evidence.

Despite brilliant research carried out on Russian eighteenth-century language by generations of scholars, our knowledge of this period remains incomplete. The principal reason is that certain spheres of the language have been investigated in detail, while others have attracted less attention (cf. chapter 2). As a result, we are left with a biased image of eighteenth-century Russian.

This investigation aims to expand this image, reveal this bias, and provide contrasting examples. It has three principal goals. First, to offer a sociolinguistic analysis of the Russian language during the 1740s, based on a broad selection of sources (the reasons for my choice of this period are detailed in section 1.4). Second, to study what forces may have caused linguistic change, or lack thereof, in the 1740s. Third, to determine how the usage observed in the textual material corresponds to the *linguistic registers*, varieties of a language associated with a particular situation of use, of the Russian language prevalent in the eighteenth century.[9]

---

7   L. P. Krysin, "Sotsial'naia markirovannost' iazykovykh edinits," in *Sovremennyi russkii iazyk: sotsial'naia i funktsional'naia differentsiatsiia*, ed. L. P. Krysin (Moscow: Iazyki slavianskoi kul'tury, 2003), 81 (and the task of a sociolinguistic investigation consists in exactly this: to get an idea of people's real linguistic life).

8   Jiří V. Neustupný, "Sociolinguistic Aspects of Social Modernization," in *Sociolinguistics: An International Handbook of the Science of Language and Society*, ed. U. Ammon, N. Dittmar, K. J. Mattheier, and P. Trudgill, 2nd rev. and ext. ed., vol. 3 (Berlin and New York: Walter de Gruyter, 2006), 2210.

9   Douglas Biber and Susan Conrad, *Register, Genre, and Style*, 2nd ed. (Cambridge: Cambridge University Press, 2019), 6; V. M. Zhivov, *Istoriia iazyka russkoi pis'mennosti*, vol. 1 (Moscow: Universitet Dmitriia Pozharskogo, 2017), 26–31.

1.2 Language and Society in Eighteenth-Century Russia

The transformation of the linguistic situation in Russia may have been quite radical for a limited group of speakers, but far less so for others. This argument is based on considerations of the nature of *language management*,[10] explained below.

The ways in which people think about the functions of language in their society, and the steps taken to influence or modify these functions are known collectively as *language policy*. A language policy, in the words of Bernard Spolsky,

> … operates within a speech community, of whatever size. The domain of language policy may be any defined or definable social or political or religious group or community, ranging from a family through a sports team or neighborhood or village or workplace or organization or city or nation state or regional alliance.[11]

Language policy, in the Spolskyan sense, has three components: *language practices, ideology,* and *management*.[12] Language practices are described as "the linguistic features chosen, the variety of language used. They constitute policy to the extent that they are regular and predictable."[13] Ideology consists of "the values, or statuses assigned to named languages, varieties and features."[14] Language management, previously known as *language planning*, is "the explicit and observable effort by someone or some group that has or claims authority over the participants in the domain to modify their practices or beliefs."[15]

Spolsky's use of the term *language management* differs from that suggested by Jiří V. Neustupný and Björn H. Jernudd, who define *language management* in the following way:

> The term language management covers what has often been referred to as language planning but its boundaries are wider. It comprises all behaviour that has language as its target, including language policy, the cultivation of language, language teaching

10 Bernard Spolsky, *Language Management* (Cambridge: Cambridge University Press, 2009).
11 Idem, *Language Policy* (Cambridge: Cambridge University Press, 2004), 40.
12 Ibid., 5.
13 Bernard Spolsky, *Language Management* (Cambridge: Cambridge University Press, 2009), 4.
14 Ibid.
15 Ibid.

and language acquisition, interpreting/translation, speaker's correction of language in discourse and speech therapy. One could also say *metalinguistic* behaviour, especially as linguistics is also one of the genres of language management.[16]

While recognizing the differences between the definitions of language management described above, this investigation draws on both. The term *language management* is used here in the sense of explicit and observable efforts to modify linguistic practices or beliefs. For these functions, Neustupný uses the term *organized management*.[17] The term language planning will not be used in this investigation.

Having reserved the term *language management* for the explicit and observable efforts to modify linguistic practices or beliefs, we must also consider the implicit and non-observable activities by which people have wielded authority over language. Where no policy or planning can be discerned, the term *simple* or *discourse-based management* can be used. An example of simple management is when a speaker corrects his or her own speech "here and now."[18] For a diachronic investigation such as this, the discourse-based management remains beyond reach.

Neustupný offers a typology for language management based on *modernity*, for which not all features need to be present simultaneously. The typology has four stages: premodern, early modern, modern, and postmodern. Although it is never explained what exactly characterizes the premodern period, this can be defined as the stage when the conditions characteristic of the next stage, the early modern, have not yet been reached. The latter are: a) the beginning of machine-assisted production; b) the emergence of new social structures; c) the appearance of modern national societies; d) the limitation of the power of the aristocracy, and e) the birth of the modern ideology of nationalism.[19]

It becomes immediately apparent that language management activities in mid-eighteenth-century Russia belonged to the premodern stage when evaluated

---

16 Neustupný, "Sociolinguistic Aspects," 2210. Cf. also "Language Management Theory," accessed June 26, 2019, http://languagemanagement.ff.cuni.cz/en/LMT; Jiří Nekvapil, "From Language Planning to Language Management," *Sociolinguistica* 20 (2006); idem, "Prologue: The Integrative Potential of Language Management Theory," in *Language Management in Contact Situations: Perspectives from Three Contintents*, ed. J. Nekvapil, T. Sherman, P. Kaderka (Frankfurt am Main: Peter Lang, 2009), 1.

17 Neustupný, "Sociolinguistic Aspects," 2210.

18 Nekvapil, "From Language Planning to Language Management," 96.

19 Neustupný, "Sociolinguistic Aspects," 2210–2211.

according to Neustupný's typology. None of the criteria suggested for early modern societies were as yet fulfilled. Indeed, when historian Simon Dixon writes about Russia in 1825, he concludes that it was by no means a modern state:

> Nowhere in Europe was popular participation in politics so severely discouraged; nowhere was subsistence agriculture so widely practised; nowhere did the workings of the world remain so mysterious to so many. Behind the façade of its rationally ordered bureaucratic hierarchy, and beneath the level of the cosmopolitan nobility, the Russian empire remained a peasant society ruled by autocrats who never relinquished their personal grip on the impersonal state authority they were so anxious to develop.[20]

Russia must have been even less modern seventy-five years earlier. However, there is only a partial overlap between the characteristics listed by Neustupný and Dixon. Sue Wright finds that

> although formal language policy making and language planning is a relatively recent development in terms of human history, as an informal activity it is as old as language itself, plays a crucial role in the distribution of power and resources in all societies. ...[21]

In accordance with Wright's argument, I regard the study of language management in eighteenth-century Russia as a possible endeavor—at least as available sources allow—despite the fact that it chronologically belongs to the premodern period.

It is reasonable to question whether the eighteenth-century Russian state and its institutions possessed the means by which they could influence the majority—let alone all—of their subjects. On the whole, the majority of Russian speakers had very limited access to education during the eighteenth century. A transformation of the linguistic situation powerful enough to permeate all of

---

20 Simon Dixon, *The Modernisation of Russia 1676–1825* (Cambridge: Cambridge University Press, 1999), 256.

21 Sue Wright, *Language Policy and Language Planning: From Nationalism to Globalisation* (Houndmills, Basingstoke: Palgrave Macmillan, 2004), 1.

society would require the force behind it to have vast resources of information and education. Modern hi-tech societies have this in the form of mass media and universal public education. The eighteenth-century Russian state, however, had far fewer and weaker resources at its disposal.

The Imperial Academy of Sciences was, in effect, the only institution that had such resources. Viktor Zhivov often returns to its role in linguistic matters.[22] He finds that, for as long as its monopoly on civil printing lasted, this organization was the only institution in Russia to actively engage in attempts to normalize the language. Although only a limited group of people read the academy's publications and adhered to its norms, the monopoly of the academy existed until the 1750s, when it began to deteriorate. This deterioration occurred in conjunction with the rapid development of literary culture during this period. Also during to the 1750s, "расхождение между реальным узусом и конструируемым Академией стандартом остается скрытым, существующим вне публичной сферы."[23] Therefore, in order to get a more accurate picture of the real linguistic landscape, it is crucial to look beyond the public sphere and consult a broad selection of relevant documents that have survived from the eighteenth century.

1.3 Historical Sociolinguistics?

Many aspects of "people's real linguistic life" in the distant past cannot be studied because tangible evidence is no longer available. In contrast to sociolinguists concerned with contemporary language, the linguist who wishes to carry out a diachronic investigation has no way of interacting with a statistically representative group of speakers in order to request additional information. Instead, he or she must observe and draw conclusions based exclusively on written evidence that has survived, sometimes by pure chance. This uneven preservation of data led William Labov to describe historical linguistics as "the art of making the best use of bad data."[24]

Notwithstanding this "bad data problem," as it is universally known, the desire to widen our knowledge of language in past societies has resulted in the gradual

---

22 Viktor Zhivov, "Literaturnyi iazyk i iazyk literatury v Rossii XVIII stoletiia," *Russian Literature* 52 (2002): 1–53; idem, *Ocherki istoricheskoi morfologii russkogo iazyka XVII–XVIII vekov* (Moscow: Iazyki slavianskoi kul'tury, 2004), 544–552.

23 Zhivov, *Ocherki*, 552 (the divergence between real usage and the standard constructed by the academy remains hidden, existing beyond the public sphere).

24 William Labov, *Principles of Linguistic Change*, vol. 1: *Internal Factors* (Oxford: Blackwell, 1994), 11.

evolution of a discipline known as *historical sociolinguistics*.[25] It developed during the last four decades, and its theoretical aspects lend themselves well to the investigation of eighteenth-century Russian language material.

1.4 Chronological Delimitations

Analyzing the entire eighteenth century would be a gigantic undertaking. Rather than maintaining a wide perspective, this study narrows in on a single decade in order to investigate the details and learn what new information they provide. But why the 1740s? Why not the 1720s or 1780s?

One reason to examine the 1740s is that this decade has long been neglected in the study of the Russian language in the eighteenth century.[26] The decade tends to be overshadowed by expositions on the Petrine reforms and the times of Lomonosov and Catherine the Great.

The 1740s are also chronologically situated halfway between the reforms of the Petrine period and the publication of M. V. Lomonosov's *Rossiiskaia grammatika* in 1757.[27] Since Lomonosov's work was the first Russian grammar book aimed at domestic consumption, the 1740s represent the last period in history when no such grammatical instruction was available to the general public.[28]

---

25 Cf. J. M. Hernández-Campoy and J. C. Conde-Silvestre, eds., *The Handbook of Historical Sociolinguistics* (Oxford: Wiley-Blackwell, 2012).

26 Anna Kretschmer, *Zur Geschichte des Schriftrussischen. Privatkorrespondenz des 17. und frühen 18. Jahrhunderts* (Munich: Otto Sagner, 1998), 255. Cf. also Ingrid Maier, review of *Zur Geschichte des Schriftrussischen. Privatkorrespondenz des 17. und frühen 18. Jahrhunderts* by Anna Kretschmer, *Zeitschrift für Slavische Philologie* 1 (2000): 186–193.

27 Mikhailo Lomonosov, *Rossiiskaia grammatika* (St. Petersburg: Imperatorskaia akademiia nauk, 1755; rpt. Leipzig: Zentralantiquariat der Deutschen Demokratischen Republik, 1972). The book was in fact published in January of 1757: V. B. Evtiukhin, "'Rossiiskaia grammatika' M.V. Lomonosova," accessed March 19, 2021, http://www.ruthenia.ru/apr/textes/lomonos/add02.htm.

28 Although not printed, grammar compilations of Russian were published prior to Lomonosov: B. A. Uspenskii, "Dolomonosovskie grammatiki russkogo iazyka (itogi i perspektivy)," in *Dolomonosovskii period russkogo literaturnogo iazyka / The Pre-Lomonosov Period of the Russian Literary Language*, ed. A. Sjöberg, Ľ. Ďurovič, and U. Birgegård (Stockholm: Kungl. vitterhets-, historie- och antikvitetsakademien, 1992), 63–169; B. A. Uspenskii, *Vokrug Trediakovskogo: Trudy po istorii russkogo iazyka i russkoi kul'tury* (Moscow: Indrik, 2008); O. L. Ariskina, "Izlozhenie ucheniia o morfemike i slovoobrazovanii v 'grammatike …' V. E. Adodurova," *Vestnik Mordovskogo universiteta* 1 (2011): 1–16; K. A. Filippov, N. V. Kareva, and S. S. Volkov, eds., *Vasilii Evdokimovich Adodurov: "Anfangs-Gründe der rußischen Sprache" ili "Pervye osnovania rossiiskogo iazyka". Formirovanie russkoi akademicheskoi grammaticheskoi traditsii* (St. Petersburg: Nauka and Nestor-Istoriia, 2014). For a recent investigation of grammars in languages other than Russian, cf. S. Mengel', S. Arshembo, M. K. Bragone, S. V. Vlasov, D. Grbich, L. V. Moskovkin, and T. Chelbaeva, eds., *Al'ternativnye puti formirovaniia*

1.5 Was Post-Petrine Russian in Disarray?

Pursuing an investigation of the Russian language in the 1740s is important for many reasons. First, it provides a deeper understanding of the Russian linguistic situation in the 1740s, since it is understudied. Secondly, we must correct, whenever possible, erroneous images of the past that have may have arisen. Such misunderstandings are not uncommon and may have various causes: biased or insufficient source information, ideological notions, and so forth. A few examples may help to illustrate this point. One author has the impression that all official business in Russia before 1750 was conducted in Church Slavic, not Russian:

> Obviously, Muscovian merchants did business in the vernacular, not Church Slavonic, which they used passively in church. The official switch to the vernacular as a written language began only with the linguistic works authored by Mikhail Vasilevich Lomonosov (1711–65). ...[29]

Another specialist suggests that post-Petrine Russian was somehow in a state of imbalance:

> Church Slavonic was losing its function as a language of literature and culture and vernacular Russian was in disarray, struggling to absorb the influx of foreign words and adapt itself to the needs of the emerging high society and the growing bureaucracy, of science and literature.[30]

1.6 Research Questions

The objectives of this investigation outlined in section 1.1 give rise to individual research questions. These questions can be further divided into two groups: 1) a group of extralinguistic issues about how Russian society was organized

---

russkogo literaturnogo iazyka v kontse XVII–pervoi treti XVIII veka: Vklad inostrannykh uchënykh i perevodchikov (Moscow: Iazyki slavianskikh kul'tur, 2021).

29 Tomasz Kamusella, *The Politics of Language and Nationalism in Modern Central Europe* (Basingstoke: Palgrave MacMillan, 2009), 161.

30 Irina Reyfman, *Vasily Trediakovsky: The Fool of the "New" Russian Literature* (Stanford: Stanford University Press, 1990), 31–32.

and how this organization impacted language, and 2) a group of purely linguistic questions.

1.6.1 Extralinguistic Questions

a) What was the societal structure of the Russian Empire during the 1740s, and what events and processes in that society may have impacted the language?
b) How was the educational system organized? What can be said concerning the levels of literacy?
c) What concrete measures did organizations and authorities take relating to linguistic matters?

1.6.2 Linguistic Questions

a) How do printed and handwritten documents in Russian from the 1740s differ significantly from each other?
b) If significant differences between printed and handwritten documents exist, how can they be interpreted from a sociolinguistic perspective?
c) Are efforts of linguistic standardization visible in printed texts from the 1740s?
d) Do handwritten documents contain evidence of linguistic standardization?
e) Is there evidence of linguistic change in the 1740s?

1.7 Outline of the Investigation

In order to meet the objectives of this investigation and to answer the research questions, this monograph is organized as follows. Chapter 1 introduces the study and its objectives. Chapter 2 outlines the current state of research on Russian in the first half of the eighteenth century, particularly the language of the 1740s. It also contains a section on sociolinguistic studies of eighteenth-century Russian language. Chapter 3 examines how Russian eighteenth-century society impacted the language. Chapter 4 presents the textual sources available for research on Russian in the 1740s. Chapter 5 discusses research methods. As a result of the methodological choices made in chapter 5, chapters 6, 7, and 8 contain respectively a situational, a linguistic and a functional analysis. Chapter 9 summarizes the conclusions of this study.

CHAPTER 2

Survey of Existing Research

Bibliographic searches reveal that linguists have given little attention to the Russian language of the 1740s. This decade constitutes the tail end of a period that was disparagingly labelled a "literary and linguistic wasteland" by a past generation of scholars.[1] For example, the author of a well-known handbook from the 1980s chose to dismiss the period in a few words: "French achieved undisputed pre-eminence in literature and the intellectual field (thought, criticism, history) from the accession of Elizabeth (1740). Everything French was worthy of imitation."[2]

In order to properly contextualize research about the Russian language during the 1740s, this discussion will present relevant issues within a wider chronological and thematic framework. This will be achieved by surveying the entire first half of the eighteenth century.

This chapter begins with a survey of research on the 1740s and then situates this decade within the overall eighteenth-century context. Because various aspects of the functions of language in society is the focus of this study, this survey of existing research will also include an assessment of research relevant to Russian historical sociolinguisticts.

2.1 Russian Language from the 1740s as a Field of Study

Research on Russian language from the 1740s has mostly revolved around religious language and business language (Ru. деловой язык).[3] Ekaterina Kislova

---

1 A. Issatschenko, "Vorgeschichte und Entstehung der modernen russischen Literatursprache," *Zeitschrift für slavische Philologie* 2 (1974): 272 (… literarische und sprachliche Wüste).

2 A. P. Vlasto, *A Linguistic History of Russia to the End of the Eighteenth Century* (Oxford: Clarendon Press, 1986), 290.

3 For a general introduction to the study of business language with a rich bibliography of Soviet and Russian literature, cf. O. V. Nikitin, *Delovaia pis'mennost' v istorii russkogo iazyka (XI–XVIII vv.): lingvisticheskie ocherki,* 3rd ed. (Moscow: Flinta, 2017). Nikitin does, however, not discuss the 1740s.

has investigated the language of sermons from the 1740s, a topic previously touched on by V. M. Zhivov.[4] Kislova finds that, despite the frequent occurrence of Russianisms in sermons, their language is

[ч]етко противопоставлен русскому языку светской литературы, в которой только отдельные грамматические церковнославянизмы допустимы как «поэтические вольности», но наиболее яркие формы (аорист, имперфект, плюсквамперфект) маркированы как чужеродные. Язык проповеди не осознается, очевидно, как русский, т. к. яркие грамматические церковнославянизмы из него не изгоняются.[5]

Research suggests that in 1750, the majority of literate people read texts that were largely similar to those read a century earlier.[6] Given the crucial importance of religion for the vast majority of people during the eighteenth century, literate Orthodox Christian Russians most likely considered texts with a significant admixture of Church Slavic as natural. The secular language had not yet incorporated the domain of religion. V. M. Zhivov writes:

---

4 V. M. Zhivov, *Kul'turnye konflikty v istorii russkogo literaturnogo iazyka XVIII–nachala XIX veka* (Moscow: IRIa, 1990); E. I. Kislova, "Grammaticheskaia norma iazyka propovedi elizavetinskogo perioda (1740-e gg.)" (Kand. nauk diss., Moskovskii gosudarstvennyi universitet, Moscow, 2007); idem, "Propoved' 1740-x godov v istorii russkogo iazyka," in *Okkazional'naia literatura v kontektste prazdnichnoi kul'tury Rossii XVIII veka*, ed. P. E. Bukharkin, U. Ekuch, and N. D. Kochetkova (St. Petersburg: Filologicheskii fakul'tet SPbGU, 2010), 33–52; idem, "'Grazhdanskoe' i 'tserkovnoslavianskoe' izdanie propovedei v XVIII v.: K voprosu o statuse dvukh tipov orfografii," in *Problemy izuchenia russkoi literatury XVIII veka* 15 (2011): 78–89; E. I. Kislova and E. M. Matveev, *Khronologicheskii katalog slov i rechei XVIII veka* (St. Petersburg: Filologicheskii fakul'tet SPbGU, 2011); E. I. Kislova, "Sermons and Sermonizing in 18th-Century Russia: At Court and Beyond," *Slověne* 2 (2014): 175–193. Kislova also maintains a website dedicated in part to the eighteenth century. The site contains, besides her own publications, a rich selection of scholarly literature: http://ekislova.ru/, accessed February 11, 2019.

5 Kislova, "Propoved' 1740-x godov," 52 (… is clearly opposed to the Russian language of secular literature, in which only individual grammatical Slavonicisms were allowed as "poetic licenses," whereas the most conspicuous forms [aorist, imperfect, pluperfect] were marked as alien. The language of the sermon is, obviously, not recognized as Russian since the glaring grammatical slavonicisms are not banished from it.).

6 Max J. Okenfuss, *The Rise and Fall of Latin Humanism in Early-Modern Russia* (Leiden: Brill, 1995), 239.

Следует иметь в виду при этом, что духовная литература XVIII в. имела никак не меньшую читательскую аудиторию, чем литература светская. Жития святых пользовались неизмеримо большим читательским спросом, чем сочинения Ломоносова. Это обстоятельство не могло не сказываться на социальных параметрах усвоения светского языкового стандарта.[7]

Research is scarce when it comes to other varieties of the language, although studies of regional business documents from the 1740s have been undertaken by Nikolai Chugaev and Larisa Belova.[8] Individual texts from the 1740s occur in academic editions.[9]

Studies that claim to deal with the history of the eighteenth-century language are very similar to descriptions of the history of Russian literature. This becomes evident when the former is compared with the latter, as has been pointed out by Helmut Keipert.[10]

Genres of imaginative literature were a recent phenomenon in the 1740s. They had very limited distribution in Russian society and "occupied an insignificant

---

7   Zhivov, *Ocherki*, 553–554 (Here one must not forget that, in the eighteenth century, spiritual literature enjoyed a readership much larger than that of secular literature. Saints' lives were vastly more popular than the writings of Lomonosov. This condition could not help but influence the social parameters of the adoption of the secular linguistic standard.)

8   N. V. Chugaev, "Paleografiia dvukh dokumentov Pyskorskogo medeplavil'nogo zavoda 1741 g.," in *Zhivaia rech' Permskogo kraia v sinkhronii i diakhronii: materialy i issledovania*, ed. I. I. Rusinova (Perm': Permskii gosudarstvennyi universitet, 2009), 257–269; L. A. Belova, *Kniga sekretnykh del Glavnogo zavodov pravleniia 1738–1740: Pamiatniki delovoi pis'mennosti I poloviny XVIII veka* (Perm': Permskii gosudarstvennyi pedagogicheskii universitet, 2011); N. V. Chugaev, ed., *Stolp prikhodnoi denezhnoi kazny pyskorskoi zavodskoi kantory 1741 godu* (Perm': PGNIU, 2016); N. V. Chugaev, "O nekotorykh osobennostiakh chislitel'nykh v prikamskom pis'mennom pamiatnike XVIII veka," *Acta linguistica petropolitana. Trudy Instituta lingvisticheskikh issledovanii* 13, no. 2 (2017): 630–659; idem, "'Stolp prikhodnoi denezhnoi kazny pyskorskoi zavodskoi kantory 1741 godu' kak istochnik izucheniia russkogo iazyka XVIII v." (Kand. nauk diss., Permskii universitet, Perm', 2019).

9   Cf., for example, Sumkina and Kotkov, *Pamiatniki*.

10 Helmut Keipert, "Die Christianisierung Rußlands als Gegenstand der russischen Sprachgeschichte," in *Tausend Jahre Christentum in Rußland: Zum Millenium der Taufe der Kiever Rus'*, ed. K. C. Felmy, G. Kretschmar, F. von Lilienfeld, and C.-J. Roepke (Göttingen: Vandenhoeck & Ruprecht, 1988), 313–346; G. Kaipert (Helmut Keipert), "Kreshchenie Rusi i istoriia russkogo literaturnogo iazyka," *Voprosy iazykoznaniia* 5 (1991): 85–112. Cf. also Alexander Issatschenko, *Geschichte der russischen Sprache*, vol. 2: *Das 17. und 18. Jahrhundert*, ed. H. Birnbaum, Ľ. Ďurovič, and E. Salnikow-Ritter (Heidelberg: Winter, 1983); Vlasto, *A Linguistic History of Russia*; Ian Press, *A History of the Russian Language and Its Speakers* (Munich: Lincom, 2007); A. M. Kamchatnov, *Istoriia russkogo literaturnogo iazyka XI–pervaia polovina XIX veka*, 2nd ed. (Moscow: Academia, 2013); Andrew Kahn, Mark Lipovetsky, Irina Reyfman, and Stephanie Sandler, *A History of Russian Literature* (Oxford: Oxford University Press, 2018).

place in publishing schedules."[11] Between 1725 and 1755, *belles-lettres* and odes constituted fifteen percent of all titles published. During the same period, religious content accounted for forty-one percent of published titles and laws, manifestos and official information represented eighteen percent.[12]

2.2 General Studies of Eighteenth-Century Russian

In the scholarly literature on the history of Russian, the eighteenth century constitutes a watershed, separating the traditions of seventeenth-century Muscovy from those of the Russian Empire. There is universal agreement about the importance of the period, as one prominent researcher described:

> ... и сегодня еще наши знания о языке этой эпохи, за которой традицией закреплен статус переходного этапа между т.н. древнерусским периодом и современным русским литературным языком (понятия и феномены, до сих пор не имеющие дефиниции в строгом смысле слова), в значительной степени фрагментарны.[13]

The main research focus of eighteenth-century Russian has concentrated on the creation and development of what is known today as the *Russian literary language* (русский литературный язык), or *contemporary standard Russian*.[14] In

---

11 Lindsey Hughes, "Russian Culture in the Eighteenth Century," in *The Cambridge History of Russia*, ed. D. Lieven, vol. 2: *Imperial Russia, 1689–1917* (Cambridge: Cambridge University Press, 2006), 79–80.

12 Gary Marker, *Publishing, Printing, and the Origins of Intellectual Life in Russia, 1700–1800* (Princeton, NJ: Princeton University Press, 1985), 59.

13 Anna Kretschmer, review of *V. K. Trediakovskijs "Gespräch zwischen einem Fremden und einem Russen über die alte und neue Orthographie und alles, was zu dieser Materie gehört": eine philologisch-kritische Darstellung* by Marianne Müller, *Russian Linguistics* 21, no. 3 (1997): 327 (... even today, our knowledge of the language of this period, to which tradition has fixed a status of transitional phase between the so-called Old Russian period and the modern Russian literary language (concepts and phenomena that are still lacking definitions in the strict meaning of the word), to a considerable degree, remains fragmentary).

14 For a definition of the characteristics of literary languages according to the Prague school, cf. A. V. Isachenko, "Vopros № 3: Kakova spetsifika literaturnogo dvuiazychiia v istorii slavianskikh narodov?," *Voprosy iazykoznaniia* 7, no. 3 (May–June 1958): 42–45. Henrik Birnbaum later rephrased the characteristics of literary languages even more succinctly: multivalence, standardization, nationwide binding force, and stylistic differentiation, cf. Henrik Birnbaum, "Fact and Fiction Concerning the Genesis of Literary Russian," *Russian Linguistics* 2 (1976): 168. For analyses of the term "literary language," cf. I. A. Podtergera, "Chto takoe istoriia

modern scholarly literature, the emerging idiom is referred to as a *new type of Russian literary language* (русский литературный язык нового типа) or *new Russian literary language* (новый русский литературный язык).[15]

"Codification of this new literary language began in the 1730s," writes V. M. Zhivov, who dates the earliest beginnings of standardization activities by the ·St. Petersburg Academy of Sciences to the middle of 1728.[16] By the 1740s, the new literary language had lost some of its novelty, and writing in it was no longer considered as "беспрецедентная смелость."[17] Certain syntactical, lexical and morphological elements that were previously separated, were now being integrated in the new written Russian.[18] In printed texts from the period, scholars have identified evidence suggesting that a process of standardization had begun. However, due to lack of research, little can be said about the extent to which the standardization had actually advanced in printed texts. Even less can be said about the varieties of the language used in texts that were never printed.

In 1984, Helmut Keipert published a survey that has since become an important key to the understanding of research on eighteenth-century Russian.[19] In the 1999 revised version, he examines the ways in which the Russian literary language has been studied and identifies four basic models, or "main foci of interest" (Germ. *Interessenschwerpunkte*):

> 1. als Geschichte der Sprache von Texten, vorzüglich der von Originalwerken [istorija literaturnogo jazyka = istorija jazyka literatury/pis′mennosti = istorija tekstov]; oder 2. als Geschichte der (literatur)sprachlicen Norm; oder 3. als Geschichte der

---

iazyka? / What is Language History?," *Slověne* 1 (2015): 394–455 (the article contains a rich bibliography relevant to the discussion); Margarita Schoenenberger, "Une sociolinguistique prescriptive: la théorie des langues 'littéraires' dans la linguistique soviétique des années 60–90," *Langage et société* 4 (2004): 28–34; N. N. Germanova, *Teoriia i istoriia literaturnogo iazyka v otechestvennom i angloiazychnom iazykoznanii* (Moscow: URSS, 2011).

15 Gerta Hüttl-Folter, "Russkii literaturnyi iazyk novogo tipa. Innovatsii v sintaksise 30-ykh godov XVIII v.," *Wiener Slavistisches Jahrbuch* 38 (1992): 21; B. A. Uspenskii, *Kratkii ocherk istorii russkogo literaturnogo iazyka (XI–XIX vv.)* (Moscow: Gnozis, 1994), 115. V. M. Zhivov, *Iazyk i kul′tura v Rossii XVIII veka* (Moscow: Iazyki russkoi kul′tury, 1996), 13.

16 Zhivov, *Language and Culture*, 3; V. M. Zhivov, "Problemy formirovaniia russkogo literaturnogo iazyka," in *Trudy Otdeleniia istoriko-filologicheskikh nauk Rossiiskoi akademii nauk 2007*, ed. A. P. Derevianko (Moscow: Nauka, 2009), 57.

17 Zhivov, *Istoriia iazyka russkoi pis′mennosti*, vol. 2, 1027 (an unprecedented audacity).

18 Kretschmer, *Zur Geschichte des Schriftrussischen*, 233.

19 Helmut Keipert, "Geschichte der russischen Literatursprache," in *Handbuch des Russisten. Sprachwissenschaft und angrenzende Disziplinen*, ed. H. Jachnow, K. Hartenstein, and W. Jachnow (Wiesbaden: Harrassowitz, 1984): 444–481.

Einstellungen von Russischsprechern zu den Problemen ihrer L(iteratursprache); oder 4. als Geschichte der Ausbildung der literatur- bzw. schriftsprachlichen Merkmale insgesamt.[20]

Keipert concludes that a strong emphasis has been placed on the first two areas of interest, but not the third and fourth. One reason suggested by Keipert is that few meta-linguistic statements by Russians have been preserved from the past.

It has long been acknowledged within the scholarly community that the general scope of eighteenth-century research has been rather narrow. Already in the 1960s, Iurii Sorokin, a Soviet specialist in historical lexicography, wrote:

> Итак, исследование языка XVIII в. до сих пор было в известной степени односторонне привлечено к памятникам собственно литературным. Но и здесь оно было сосредоточено по преимуществу на произведениях нескольких писателей (Кантемира, Ломоносова, Сумарокова, Фонвизина, Радищева, Карамзина, Дмитриева, Державина, отчасти Тредиаковского, комедий второй половины XVIII и начала XIX в., в частности Плавильщикова и некоторых других),— на произведениях очень симптоматичных и важных, но не создающих полной картины.[21]

In the West, Keipert also criticized higher education courses on the history of the Russian literary language of their "shameful neglect" of the socio-historical aspects of their subject.[22] However, equating Russian linguistic history with that

---

20 Helmut Keipert, "Geschichte der russischen Literatursprache," in *Handbuch der sprachwissenschaftlichen Russistik und ihrer Grenzdisziplinen*, ed. H. Jachnow (Wiesbaden: Harrassowitz, 1999), 727 ([1] the history of individual texts; [2] the history of the (literary) language norm; [3] the history of attitudes of Russian speakers towards their literary language; and [4] an integrated history of the evolution of the characteristics of literary and written language).

21 Iurii S. Sorokin, ed., *Protsessy formirovaniia leksiki russkogo iazyka (ot Kantemira do Karamzina)* (Moscow and Leningrad: Nauka, 1966), 13 (Thus far, the investigation of the eighteenth-century language has, to a certain extent, focused only on the great works of literature in the narrow sense. And even here it concentrated on the works of a few writers [Kantemir, Lomonosov, Sumarokov, Fonvizin, Radishchev, Karamzin, Dmitriev, Derzhavin, Trediakovskii, the comedies of the second half of the 18th and early 19th centuries, particularly Plavil'shchikov and a few others], on works that are indicative and important, but that do not provide the full picture).

22 Helmut Keipert, review of *Teoreticheskie osnovy istorii russkogo literaturnogo iazyka* by A. I. Gorshkov, *Russian Linguistics* 8 (1984): 162.

of imaginative literature has endured in practice, if not in theory.[23] Keipert concludes that the image of the eighteenth-century language does contain certain "notorische Lücken."[24]

In 2015, Irina Podtergera published an article that has proven valuable for explaining the causes underlying the situation described above by Keipert. According to her, the term *literary language* has been interpreted in two different ways by scholars working in different historical periods, resulting in a confusion of the concepts. The first definition of *literary language* was employed by A. I. Sobolevskii and other scholars in the late nineteenth and early twentieth centuries: "литературный язык 1—письменный язык, язык литературных произведений и документов." The second definition, used during the twentieth century by representatives of the Prague linguistic circle, reads: "литературный язык 2—стандартный язык, который в том числе может функционировать как язык литературных произведений."[25] Podtergera continues:

> На самом же деле мы имеем дело со смешением, возникшим в результате наложения друг на друга двух омонимичных терминов и двух стоящих за ними традиций. Чтобы ликвидировать это досадное смешение, нужно прежде всего признать наличие первой, более ранней традиции в отечественном языкознании как полноценной и завершенной в себе. Отдав дань уважения Соболевскому как одному из крупнейших ученых своего времени и признав его вклад в мировую лингвистику, нам, вероятно, следует прекратить попытки во что бы то ни стало вписать его линию в актуальный научный опыт.[26]

---

23 Cf. S. O. Savchuk and D. V. Sichinava, "Korpus russkikh tekstov XVIII veka v sostave Natsional'nogo korpusa russkogo iazyka: problemy i perspektivy," in *Natsional'nyi korpus russkogo iazyka: 2006–2008. Novye rezul'taty i perspektivy*, 52–70, accessed January 19, 2019, http://ruscorpora.ru/sbornik2008/04.pdf; Kislova, "Propoved' 1740-x godov," 33.

24 Keipert, "Geschichte der russischen Literatursprache," 728 (notorious gaps).

25 Podtergera, "Chto takoe istoriia iazyka?," 420–421 (literary language 1—written language, the language of literary works and documents; … literary language 2—a standard language that, among other things, can function as the language of literary works).

26 Ibid., 424 (In fact we are dealing with a confusion that occurred as a result of an imposition one on top of the other of two homonymous terms and of the two traditions behind them. In order to liquidate this annoying confusion, it is first necessary to recognize the existence of the first, earlier tradition in linguistics in Russia as valuable and complete in itself. Having paid tribute to Sobolevskii as one of the greatest scholars of his time and having recognized his contribution to world linguistics, we probably should discontinue the efforts to insert his line in the current scholarly experience).

Podtergera finds that the position according to which *literary language* is under-stood as the language of literature maintains a strong position in the syllabi of higher education (presumably in the Russian Federation, although this is not stated—T.R.), thus reducing the history of the literary language to historical stylistics.

During the last decade of the twentieth century, however, something started to shift in the diachronic research on Russian. In their review of Keipert's 1999 survey article, V. M. Zhivov, Elena Zemskaia, and Leonid Krysin conclude that

> Историю литературного языка нового времени невозможно написать, не представляя себе, каков был круг пользователей этого языка, как и когда он начал утрачивать свою элитарность, как воспринимался этот язык большинством населения, остававшимся к этому языку во многом непричастным.[27]

By the late 1990s, a steady flow of works had begun to contribute to a more complete picture of the eighteenth-century language, as desired by Iurii Sorokin in the 1960s (see above). Important contributions made during the 1990s and 2000s include work by Gerta Hüttl-Folter, Anna Kretschmer, V. M. Kruglov, B. A. Uspenskii, V. M. Zhivov, and many others.[28]

The latest comprehensive treatment of the eighteenth century is V. M. Zhivov's monumental two-volume *Istoriia iazyka russkoi pis'mennosti*. It was published posthumously in 2017 and is likely to remain influential for the foreseeable future. Concerning the first half of the eighteenth century Zhivov writes:

---

27 V. M. Zhivov, E. A. Zemskaia, and L. P. Krysin, review of *Geschichte der russischen Literatursprache* by H. Keipert, *Voprosy iazykoznaniia* 5 (2000): 127 ([t]he history of the literary language of the modern period cannot be written without imagining what the circle of users of this language was like, how and when it began to lose its elite status, and how this language was received by the majority of the population who, generally, did not contribute to it).

28 Gerta Hüttl-Folter, *Syntaktische Studien zur neueren russischen Literatursprache. Die frühen Übersetzungen aus dem Französischen* (Vienna: Böhlau, 1996); Kretschmer, *Zur Geschichte des Schriftrussischen*; V. M. Kruglov, "O kharaktere normy v russkom iazyke pervoi chetverti XVIII veka," in *Petra philologica, Literaturnaia kul'tura Rossii XVIII veka*, vol. 6, ed. N. A. Gus'kov, E. M. Matveev, M. V. Ponomarëva (St. Petersburg: Nestor-Istoriia, 2015), 167–180; Nikita Mikhaylov, "Tvoritel'nyi padezh v russkom iazyke XVIII veka" (PhD diss., Uppsala University, Uppsala, 2012); B. A. Uspenskii, *Vokrug Trediakovskogo* (Moscow: Indrik, 2008); Zhivov, *Iazyk i kul'tura*; idem, "Literaturnyi iazyk i iazyk literatury v Rossii XVIII stoletiia"; idem, *Ocherki*.

Языковая ситуация радикально меняется в эпоху Петра Великого: культурная революция, устроенная царем-преобразавателем, сопровождается и лингвистической революцией. Она состоит прежде всего в отказе от старой регистровой организации языковой деятельности. На смену языку, фрагментированному по регистрам, приходит—по крайней мере, в идее, в идеале—единый полифункциональный письменный язык, парадоксальным образом являющийся в то же время «гражданским наречием».[29]

However, until the end of the 1750s,

[н]овый языковой стандарт остается достоянием небольшой части образованной элиты, а возникшие за этот период образовательные институции (Академическая гимназия, Шляхетный корпус, Московский университет) существенной экспансии нового идиома пока еще не дают.[30]

In addition, during the mid-1740s, Zhivov identifies signs of a new cultural-historical situation affecting the literary language. The new idiom had acquired additional features characteristic of literary languages.[31] This process, however, came to fruition after the 1740s, and thus lie beyond the scope of this investigation.

Is it then reasonable to talk of a linguistic "revolution" during the first half of the eighteenth century? Yes, but only from the position of elite culture, as Aleksandra Pletnëva has pointed out.[32]

---

29 Zhivov, *Istoriia*, vol. 1, 73–74 (The linguistic situation changes radically in the time of Peter the Great: the cultural revolution organized by the tsar-reformer is accompanied by a linguistic revolution. This means, in the first place, the renunciation of the old, register-based organization of linguistic activity. A language fragmented into registers is supplanted—at least conceptually—by a unified polyfunctional written language, which is, paradoxically, at the same time the "civil dialect").

30 Zhivov, *Istoriia*, vol. 2, 1060 ([t]he new linguistic standard remains the property of a small portion of the educated elite, whereas the educational institutions that appeared during this period [the Academy Grammar School, the Cadet Corps, the Moscow University] do not yet result in any significant expansion of the new idiom). The English renderings of the names of these institutions are taken from Geoffrey Hosking's *Russia and the Russians. A History*, 2nd ed. (Cambridge, MA: The Belknap Press of Harvard University Press, 2011), 207–208.

31 Zhivov, *Istoriia*, vol. 2, 1027–1028.

32 A. A. Pletnëva, "Sotsiolingvistika i problemy istorii russkogo iazyka XVIII–XIX vekov," in *Zhizn' iazyka: Sbornik statei k 80-letiiu Mikhaila Viktorovicha Panova*, ed. S. M. Kuz'mina (Moscow: Iazyki slavianskoi kul'tury, 2001), 269.

Where does the lasting value of Zhivov's *Istoriia iazyka russkoi pis'mennosti* lie? Partly, the answer is found in its title. Zhivov explains:

> Существенно лишь иметь в виду, что ситуация с письменным языком в эпоху до появления языкового стандарта (литературного языка) была принципиально иной, чем та, к которой мы привыкли. … Такая ситуация во всех европейских обществах возникла сравнительно недавно.[33]

2.3 Sociolinguistically Oriented Studies of Eighteenth-Century Russian

Historical sociolinguistics is an important part of our current understanding of language history.[34] As previously mentioned, eighteenth-century Russian was often studied on the basis of literary and other printed texts. Another traditional focus has been on the language use of individual members of the elite of Russian society. An example is the following recommendation, taken from a historical grammar published in the early 1960s: "[t]he phonology of eighteenth-century Russian may be studied at the beginning of this period in the private correspondence and official papers of Peter the Great and in the middle of it in the data pertaining to the three styles recommended by Lomonosov."[35]

The 1960s saw a broadening of the base for diachronic investigations when S. I. Kotkov and his fellow scholars began to prepare editions and studies of private letters, business and administrative documents, providing researchers with a larger variety of texts than had previously been available.[36] Today, busi-

---

33 Zhivov, *Istoriia*, vol. 1, 35 ([i]t is essential to keep in mind that the written language situation during the period preceding the emergence of the linguistic standard (the literary language) was fundamentally different from what we are used to. … Such a situation appeared relatively recently in all European societies).

34 Podtergera, "Chto takoe istoriia iazyka?," 427.

35 W. K. Matthews, *Russian Historical Grammar* (London: The Athlone Press, 1960), 170.

36 For example, S. I. Kotkov, "Russkaia chastnaia perepiska XVII–XVIII vv. kak lingvisticheskii istochnik," *Voprosy iazykoznaniia* 6 (1963): 107–116; A. I. Sumkina, *Sintaksis moskovskikh aktovykh i epistoliarnykh tekstov XVIII v.*, ed. S. I. Kotkov (Moscow: Nauka, 1987); A. P. Maiorov, *Ocherki leksiki regional'noi delovoi pis'mennosti XVIII veka* (Moscow: Azbukovnik, 2006); O. V. Nikitin, *Problemy ėtnolingvisticheskogo izucheniia pamiatnikov delovoi pis'mennosti*, 3rd ed. (Moscow: Flinta, 2017), 76.

ness documents are attracting increasing scholarly interest, including those from Russia's regions.[37]

In the West, historical sociolinguistics has established itself as a discipline within diachronic linguistics during the last half-century or so.[38] Thanks to this discipline, we now understand that Russian language history was more heterogeneous than was previously assumed, and the interest in historical sociolinguistics is growing.[39]

Historical sociolinguistics is a term used in the Soviet Union/Russia since the early 1980s. In 1983, the historian V. B. Kobrin read a paper at a conference in Dnepropetrovsk, the theme of which translates into English as "The Fourth All-Union Conference 'Current Problems of Source Criticism and Special Historical Disciplines.'" Kobrin contributed a paper entitled "Historical Sociolinguistics as a Special Historical Discipline."[40] In it, he suggests that new information could be gained from studying changes in the "social codes" of languages:

> Коротко можно сказать, что крестьянин XVII в., переодевшийся боярином, вряд ли был бы разоблачен по языку, а крестьянин XVIII не имел шансов не выдать себя, если бы вздумал вырядиться генералом.[41]

---

37 See, for example, L. A. Glinkina and E. A. Sivkova, eds., *Delovoi iazyk XVIII–nachala XIX vekov na Iuzhnom Urale i v Zaural'e* (Cheliabinsk: Poligraf-Master, 2006); T. P. Rogozhnikova, ed., *Istoriia russkogo literaturnogo iazyka: regional'nyi aspekt* (Moscow: Flinta, 2016).

38 Cinzia Russi, ed., *Current Trends in Historical Sociolinguistics* (Warsaw and Berlin: DeGruyter Open, 2016); Terttu Nevalainen and Helena Raumolin-Brunberg, "Historical Sociolinguistics: Origins, Motivations, and Paradigms," in *The Handbook of Historical Sociolinguistics*, ed. J. M. Hernández-Campoy and J. C. Conde-Silvestre (Oxford: Wiley-Blackwell, 2012), 22–40.

39 Kretschmer, *Zur Geschichte des Schriftrussischen*; Nikitin, *Problemy ėtnolingvisticheskogo izucheniia*, 77; Podtergera, "Chto takoe istoriia iazyka?," 437. The use of foreign languages in eighteenth-century Russia is the object of several recent studies: May Smith, *The Influence of French on Eighteenth-Century Literary Russian: Semantic and Phraseological Calques* (Oxford: Peter Lang. 2006); Gesine Argent, Derek Offord, and Vladislav Rjéoutski, "The Functions and Value of Foreign Languages in Eighteenth-Century Russia," *The Russian Review* 1 (2015): 1–19; Derek Offord, Vladislav Rjéoutski, and Gesine Argent, *The French Language in Russia: A Social, Political, Cultural and Literary History* (Amsterdam: Amsterdam University Press, 2018); Derek Offord, "Sociolinguistics and History: An Interdisciplinary View of Bilingualism in Imperial Russia," *Journal of Historical Sociolinguistics* 1 (2020): 1–33.

40 V. B. Kobrin, "Istoricheskaia sotsiolingvistika kak spetsial'naia istoricheskaia distsiplina," in *Oprichnina, genealogiia, antroponimika: izbrannye trudy,* ed. E. G. Astvatsaturian, A. G. Makarov, and Iu. M. Eskin (Moscow: RGGU, 2008), 246–254.

41 Ibid., 249 (In short, one could say that a seventeenth-century peasant dressed up as a boyar would hardly be exposed on linguistic grounds, whereas an eighteenth-century peasant would certainly betray himself if he tried to pass himself off as a general).

Kobrin briefly describes the status of sociolinguistics in the Soviet Union and how it had begun to be used synchronically, and scholars such as Iu. D. Desheriev had written about how "retrospective sociolinguistics" still lacked a conceptual apparatus, but no development had as yet taken place in the field.[42]

According to Kobrin, the Soviet Union was the birthplace of sociolinguistics, and its father was E. D. Polivanov.[43] Sociolinguistic studies were halted during Stalinism, and later Soviet linguists paid less attention to the social factors in linguistic development. However, after the fall of the Soviet Union, interest in historical sociolinguistics surfaced once again.[44]

Today, approximately three decades later, the importance of certain types of texts for our understanding of Russian linguistic developments during the eighteenth century is becoming increasingly apparent. These texts include business texts, private correspondence, and other kinds of domestic (бытовые) texts.[45] However, leading scholars conclude that methods suitable for investigation of the Russian material require design and development.[46] The present investigation represents one such development.

---

42 Ibid., 247.

43 L. P. Krysin, "Evgenii Dmitrievich Polivanov," in *Stat'i o russkom iazyke i russkikh iazykovedakh*, 2nd ed. (Moscow: Flinta, 2016), 496; E. D. Polivanov, "Fonetika intelligentskogo iazyka," in *Izbrannye raboty: Stat'i po obshchemu iazykoznaniiu*, ed. A. A. Leont'ev (Moscow: Nauka, 1968), 225–235.

44 V. M. Alpatov, A. N. Baskakov, and G. K. Venediktov, *Diakhronicheskaia sotsiolingvistika* (Moscow: Nauka, 1993); V. I. Belikov and L. P. Krysin, *Sotsiolingvistika: Uchebnik dlia vuzov* (Moscow: RGGU, 2001). Neither of these publications have new things to say about developments during the eighteenth century. For a brief history of sociolinguistics in the East Slavic area, cf. Karl Gutschmidt, "Die ostslawische Region / The East-Slavic Area," in *Sociolinguistics/Soziolinguistik: And International Handbook of the Science of Language and Society*, ed. U. Ammon, N. Dittmar, K. J. Mattheier, and P. Trudgill, 2nd ed., vol. 3 (Berlin and New York: Walter de Gruyter, 2006), 1852–1853.

45 L. L. Kasatkin, *Sovremennaia russkaia dialektnaia i literaturnaia fonetika kak isthochnik dlia istorii russkogo iazyka* (Moscow: Nauka and Iazyki russkoi kul'tury, 1999), 22; Anna Kretschmer, "Chelovek za pis'mom (russkii chelovek Petrovskogo vremeni v chastnoi perepiske)," in *Die russische Sprache und Literatur im 18. Jahrhundert: Tradition und Innovation. Gedenkschrift für Gerta Hüttl-Folter*, ed. Juliane Besters-Dilger and Fedor B. Poljakov (Frankfurt am Main and New York: Peter Lang, 2009), 267; A. P. Maiorov, "Sverkhtekst v Zabaikal'skoi delovoi pis'mennosti XVIII v. kak istochnik rekonstruktsii regiolekta togo vremeni," *Izvestiia Iuzhnogo federal'nogo universiteta* (series: Filologicheskie nauki) 3 (2019): 34–45.

46 Nikitin, *Problemy ètnolingvisticheskogo izucheniia*, 77–78.

2.4 Language and Politics in the 1740s

Language management (cf. above, section 1.2) is the conscious and explicit effort to control people's choices in linguistic matters, whether done by members of the family, communities or the state. Even though the Russian Empire lacked a state language agency in the modern sense of the word during the 1740s, state organized language management activities did take place.

In the 2009 preface to the English translation of *Language and Culture in Eighteenth-Century Russia*, V. M. Zhivov comments on what he considers a weakness in his original investigation. He finds that it is lacking "an institutional component". The "institutional component" he is referring to is the role of the Academy of Sciences in the codification of the language,[47] on which he elaborates in later publications.[48] Today, most scholars will agree that the Academy of Sciences was a crucial component in the development of the Russian literary language during the eighteenth century.

Throughout the 1740s, the Russian state was uncontested in institutional language management. Through its various administrative branches and its effective control of Russia's printing presses, the state exercised power over both religious and secular language.[49] Until the end of the 1750s, the academy was the sole body responsible for printing texts in the civil typeface, which was used for printing secular texts.[50]

The developments in the Academy of Sciences during the 1740s deserve to be investigated, as do other forms of language management in Russia during this period. Much has been written about the initiative to form a translators' conference, known as the Russian Conference (Российское собрание) in 1735.[51] Less is known about its real impact, and the impact of the work of individuals such as V. K. Trediakovskii, and the "linguistic programs" ascribed to him and other persons associated with the academy.[52]

---

47 Zhivov, *Language and Culture*, xiii.
48 Zhivov, "Literaturnyi iazyk"; idem, *Ocherki*; idem, *Istoriia*.
49 Marker, *Publishing, Printing*, 233.
50 Zhivov, *Language and Culture*, xiii.
51 Marker, *Publishing, Printing*, 52; Evgenii G. Pivovarov, "K istorii sozdaniia Rossiiskogo sobraniia Akademii nauk," *Sotsiologiia nauki i tekhnologii* 4 (2018): 7–20. This gathering is sometimes referred to in English as the *Russian convocation*, cf. Ilya Serman, "The Eighteenth Century: Neoclassicism and the Enlightenment, 1730–90," in *The Cambridge History of Russian Literature*, ed. C. A. Moser, rev. ed. (Cambridge: Cambridge University Press, 1992), 55.
52 Cf. Uspenskii, *Kratkii ocherk*; idem, *Vokrug Trediakovskogo*; Zhivov, *Istoriia*, vol. 2, 1012–1025.

2.5 Assessing the Situation

Whether it is the result of how the term *literary language* has been interpreted, or through some combination of other reasons, descriptions of the development of Russian are strongly reminiscent of the *funnel view* of language history.[53] Heavily summarized, this theory can be described in the following manner: at the wide end of the funnel (that is, at an early stage in the development), a number of coexisting varieties of a language are "poured into" the funnel, and at the narrow end of the funnel (a later stage), a *standard language* emerges: "[t]he fate of the original varieties poured in at the top and others that may have arisen at a later stage are generally not taken into consideration."[54]

The funnel view results in a norm-oriented perception of language history. This brings to mind the "sanitized language history," which has earlier characterized the studies of the development of the French language: "Until recent years, histories of the French language were based primarily on literary texts. This has resulted in a sanitized version that makes the language history appear more homogeneous than it surely was."[55] A situation similar to this can be said to exist also in the historiography of the Russian language, likely a result of reverence for the standard language throughout the modern period:

> В отечественной культуре авторитет литературного языка весьма высок. Отклонения от литературной нормы оцениваются обществом негативно как показатель низкого культурного уровня говорящих. Это связано с тем, что в отечественной культуре литературный язык ассоциируется, прежде всего, нес социальным положением говорящего, но с его культурно-образовательным уровнем. Более того, учению о русском литературном языке нередко придается политико-патриотическая окраска.[56]

---

53 Richard J. Watts, *Language Myths and the History of English* (Oxford: Oxford University Press, 2011), 290.

54 Watts, *Language Myths*, 291–293.

55 William J. Ashby, review of *Sociolinguistic Variation in Seventeenth-Century France* by W. Ayres-Bennett, *The French Review* 6 (2006): 1403.

56 Germanova, *Teoriia i istoriia*, 200 (In domestic culture, the authority of the literary language is very high. Deviations from the literary norm are judged negatively by society as an indicator of a low cultural level on the part of the speakers. This is linked to the association, in domestic culture, of the literary language not with the social position of the speaker, but with his level of culture and education. Furthermore, the doctrine of the Russian literary language is often coloured by politics and patriotism).

Nationalism can thus be a consideration in the analysis of the ways in which language history has been written during the past century. Anna Kretschmer finds this to be one of the defining characteristics of diachronic Slavic studies:

> Zu dem Erbe der Romantik gehört auch die Überbetonung des Nationalen, des Autochtonen, die bis zum heutigen Tag gerade für die diachrone Slavistik so prägend ist. Dabei wird nur zu häufig vergessen, daß die Grenze zwischen dem Autochtonen und dem Autarken, dem zum Prinzip erhobenen Anspruch, auch im Hinblick auf die Schrift- bzw. Standardsprache sich selbst zu genügen, fließend ist und leicht überschritten werden kann. Die Ausrichtung auf das Eigene birgt immer die Gefahr eines xenophoben Purismus in sich. In der diachronen Slavistik hat sie u. a. dazu geführt, daß über die Grenzen der nationalen Schulen hinweg so gut wie keine Koordinierung der Forschung stattfindet.[57]

2.6 Conclusions

As this survey of existing research illustrates, the linguistic situation in Russia during the 1740s has never been subject to detailed investigation. There are investigations of individual genres, notably sermons, and some information can be extracted from general treatments of the eighteenth century. However, it remains difficult to understand the various forms of written Russian and how they differed from one another.

Many scholars have reacted against the bias towards imaginative literature, which prevails in the existing research on Russian in the eighteenth century. In the 2000s, these critical opinions resulted in a growing research interest related to previously neglected linguistic domains, such as regional business texts.

However, despite much new research, the image of the second quarter of the eighteenth century remains unclear. This is partially due to the fact that certain

---

57 Kretschmer, *Zur Geschichte des Schriftrussischen*, 5–6 (The legacy of Romanticism also includes an overemphasis on the national, the autochthonous, which to date has been so characteristic of diachronic Slavic studies. It is all too often forgotten that the boundary between the autochthonous and the autarchic can escape the claim, made into a principle, that it is also self-sufficient with regard to the written and standard language, and can easily be crossed. The focus on one's own always carries with it a risk of xenophobic purism. In diachronic Slavic studies, this has, among other things, resulted in the almost complete absence of research coordination across the boundaries of national schools).

functional spheres of the language remain understudied. To put it simply: several pieces of the puzzle are missing.

In order to remedy the current situation, several issues need to be addressed. First of all, an improved understanding of the linguistic situation calls for broadening the textual base to include greater variety.

Secondly, several remaining problems deserve renewed scrutiny: What was the literate culture like in the eighteenth century for the majority of the population of the Russian Empire? Who could read and write? What can be said about the literacy rates for men and women, and for people from diverse social backgrounds? How did literate people use their skills? How is the literacy level of the period reflected (or revealed) in preserved documents?

Thirdly, with the broadening of the field of vision comes a need to consider how "new" areas of research have been perceived intellectually in Russia and other countries. Although the subject does not strictly belong to linguistics, an investigation of Russian in the 1740s would be incomplete if it did not take into account the ideological considerations at the base of current perceptions of history.

The remaining chapters of this book are dedicated to answering these questions and finding solutions to these problems.

CHAPTER 3

The Impact of Society on Language

In chapters 6 to 8 of the present investigation, a number of texts in Russian from the 1740s will be subject to analysis. However, before determining the significance of the linguistic information found in these texts, it seems logical first to examine the sociocultural context of Russian in the 1740s. This will be done in the form of a brief survey of extralinguistic evidence.

In order to make the exposition as accessible as possible, a very brief introduction to Russian society in the 1740s is provided below. Such an introduction must, by necessity, draw on work done by others—mainly the work of historians—and there is an evident risk of reiterating facts already familiar to many readers. For this reason, the introductory remarks below are kept to a minimum.

3.1 Introductory Remarks

After a reform promulgated in 1727, the Russian Empire consisted of 14 provinces (губерния) and approximately 250 counties (уезд). The territorial expansion during the 1740s was modest. Following the Peace of Turku in 1743, a portion of Eastern Finland was annexed. In 1744, a reform of the gubernii led to the addition of two new provinces: Vyborg and Orenburg.[1]

---

1   B. Tarkhov, "Izmenenie administrativno-territorial'nogo deleniia Rossii XIII–XIX vv.," *Logos* 1 (2005): 65–66.

3.1.1 Peoples and Languages

Between 1719 and 1857, Russian authorities levied ten tax revisions (ревизия).[2] The second revision was undertaken in 1744 and 1745. According to its findings, the male population comprised a little over nine million individuals.[3] Multiplied by 1.02—since there were slightly more females than males—the grand total amounted to almost nineteen million individuals, that is, slightly less than France of the same period.[4] Between the second and third revisions (1744–1762), the population of the Russian Empire increased by some sixteen percent.[5] While the majority of the population of Russia in the 1740s was ethnically Russian (over sixty-nine percent), the empire was characterized by great ethnic diversity.[6] Fascinating as they may seem, questions about the empire's ethnic composition are not immediately relevant to the present investigation, which focuses on the language of the majority: Russian.

This investigation is concerned with varieties of Russian in the first half of the eighteenth century. However, in order to avoid unwanted repetition, detailed discussions of these varieties will be presented in the chapters below. At this stage, a general observation must suffice: contemporary standard Russian is closely related to the varieties of spoken and written language employed during the 1740s, although the spheres of existence of these varieties differed from what we can observe today (cf. below, section 5.2.2). For the most part, the Russian-speaking population communicated amongst themselves in their local dialects. The development of the latter is the object of historical dialectology.[7] The distribution of Russian dialects during the early modern period is of great interest for the research on regional business language (cf. above, section 2.3).

---

2   B. N. Mironov, *Rossiiskaia imperiia: Ot traditsii k modernu*, vol. 1 (St. Petersburg: Dmitrii Bulanin, 2014), 530.

3   V. M. Kabuzan, *Narodonaselenie Rossii v XVIII–pervoi polovine XIX v. (po materialam revizii)* (Moscow: Izdatel'stvo Akademii nauk SSSR, 1963), 163. Kabuzan reports the figure 9,103,387. The figures have since been reinterpreted by Arcadius Kahan, whose estimation is 9,105,017: Arcadius Kahan, *The Plow, the Hammer and the Knout: An Economic History of Eighteenth-Century Russia* (Chicago and London: The University of Chicago Press, 1985), 8.

4   Mironov, *Rossiiskaia imperiia: Ot traditsii k modernu*, 512. The population of France in 1740 was 24.6 million: Louis Henry and Yves Blayo, "La Population de la France de 1740 à 1860," *Population* 30, no. 1 (1975), 95.

5   V. M. Kabuzan, *Narody Rossii v XVIII veke: chislennost' i ètnicheskii sostav* (Moscow: Nauka, 1990), 116.

6   Ibid., 132; Andreas Kappeler, *Rußland als Vielvölkerreich: Entstehung, Geschichte, Zerfall*, 2nd ed. (Munich: C. H. Beck, 2008), 100–108.

7   K. V. Gorshkova, *Istoricheskaia dialektologiia russkogo iazyka* (Moscow: Prosveshchenie, 1972).

3.1.2 Social Stratification

The social stratification of Russian society increased during the seventeenth and early eighteenth centuries, resulting in the development of society based on the *soslovie* (сословие [plural *sosloviia*, сословия], a term often rendered in English as "estate"—T.R.).[8] While as a term *soslovie* is well established, certain aspects of the concept itself are not. Alison K. Smith points out that the use of the term *soslovie* is slightly anachronistic for the eighteenth century prior to the reforms launched by Catherine the Great in 1767.[9] A recent volume by historians N. A. Ivanova and V. P. Zheltova presents a number of key issues of *soslovie* society that remain unresolved. One such issue concerns the chronology of formation. While some researchers favor the beginning of the eighteenth century, others claim that the formation process of the *sosloviia* reached its culmination as late as the 1830s.[10] Another discussion has as its goal to define the relationship between the Russian state and the *sosloviia*, whether or not this relationship should be considered "serflike" for all social categories.[11] While the outcome of such discussions are of great interest, further treatment of them clearly lies beyond the framework of the present investigation. Instead, focus will be shifted to the distribution of the *sosloviia* in the population.

The second revision reports that, of the approximately nineteen million Russians, about ninety percent were peasants (крестьяне).[12] The peasants were not a homogeneous group, but rather belonged to various categories with different judicial status: state serfs, estate serfs, monastery serfs, and others.[13] Their economic conditions also varied. While the overwhelming majority worked in agriculture, a few—like the serf Kondratii, who began his career as a

---

8 N. A. Ivanova and V. P. Zheltova, *Soslovnoe obshchestvo Rossiiskoi imperii (XVIII–nachalo XX veka)*, 2nd ext. ed. (Moscow: Novyi khronograf, 2019), 7.

9 For a discussion of this term and its possible translations (estate, caste, class, and so forth), see Alison K. Smith, *For the Common Good and Their Own Well-Being: Social Estates in Imperial Russia* (Oxford and New York: Oxford University Press, 2014), 5.

10 Ivanova and Zheltova, *Soslovnoe obshchestvo*, 7–8.

11 Ibid., 8; B. N. Mironov, *Sotsial'naia istoriia Rossii perioda imperii (XVIII–nachalo XX v.)*, 3rd rev. and ext. ed. (St. Petersburg: Dmitrii Bulanin, 2003), vol. 1, 77–78.

12 Figures pertaining specifically to social stratification during the 1740s are unavailable. However, since figures reported by Ia. E. Vodarskii, *Naselenie Rossii v kontse XVII–nachale XVIII veka (chislennost', soslovno-klassovyi sostav, razmeshchenie)* (Moscow: Nauka, 1977), 56 for the years 1719 and 1795 are identical, we may assume that they are valid also for the years 1740–1749. Mironov concludes that the social composition of the empire changed at a very slow pace. Peasants made up 89.1% of the population in 1719, falling slowly to 80.1% in 1913, cf. Mironov, *Rossiiskaia imperiia: Ot traditsii k modernu*, 476.

13 Mironov, *Rossiiskaia imperiia: Ot traditsii k modernu*, 398.

cottage-industry weaver on the estates of the nobleman Bibikov—became successful industrialists.[14]

The remainder of the population fell into a number of groups. Approximately 3–4% were counted as town dwellers (городское сословие), another 1.5–2% belonged to the clergy, and between 1 and 1.5% were made up of the service personnel of the army and navy.[15]

The most influential group in Russian eighteenth-century society was the nobility. During the reign of Empress Elizabeth, this *soslovie* was often referred to as the *shliakhetstvo* (шляхетство), or *dvorianstvo* (дворянство).[16] During the inital decades of the eighteenth century, the nobility doubled in number. In 1700, it had counted "little more than 15,000 men."[17] According to the second revision, the nobility constituted 0.5% of the population.[18] In absolute numbers this amounted to 37,326 males.[19]

3.1.3 Politics and Administration

Historian Aleksandr Kamenskii characterizes the reign of Elizabeth (1741–1761) as a period of stabilization of the political and social life compared to the preceding decades. The leading figures of the era belonged to a generation that had grown up in the midst of the Petrine transformations.[20]

Following a peace treaty with the Ottoman Empire in 1739, Russia enjoyed a comparatively peaceful decade as far as external military engagements were concerned. A minor war with Sweden between 1741 and 1744 was merely

---

14 B. B. Gorshkov, *Peasants in Russia from Serfdom to Stalin: Accomodation, Survival, Resistance* (London: Bloomsbury Academic, 2018), 73.

15 Mironov, *Rossiiskaia imperiia: Ot traditsii k modernu*, 444–445; cf. also Elise Kimerling Wirtschafter, "The Groups Between: *Raznochintsy*, Intelligentsia, Professionals," in *The Cambridge History of Russia*, ed. D. Lieven, vol. 2: *Imperial Russia, 1689–1917* (Cambridge: Cambridge University Press, 2006), 245–263.

16 Ivanova and Zheltova, *Soslovnoe obshchestvo*, 79.

17 Dominic Lieven, "The Elites," in *The Cambridge History of Russia*, ed. D. Lieven, vol. 2: *Imperial Russia, 1689–1917* (Cambridge: Cambridge University Press, 2006), 230.

18 Kabuzan, *Narodonaselenie*, 154.

19 Walter Leitsch, "The Russian Nobility in the Eighteenth Century," *East European Quarterly* 3 (1977): 317.

20 Éduard Épshtein, "Opyt XVIII veka nel'zia vziat' i perenesti v XXI vek," *Gazeta.ru*, July 08, 2016, accessed April 22, 2021, https://www.gazeta.ru/science/2016/07/08_a_8372981.shtml.

"peripherally important."[21] Also, the Russian Empire took little part in the great European military conflict of the period, the War of the Austrian Succession (1740–1748).[22]

Real power in Russia, during the eighteenth century, fluctuated among three groups of institutions: (1) the visible state: Senate, Holy Synod, *kollegii*;[23] (2) the monarch's advisory council (under various names); and (3) the monarch's personal favorites.[24] Towards the middle of the century, a clearer understanding emerged between the sovereign (государь) and the state (государство). The state was no longer perceived as the fiefdom of the sovereign.[25] Nonetheless, the empire's center of power was the sovereign, who was aided by small groups of advisers.[26] No constitutional assembly or other popular representation existed, rather "the Russian monarchy consulted representatives of social groups, local communities, and central institutions on an *ad hoc* basis"[27] The monarch remained the sole formal legislative authority until the introduction of the State Duma in 1906, that is, far beyond the period chosen for the present investigation.[28]

---

21 Kahan, *The Plow, the Hammer and the Knout*, 8, table 1.3. Cf. also N. Shpilëvskaia, *Opisanie voiny mezhdu Rossieiu i Shvetsieiu v Finliandii v 1741, 1742 i 1743 godakh* (St. Petersburg: Iakov Trei, 1859).

22 E. M. Sobko, "Uchastie Rossii v voine za avstriiskoe nasledstvo," *Voprosy istorii* 1 (2012): 166–172; E. M. Sobko, "Rossiisko-frantsuzskie otnosheniia v period voiny za avstriiskoe nasledstvo," *Vestnik Moskovskogo gosudarstvennogo oblastnogo universiteta* (series: Istoriia i politicheskie nauki) 3 (2017): 56–66; Francine-Dominique Liechtenhan, *La Russie entre en Europe: Elisabeth Ire et la Succession de l'Autriche (1740–1750)* (Paris: CNRS, 1997).

23 *Kollegiia* (коллегия) was the term used for an agency of the central administration, that is, a ministry, such as the Kollegiia of Foreign Affairs (Иностранная коллегия or Коллегия иностранных дел) or the Kollegiia of War (Военная коллегия), cf. Erik Amburger, *Geschichte der Behördenorganisation Russlands von Peter dem Grossen bis 1917* (Leiden: Brill, 1966), 118–120.

24 Hosking, *Russia and the Russians*, 213.

25 Evgenii Anisimov, *Derzhava i topor: tsarskaia vlast', politicheskii sysk i russkoe obshchestvo v XVIII veke* (Moscow: Novoe literaturnoe obozrenie, 2019), 15; Ivanova and Zheltova, *Soslovnoe obshchestvo*, 45.

26 Amburger, *Geschichte der Behördenorganisation*, 64; Ivanova and Zheltova, *Soslovnoe obshchestvo*, 45.

27 Elise K. Wirtschafter, "Social Categories in Russian Imperial History," *Cahiers du monde russe* 50, no. 1 (2009): 244.

28 Idem, "A State in Search of a People: The Problem of Civil Society in Imperial Russia," in *Eighteenth-Century Russia: Society, Culture, Economy*, ed. R. Bartlett and G. Lehmann-Carli (Berlin: LIT, 2007), 374.

Russia was administered by a bureaucratic apparatus that had received its basic structure through the reforms of Peter the Great.[29] By European standards, the educated and ruling cadres remained small throughout the 1740s.[30] The administrators were mostly Russians, but there was also a significant contingent of non-Russians. Thus, in 1730, the percentage of non-Russian administrators was thirty percent.[31]

3.2 Education and Literacy in Eighteenth-Century Russia

As was seen in the Introduction (cf. above, section 1.2.1), Neustupný lists a number of criteria linked to modernity, which require fulfilment in order to facilitate early modern language management. The criteria include, among other, the emergence of new social structures, the appearance of modern national societies, and the limitation of the power of the aristocracy. Based on these criteria, it was concluded that Russia in the 1740s clearly belonged to the premodern type of society as far as language management was concerned. However, in order to understand the linguistic situation on Russia, and how decisions were made that were relevant to its development, one other criterion is important: the development of the system of education.

Intended as a base for further discussion, the current section will provide an overview of education in Russian society during the 1740s.

3.2.1 Education

In the 1740s, like other European states, Russia did not possess a ministry of education. Such institutions and their legal foundations were not created until a couple of decades later. Laws on public schools began to appear in the 1760s, with Prussia's *General Regulation on Rural Schools* (*General-Landschulreglement*) from 1763 as an early example.[32] Europe's first state agency charged with public

---

29 Lindsey Hughes, *Russia in the Age of Peter the Great* (New Haven, CT: Yale University Press, 1998); Aleksandr B. Kamenskii, *Ot Petra I do Pavla I. Reformy v Rossii XVIII veka. Opyt tselostnogo analiza* (Moscow: RGGU, 2001); Amburger, *Geschichte der Behördenorganisation*.

30 Lieven, "The Elites," 230.

31 Mironov, *Sotsial'naia istoriia*, vol. 1, 32.

32 Marcelo Caruso and Daniel Töpper, "Schooling and the Administrative State: Explaining the Lack of School Acts in Nineteenth-Century Prussia," in *School Acts and the Rise of Mass Schooling: Education Policy in the Long Nineteenth Century*, ed. J. Westberg, L. Boser, and I. Brühwiler (Cham: Palgrave Macmillan, 2019), 45.

education was set up in the Polish-Lithuanian Commonwealth in 1773.[33] In Russia, the Main Commission for Public Schools (Главная комиссия училищ) was established in 1782 and the Ministry of National Education (Министерство народного просвещения) about twenty years after that.[34] The state educational initiatives took a long time to develop, and the number of state high schools remained low throughout the century.[35] In the absence of a unified educational system, three principal forms of education were available in Russia: ecclesiastical, private, and state-organized.

The educational establishments of the church were organized according to four levels: parish schools, district schools, seminaries, and academies. Basic literacy education, the main focus of parish schools, was the basis for much of the further education. This continued according to well-established traditions:

> At least during the first two-thirds of the eighteenth century elementary language learning preserved the traditional pattern, that is, it consisted of studying the Slavonic primer, prayer book and Psalter, to which might be added Feofan Prokopovich's *Russian Catechism* (*Pervoe uchenie otrokom*) …; attempts to introduce books in the civil script into primary education were not successful.[36]

In traditional Muscovite society, formal education had not been a general requirement, even for priests.[37] To cope with the lack of educated people, institutions of higher learning began to be introduced in Russia during the second half of the seventeenth century. Leading representatives of the Great Moscow Synod (Большой московский собор) of 1666–1667 concluded that the great schism in the Russian Orthodox Church in the mid-1600s had come about due to the

---

33 Danuta M. Gorecki, "The Commission of National Education and Civic Revival through Books in Eighteenth-Century Poland," *The Journal of Library History* 2 (1980): 138–166; John A. Račkauskas, "The First National System of Education in Europe: The Commission for National Education of the Kingdom of Poland and the Grand Duchy of Lithuania (1773–1794)," *Lituanus—Lithuanian Quarterly Journal of Arts and Sciences* 4 (1968).

34 Amburger, *Geschichte der Behördenorganisation*, 187–191; Patrick L. Alston, *Education and the State in Tsarist Russia* (Stanford: Stanford University Press, 1969), 18.

35 Lieven, "The Elites," 239.

36 Zhivov, *Language and Culture*, 412.

37 Wayne Dowler, *A History of Education in Modern Russia: Aims, Ways, Outcomes* (London: Bloomsbury, 2021), 15.

absence of schools in the country.[38] Most famous among the new institutions is the Moscow Slavo-Greco-Latin Academy.[39] Later, during the reforms of Peter the Great, the state sponsored the creation of several educational facilities.[40] However, these did not gain immediate popularity. E. K. Sysoeva, the author of a recent handbook on the history of Russian education, points out that coercive measures were often recommended to force people into education.[41] One explanation for the need of compulsion is that students were not well treated. Disciplinary measures included flogging and pressing into naval service.[42]

In the highest-level institutions the curriculum included theology, philosophy, literature, church history, arithmetic, geography, Greek, Latin, and modern languages, such as French and German.[43] This caused an evident inequality in terms of access to education: "While the clergy and the higher estates could be taught all manner of subjects, local parishioners (that is, the peasants) would learn, at most, their ABCs."[44] There were notable exceptions to this in Russia of the 1740s, for instance, serf children sometimes received good education to prepare for future service as estate administrators.[45]

Towards the very end of his life, in 1724, Peter signed the charter creating the Academy of Sciences. From the outset, this institution also had a "university" attached to it:

> Универзитетъ есть собраніе ученыхъ людей, которые наукамъ высокимъ, яко ѳеологія и юрисъ пруденція (правъ искусству), медицины и философіи, сирѣчь до какого состоянія оныя нынѣ дошли, младыхъ людей обучаютъ.[46]

38 B. L. Fonkich, *Greko-slavianskie shkoly v Moskve v XVII veke* (Moscow: Iazyki slavianskikh kul'tur, 2009), 65.

39 S. K. Smirnov, *Istoriia Moskovskoi slaviano-greko-latinskoi akademii* (Moscow: V. Got'e, 1855); A. A. Larionov, "Studenchestvo v Slaviano-greko-latinskoi akademii v pervoi polovine XVIII veka," *Rossiiskaia istoriia* 6 (2010): 30–40.

40 Cracraft, *The Petrine Revolution*, 132–133; E. K. Sysoeva, *Shkola v Rossii XVIII–nachalo XX vv.: vlast' i obshchestvo* (Moscow: Novyi khronograf, 2015), 31–41.

41 Sysoeva, *Shkola v Rossii*, 47.

42 D. A. Tolstoi, "Vzgliad na uchebnuiu chast' v Rossii v XVIII stoletii do 1782 goda," *Sbornik otdeleniia russkogo iazyka i slovesnosti Imperatorskoi akademii nauk* 38, no. 4 (1885): 12.

43 S. F. Egorov, ed., *Rossiiskoe obrazovanie: istoriia i sovremennost'* (Moscow: ITPIMIO, 1994), 59–60.

44 Gary Marker, "The Westernization of the Elite, 1725–1800," in *A Companion to Russian History*, ed. A. Gleason (Malden, MA: Wiley Blackwell, 2014), 190.

45 Dowler, *A History of Education*, 19.

46 M. I. Sukhomlinov, ed., *Materialy dlia istorii Imperatorskoi akademii nauk*, vol. 1 (St. Petersburg: Imperatorskaia akademiia nauk, 1885–1900), 14 (A university is an assembly of learned

The major Russian educational institutions were staffed by foreigners, and foreign teachers remained in majority at major Russian educational institutions throughout the first half of the eighteenth century. When new *Statutes* (*Регламент*) were issued in 1747 for the Academy of Sciences—and for the Gymnasium, a secondary school attached to the academy[47]—they stated that the language of instruction should be Russian. However, despite some efforts, it proved impossible to find suitable teaching staff, and it was therefore decided that instruction should continue as before, that is, not in Russian, but rather in French, German, and Latin.[48] Among the large institutions, only the Slavo-Greco-Latin Academy, which had Russians on its staff, was an exception in this respect because of its Orthodox character.[49]

Some general handbooks on the history of Russian education give the impression that the University of the Academy of Sciences was fully functional from the beginning.[50] This, in fact, was not the case. In its early stages, higher education in Russia was riddled with start-up problems and enrollment was negligible. The first class of the university had eight students and during some of the subsequent years, none were recruited. Since there were scarcely any Russians with secondary education, the first students had to be invited from abroad.[51]

Other difficulties originated within the faculty: at one point, in 1736, the professors could not be persuaded to give lectures. In the 1740s, with the university again practically dormant, the academicians were ordered to read public lectures, and posters were printed to this effect, but the expected audience failed to show up.[52] As D. A. Tolstoi, a late nineteenth-century scholar, wrote: "И так,

---

people who teach young people the high sciences, such as theology, and jurisprudence [the art of law], medicine and philosophy, that is, to such an extent as they have now reached).

47 About the Gymnasium, see L. V. Moskovkin, *Iazykovoe obrazovanie v Akademicheskom univer-sitete i gimnazii v XVIII veke* (Sankt-Peterburg: Izdatel'stvo Sankt-Peterburgskogo universiteta, 2019), 40.

48 A. I. Liubzhin, *Istoriia russkoi shkoly imperatorskoi ėpokhi*, vol. 1: *Russkaia shkola XVIII stoletiia* (Moscow: Nikeia, 2014), 572;, D. A. Tolstoi, "Akademicheskii universitet v XVIII stoletii, po rukopisnym dokumentam arkhiva Akademii nauk," *Sbornik otdeleniia russkogo iazyka i sloves-nosti Imperatorskoi akademii nauk* 38, no. 6 (1885): 15.

49 Vladislav Rjeoutski, "Migrants and Language Learning in Russia (Late Seventeenth–First Part of Eighteenth Century)," *Paedagogica historica* 6 (2018): 702.

50 For example, S. F. Egorov, ed. *Khrestomatiia po istorii shkoly i pedagogiki v Rossii (do Velikoi Oktiabr'skoi Sotsialisticheskoi Revoliutsii)*, 2nd rev. ed. (Moscow: Prosveshchenie, 1986), 42.

51 Dowler, *A History of Education*, 11.

52 Tolstoi, "Vzgliad na uchebnuiu chast'," 9–11. Cf. also P. Pekarskii, *Istoriia Imperatorskoi akademii nauk* (St. Petersburg: Imperatorskaia akademiia nauk, 1873), vol. 2, 328; William H. E. Johnson, "Russia's Edicational Heritage: Teacher Education in the Russian Empire, 1600–1917" (PhD diss., Columbia University, New York, 1950), 37.

профессора жаловались на то, что у них нет студентов, студенты на то, что профессора их не учат."[53]

The Academy University was finally brought to a standstill in 1743. Subsequent efforts to revive it during the late 1740s and 1750s by the new president of the academy, Count Kirill Razumovskii (from 1746), V. K. Trediakovskii, and M. V. Lomonosov did not result in expansion. For a time in 1746, however, Lomonosov did lecture publicly on experimental physics in Russian.[54]

A later endeavor, which proved lasting, was the foundation of Moscow University in 1755. However, at its opening, it too had a very modest body of students: 100, dropping to 82 thirty years later.[55]

The third component of the educational system in early eighteenth-century Russia was privately organized educational endeavors. Private tutors were used in all ranks of society, from peasant literacy tutors (мастера грамоты) to imported French and German tutors for the children of the more privileged.[56] Examples of peasants creating their own literacy schools exist as early as the seventeenth century.[57]

Advertisements for foreign teachers began appearing in the *Sanktpeterburgskie vedomosti* in the 1740s, and the first description of a private school run by foreigners in Russia appeared at the end of that decade. In 1746, eight French tutors were working in Moscow.[58] As for the basic schooling of their own children, foreign nationals set up their own schools in close connection with their religious communities.[59]

Finally, besides the education available within Russia, a possibility of travelling abroad also existed. Among others, this was an option for some of the graduates from the Academy University, who, upon completion of the course, were

---

53 Tolstoi, "Akademicheskii universitet," 15 (and so the professors complained that they had no student, and the students complained that the professors were not teaching them).

54 Offord, Rjéoutski, and Argent, *The French Language in Russia*, 317.

55 V. O. Kliuchevskii, *Kurs russkoi istorii*, part 5 (Moscow: Mysl', 1989), 151–152.

56 Rjéoutski, "Migrants and Language Learning," 699.

57 Elise K. Wirtschafter, *Social Identity in Imperial Russia* (DeKalb, IL: Northern Illinois University Press, 1997), 130.

58 Vladislav Rjéoutski, "Les écoles étrangères dans la sociéte russe à l'epoque des Lumières," *Cahiers du monde russe* 3 (July–September 2005): 478–479; V. S. Rzheutskii, "Frantsuzskie guvernëry v Rossii XVIII v. Rezul'taty mezhdunarodnogo issledovatel'skogo proekta 'Frantsuzy v Rossii,'" in *Frantsuzskii ezhegodnik 2011: Frankoiazychnye guvernëry v Evrope XVII–XIX vv.*, ed. A. V. Chudinov (Moscow: IVI RAN, 2011), 58–80.

59 Peter Hoffmann and V. I. Osipov, eds., *Geographie, Geschichte und Bildsungswesen in Russland und Deutschland im 18. Jahrhundert: Briefwechsel Anton Friedrich Büsching–Gerhard Friedrich Müller 1751 bis 1783* (Berlin: Akademie, 1995), 19.

promoted to adjunct professors and sent abroad for further training.[60] Groups of students were dispatched to Leiden in the Netherlands to study law, mathematics, and medicine.[61] Others were dispatched to Germany, especially to Halle, Leipzig, Jena, and Wittenberg.[62] Students who were sent abroad were selected among the most talented graduates of schools such as the Moscow Slavo-Greco-Latin Academy.[63]

Summing up this presentation of the system of education in Russia, it is clear that around the middle of the eighteenth century the church stood out as the main educational provider.[64] In this respect, Russia did not differ from other European countries.[65] Despite the fact that the reforms of Peter the Great and his successors added many new schools to Russia's educational system, it still catered to a fraction of the population and took a long time to develop.[66] The design of the educational system, largely influenced by the religious institutions, also affected its ability to teach Russian as a mother tongue. Such instruction started no earlier than the second half of the 1730s.[67]

3.2.2 Literacy

An eyewitness account of the literacy situation in Russia during the first half of the eighteenth-century is found in I. T. Pososhkov's *Book on Poverty and Wealth*. The narrative refers to the 1720s:

> Паки немалая пакость крестьянам чинитца и от того, что грамотных людей у них нет. Аще в коей деревне дворов дватцать или и трицать, а грамотнаго человека ни единаго у

60 Tolstoi, "Vzgliad na uchebnuiu chast'," 11.
61 N. Hans, "Russian Students at Leyden in the 18th Century," *The Slavonic and East European Review* 35 (85) (1957): 551–562; Marker, *Publishing, Printing*, 72.
62 Günter Mühlpfordt, "Rußlands Aufklärer und die Mitteldeutsche Aufklärung: Begegnungen, Zusammenwirken, Partnerschaft," in *Deutsch-russische Beziehungen im 18. Jahrhundert: Kultur, Wissenschaft und Diplomatie*, ed. C. Grau, S. Karp, and J. Voss (Wiesbaden: Harrassowitz, 1997), 168.
63 Liubzhin, *Istoriia russkoi shkoly*, 563.
64 Marker, *Publishing, Printing*, 72.
65 Nigel Aston, "The Established Church," in *The Oxford Handbook of the Ancien Régime*, ed. W. Doyle (Oxford: Oxford University Press, 2012), 293.
66 William T. Brickman and John T. Zepper, *Russian and Soviet Education 1731–1989: A Multilingual Annotated Bibliography* (New York and London: Garland Publishing, Inc., 1992), 9–15.
67 Zhivov, "Literaturnyi iazyk i iazyk literatury," 13; Moskovkin, *Iazykovoe obrazovanie*, 40.

них нет, и какой человек к ним ни приедет с каким указом или
и без указу, да скажет, что указ у него есть, то тому и верят …
И ради охранения от таковых напрасных убытков, видится,
не худо б крестьян и поневолить, чтоб они детей своих, кои
десяти лет и ниже, отдавали дьячкам в научение грамоты и,
науча грамоте, научили бы их писать. И чаю, не худо бы так
учинить, чтобы не было и в малой деревне без грамотнаго
человека.[68]

Viewed in a larger context, Pososhkov's account clearly does not represent the whole story. As stated in the previous section, there were schools where peasants learned to read and write, so not all peasants were analphabets. On the contrary, it is sometimes claimed that leading members of Russia's eighteenth-century elite in fact were. One name that comes up in such discussions is that of the powerful A. D. Menshikov (1673–1729); however, this is a dubious example, because Menshikov was born among the lower ranks of society and did not receive an education that would have been expected of a nobleman.[69] Claims about the analphabetism of various historical figures cannot be proven either way, and there is a strong possibility that rumors of illiteracy have been exaggerated by political enemies or a disrespectful posterity.[70] In any case, the allegations in themselves are interesting since they suggest that literacy was not to be assumed in the eighteenth century, even among members of the ruling elite.

Setting out to examine the literacy situation in eighteenth-century Russia, one soon discovers that there are no reliable statistics on literacy rates. Instead, knowledge about literacy must be gained in other ways. Historian B. N. Mironov has done much work on the issue of literacy in the Russian Empire. In 1985, he suggested a method for calculating literacy levels in the past based on

68 I. T. Pososhkov, *Kniga o skudosti i bogatstve i drugie sochineniia*, ed. B. B. Kafengauz (Moscow: Izdatel'stvo Akademii nauk SSSR, 1951), 171; the English translation is quoted from Iván Pososhkóv, *The Book of Poverty and Wealth*, ed. and transl. A. P. Vlasto and L. R. Lewitter (London: Athlone Press, 1987), 313 (The peasants also suffer no little hardship from a lack of literate men among them. A village of twenty or thirty families may not have a single literate man, so a stranger has but to flourish a written order before them, or even merely to state that he has such an order without producing it, and they will surely believe him. … To guard against this it would clearly be advisable to oblige peasants to send their children under the age of ten to the sacristan to be taught to read and, that learnt, also to write. It seems to me that it would be no bad thing to ensure that even in the smallest village all are able to read).

69 Tho. Consett, *The Present State and Regulations of the Church of Russia Establish'd by the Late Tsar's Royal Edict* (London: S. Holt, 1729), xliv; Okenfuss, *The Rise and Fall*, 123.

70 Cf. N. A. Kopanev, "Knigi imperatritsy Elizavety Petrovny," in *Kniga v Rossii XVI–serediny XIX v.*, ed. A. A. Zaitseva (Leningrad: BAN, 1990), 109–110.

retrospective prognoses.[71] For the present investigation, one of his estimates is interesting. He calculates that, in 1757, literacy in the statistical cohort of ten- to nineteen-year-olds was 19.3% for urban males and 5.1% for urban females, while for rural males and females they were 3.3% and 3.1% respectively.[72]

It was not until a century or so after the 1740s that literacy statistics began to appear. I. M. Bogdanov reports figures collected by N. P. Luppov from the marriage registry of a rural community in Viatka province for the years 1839–1848. According to these statistics, eleven percent of males were literate, while none of the females could read or write.[73]

What methods, then, are at our disposal for determining how many speakers of Russian in earlier centuries actually knew how to read, and how many knew how to write? These and related questions have been addressed by a number of scholars starting with A. I. Sobolevskii in the nineteenth century.[74]

For estimates of literacy rates during the late seventeenth century, specialists have largely relied on the analysis of signatures.[75] Using this method, combined with data from examinations of witnesses during legal proceedings, Mironov has concluded that literacy among adult townspeople did not exceed thirteen percent, and among peasants, two to four percent.[76]

Among scholars who have dealt with the topic of literacy, estimates vary from the high percentages of literacy calculated by Sobolevskii for mid-seventeenth century Muscovy—seventy-five percent or more for landlords, fifty percent for urban dwellers, and fifteen percent for the peasantry—to Gary Marker's more skeptical view that "Muscovy was characterized by a near absence of literacy and

---

71 B. N. Mironov, "Gramotnost' v Rossii 1797–1917 gg.: Poluchenie novoi istoricheskoi informatsii s pomoshch'iu metodov retrospektivnogo prognozirovaniia," *Istoriia SSSR* 4 (1985): 137–153.

72 Ibid., 148.

73 I. M. Bogdanov, *Gramotnost' i obrazovanie v dorevolutsionnoi Rossii i v SSSR (istoriko-statisticheskie ocherki)* (Moscow: Statistika, 1964), 57.

74 Gary Marker, "Literacy and Literacy Texts in Muscovy: A Reconsideration," *Slavic Review* 49, no. 1 (1990): 74–89. For a general introduction to the measurement of literacy levels in pre-modern societies, see R. S. Schofield, "The Measurement of Literacy in Pre-Industrial England," in *Literacy in Traditional Societies*, ed. J. Goody (Cambridge: Cambridge University Press, 1968).

75 For discussions of methods and difficulties associated with estimating literacy rates before the age of modern statistics, see, for example, Schofield, "The Measurement of Literacy"; Geraldine Jonçich Clifford, "Buch und Lesen: Historical Perspectives on Literacy and Schooling," *Review of Educational Research* 4 (1984): 472–500; Marker, "Literacy and Literacy Texts in Muscovy"; B. Mironov, "Uchënost'—vot chuma, uchënost'—vot prichina …," *Rodina* 6 (2006), accessed June 14, 2011, http://www.istrodina.com/rodina_articul.php3?id=1905&n=99.

76 Mironov, "Uchënost'."

a correspondingly low level of genuine learning and education."[77] Marker suggests that rudimentary literacy levels may have been from three to ten percent of the population, while intermediate literacy levels were as low as one or two percent in the late seventeenth century.[78]

In the first third of the eighteenth century, Mironov suggests that literacy among the most prosperous townspeople reached forty-two percent. Other traders and manufacturers show percentages between four and ten percent. Peasants in northern Russia, judged by signatures on collective supplications, appear to have reached literacy rates of about nine percent. He points out that literacy rates were subject to variation between, as well as within, social groups. There was also geographic variation. Estimates suggest that literacy among peasants of northern Russia was five to ten times higher than in the central regions.[79]

The figures presented by Marker correspond fairly well to those published by Mironov. According to the latter, male literacy among peasants varied between one and twelve percent towards the end of the eighteenth century. One-fifth to one quarter of the town dwellers were literate while more than three-quarters of the clergy knew how to read and write. The highest rate of literacy in eighteenth century Russia was found among male representatives of the nobility: eighty-four to eighty-seven percent.

A rare exception to the scarcity of information about the 1740s, again reported by Mironov, is the data comprising 4,306 observations of soldiers recruited to the army between the years 1732 and 1756.[80] His results suggest a literacy rate among recruits of around 0.5%.

Among officers, the situation was different. A small study conducted by the author of the present investigation on material from two regiments, the Kozlovskii Garrison Infantry Regiment and the Pavlovskii Garrison Infantry Regiment, shows that in 1740, the majority of commissioned officers knew how to read and write. The information was deemed important enough to deserve its own column in the mustering rolls: "грамоте писать умеетъ или кто не умеетъ" (knows how to write or not). Out of a total of six lieutenants enrolled in the Pavlovskii Regiment, two individuals—Zakharei Alymov and Iakov Iviakov—are reported as being illiterate. Similarly, from a total of seven ensigns, one Stepan Chepelëv did not know how to read or write. In all three cases, this

77 Marker, "Literacy and Literacy Texts in Muscovy," 75.

78 Ibid., 89.

79 B. N. Mironov, "The Development of Literacy in Russia and the USSR from the Tenth to the Twentieth Centuries," *History of Education Quarterly* 2 (1991): 233; idem, "Uchënost'."

80 Idem, *The Standard of Living and Revolutions in Russia, 1700–1917* (London: Routledge, 2012), 60.

was grounds for denial of promotion. This, in turn, was noted in a separate column: "За неумениемъ грамоте удостоит невозможно" (promotion denied due to illiteracy).[81] The three men were older than their colleagues, and they had all been in the service from twenty five to thirty years, Iviakov since 1707.

In comparing the findings by Marker and Mironov, it is reasonable to assume that the overall literacy rates for adult males in the 1740s lay somewhere slightly below five percent.

As illustrated above, Marker differentiates between rudimentary and intermediate literacy. This differentiation is important since there is an obvious difference of ability between being able to sign your name and being able to decode and/or produce structurally complicated texts. There are well-founded reasons to suggest that, in order to participate in a literate culture, one must master intermediate literacy. This immediately raises a new question: How large was the "reading public" in the 1740s? Calculations suggest that the reading public in Russia a century later, in the middle of the nineteenth century, comprised between 600,000 and 1 million people, which means between 1% and 1.5% of the population.[82] What situation was in the 1740s, we cannot say with certainty. However, given the calculated literacy rates, it is not unreasonable to imagine that the figure was considerably lower.

What about women and literacy? Mironov concludes that female literacy rates were probably significantly lower than those reported for males, but they cannot be determined due to lack of data.[83] His conclusion is supported by statistics from the second half of the nineteenth century.[84] Research on female literacy conducted after Mironov's investigation provides some insights. Calculations by Michelle Marrese suggest that literacy among provincial noblewomen varied between four and twenty-six percent at the middle of the eighteenth century, that is, a mere fraction of the percentage reported for males of this social stratum.[85] Is this the whole story? Maybe not. A different view on the issue of literacy is offered by Aleksandra Pletnёva and Aleksandr Kravetskii. In their investigation of literacy in Church Slavic in the nineteenth and twentieth centuries, they find that

81 *1740 god genvaria 1 dnia Pavlovskago garnizonnogo pekhotnogo polku Imennoi spisok" shtap" i ob̃er" afitserom"* […], Central State Historical Archives of Ukraine (TsDIAK Ukraïny), f. 1812, op. 1, no. 3.
82 Mironov, *Sotsial'naia istoriia*, vol. 1, 265.
83 Idem, "The Development of Literacy in Russia," 234.
84 Bogdanov, *Gramotnost'*.
85 M. L. Marrese, *A Woman's Kingdom: Noblewomen and the Control of Property in Russia, 1700–1861* (Ithaca: Cornell University Press, 2002), 213–215.

существенная часть населения страны, в первую очередь крестьяне, могли читать церковнославянские тексты, но не владели русским литературным языком. Уровень церковнославянской грамотности в процентном отношении был более высоким, чем уровень русской грамотности. Однако в господствующей культурной парадигме умение читать по-славянски рассматривалось не как элемент образованности, а как часть «нецивилизованной», «народной» культуры.[86]

Since the claims made by Kravetskii and Pletnëva apply to a much later period—the twentieth century—they lack immediate relevance for the eighteenth century. They do, however, undeniably offer food for thought. The existing literature supports the idea that the reading and writing skills taught by a minor church official would be in Church Slavic, and thus a considerable portion of the population who were peasants, could read Church Slavic but not Russian. So, questions to consider are: how should literacy in eighteenth-century Russia be classified? Were there different kinds of literacy?

Throughout the eighteenth century people learned to read using the Cyrillic alphabet and reading by rote (по складам). The civil alphabet was "supplementary and only learned by small social groups," such as those who came into contact with printed, secular texts.[87] In all likelihood, therefore, literacy in the civil script was limited during the first half of the eighteenth century.

Since, as was seen above, Russia did not possess a unified educational system during the 1740s, it is likely that much literacy training took place in informal circumstances, such as in people's homes.[88] Since literacy training was not

86 A. G. Kravetskii and A. A. Pletnëva, *Istoriia tserkovnoslavianskogo iazyka v Rossii: konets XIX–XX vv.* (Moscow: Iazyki russkoi kul'tury, 2001), 41 (… a considerable portion of the country's population, predominantly peasants, were able to read Church Slavic texts but did not master the Russian literary language. The level of literacy in Church Slavic was percentually higher than literacy in Russian. However, in the predominant cultural paradigm, the ability to read in Slavic was viewed not as an element of education, but as a part of an "uncivilized," "popular" culture). Cf. also A. A. Pletnëva, "K kharakteristike iazykovoi situatsii v Rossii XVIII–XIX vv.," *Russkii iazyk v nauchnom osveshchenii* 2 (12) (2006): 213–229.

87 Zhivov, *Language and Culture*, 11; cf. also Max J. Okenfuss, *The Discovery of Childhood in Russia: the Evidence of the Slavic Primer* (Newtonville, MA: Oriental Research Partners, 1980); B. A. Uspenskii, "Starinnaia sistema chteniia po skladam (glava iz istorii russkoi gramoty)," in his *Izbrannye trudy*, vol. 3 (Moscow: Iazyki russkoi kul'tury, 1997), 246–288.

88 Harvey J. Graff, "Introduction to Historical Studies of Literacy," in *Understanding Literacy in Its Historical Contexts: Socio-Cultural History and the Legacy of Egil Johansson*, ed. H. Graff, A. Mackinnon, B. Sandin, and I. Winchester (Lund: Nordic Academic Press, 2009), 16.

centrally organized, there is a high likelihood that it varied in content and depth. Any general conclusions concerning literacy in mid-eighteenth-century Russia must therefore be circumspect.

A serious problem is that so much of the research is based on signatures. Mironov recognizes the risks associated with overestimations of literacy data based exclusively on signatures.[89] He sees three principal drawbacks: the number of signatures is low; signatures do not provide stable and exact data on the level of literacy; and the use of the signature method tends to raise the level of literacy, since there was a tendency to invite literate people as signatories when possible. His work clearly demonstrates that no single type of source can provide trustworthy data about the literacy situation in eighteenth-century Russia. Instead, a clear picture may be found using a combination of data from multiple sources. This is the case also in other countries, where scholars have gathered information from a variety of sources in order to assess literacy rates: in Sweden it has been church registers; in France, marriage and military records; in Britain, marriage and census records; and in North America, manuscript census records.[90]

3.3 Language Management

Above, in section 1.2, the term *language management* was introduced, and a brief comparison was made of its uses by different scholars. This term was chosen for the present investigation to describe observable efforts to control and influence language. The opposite of this was termed *discourse, simple* or *discourse-based management*, that is, implicit language management activities.

Language management takes place today all around us and we can safely assume that the same was true during the 1740s. People influence each other's language within the family, the community, and in interactions with people from the outside. We must also assume that language management, especially of the discourse-based variety, took place in all languages spoken across the Russian Empire during the eighteenth century. For the purposes of the present investigation, however, the latter topic must be left unaddressed. The evidence of discourse-based management when speaking of Russia in the 1740s, is, if not irretrievably lost, then scant to the point of near-nonexistence. In other words, we must focus on traces of language management that are observable in texts from the examined period.

---

89 Mironov, "Uchënost'."
90 Graff, "Introduction," 15.

The present investigation is concerned with Russian. While maintaining a strictly Russian-centric perspective, however, one other culturally important language deserves mentioning: Church Slavic. Texts in Church Slavic were being composed in Russia during the 1740s, enjoyed prestige in the society of the period, and are preserved in great numbers.[91] Foremost among them is the Bible. The Russian state, through the offices of the Holy Synod, carried out a revision of the Bible during the 1740s, a task of great relevance to many people, and with an effect that lasts up to the present day. The revision, which resulted in a "reasonably accurate rendering of the Septuagint text," is known in Russian as the *Елизаветинское издание Библии* and in English as the *Elizabethan Bible*.[92] The history of Church Slavic in eighteenth-century Russia is, however, the subject of an entirely different investigation.

3.3.1 Examining Language Management in Handwritten Documents from the 1740s

Texts were produced in every corner of the Russian Empire and language produced in the provinces developed slightly differently compared to the center. One explanation of this is that old administrative structures remained longer in the provinces, continuing to influence administrative usage. Oleg V. Nikitin finds that

> Даже во второй половине XVIII столетия, когда система государственного судебного производства функционировала в ее гражданских формах самостоятельно, монастырь оставался одним из главных «действующих лиц», поддерживающих старые приказные традиции в глубинке.[93]

---

91 A. A. Guseva, *Svod russkikh knig kirillovskoi pechati XVIII veka tipografii Moskvy i Sankt-Peterburga i universal'naia metodika ikh identifikatsii* (Moscow: Indrik, 2010).

92 Francis J. Thomson, "The Three Slavonic Translations of the Greek Catena in Job. With an Appendix on the Author of the First Prologue to the First Translation: Polychronius or Photius?," in *The Bible in Slavic Tradition*, ed. A. Kulik, C. M. MacRobert, S. Nikolova, M. Taube, and C. M. Vakareliyska (Leiden: Brill, 2016), 157.

93 Nikitin, *Delovaia pis'mennost'*, 177 (Even in the second half of the eighteenth century, when the state judicial system functioned independently in its secular forms, the monastery remained one of the principal "actors," supporting the old administrative [*prikaz*—T.R.] traditions in remote places).

Nikolai Chugaev's investigation of administrative documents, stemming from the early 1740s, from the Prikam'e region of the western Urals, support Nikitin's conclusions. Chugaev finds that the texts in his investigation display a greater number of archaisms than texts produced in the center.[94]

One way of studying the effects of language management in eighteenth-century Russia is thus to examine texts from a certain period, looking for features of the language (in vocabulary, morphology, syntax, formulas, and so forth), known from existing research to be typical. Another way is to observe how closely the language in a document adheres to codified norms. As far as the 1740s are concerned, this presents considerable difficulties due to the fact that the number of such codified norms was very small indeed. While grammars of Church Slavic and Russian had been published in far away places, such as England, no normative grammar was widely available for Russian domestic use.[95] The discussion of доломоносовские (pre-Lomonosov) grammars ran high in the 1970s–1990s (for some of the most important contributions, cf. above, section 1.4). In short, the only reasonably contemporary printed grammar of Russian—written in German—was the one found in Ehrenreich Weismann's German-Latin-Russian dictionary from 1731.[96] The *Anfangs-Gründe*, as the grammar is known, was compiled by the then student at the Academy University, Vasilii Evdokimovich Adodurov, apparently from a variety of sources.[97] Other codified norms, concerning the use of certain characters in print, had been issued by the Academy of Sciences.[98]

---

94 Chugaev, "Stolp prikhodnoi denezhnoi kazny," 20.

95 Boris O. Unbegaun, ed., *Henrici Wilhelmi Ludolfi Grammatica Russica, Oxonii A. D. MDCXCVI* (Oxford: Oxford University Press, 1959); Anders Sjöberg, Ľubomir Ďurovič, and Ulla Birgegård, eds., *Dolomonosovskii period russkogo literaturnogo iazyka / The Pre-Lomonosov Period of the Russian Literary Language* (Stockholm: Kungl. Vitterhets-, historie- och antikvitetsakademien, 1992).

96 E. Weissmann, *Teutsch-lateinisch- und russisches Lexicon, samt denen Anfangs-Gründen der russischen Sprache / Nemetsko-latinskii i russkii leksikon kupno s pervymi nachalami ruskago iazyka* (St. Petersburg: Imperatorskaia akademiia nauk, 1731). A facsimile edition is available in Filippov, Kareva, and Volkov, *Vasilii Evdokimovich Adodurov*, 45–90.

97 Helmut Keipert and Andrea Huterer, eds., *Compendium Grammaticae Russicae (1731). Die erste Akademie-Grammatik der russischen Sprache* (Munich: Verlag der Bayerischen Akademie der Wissenschaften, 2002), 122; A. A. Kostin, "Akribiia i ameleia, ili Gde byt' dobroi zemle? (grammatika V. E. Adodurova v kontekste i bez)," *Slověne* 1 (2016): 263–299.

98 V. A. Istrin, *1100 let slavianskoi azbuki*, 3rd ed., ed. L. P. Zhukovskaia (Moscow: LKI, 2010), 161.

3.3.2 The Imperial Academy of Sciences, a Language Management Agency

In the modern world, many countries have official or semi-official language management agencies, known variously as academies, boards, councils, or commissions. Such language agencies began appearing in Europe between the sixteenth and eighteenth centuries: the Accademia della Crusca in Florence, Italy, in 1583, the Académie française in Paris, France, in 1635, and the Real Academia Española in Madrid, Spain, in 1713.[99] Russia received its own national language academy in 1783 through the establishment of the Императорская российская академия (Imperial Russian Academy) headed by Princess Ekaterina Vorontsova-Dashkova.[100] Thus, strictly speaking, Russia did not have its own language academy during the 1740s. However, this did not mean that centrally organized language management activities did not take place.

The Императорская академия наук (Imperial Academy of Sciences) was founded by Peter the Great on January 22, 1724. It consisted of three sections, known as "classes": (1) a mathematical class including theoretical mathematics, astronomy, geography, navigation, and mechanics; (2) a physics class that included theoretical and experimental physics, anatomy, chemistry, and botany; (3) a humanities class with three departments (rhetoric and antiquities, ancient and modern history and law, and politics and ethics).[101] In addition, a fourth, administrative branch with a secretary and a librarian is sometimes also referred to as a "class."[102] None of these was formally charged with the task of managing the Russian language, however. The St. Petersburg academy was intended to be similar to learned institutions abroad:

> И понеже сіе учрежденіе такой академіи, которая въ Париже обрѣтается, подобна есть (кромѣ сего различія и авантажа, что сія академія и то чинитъ, которое универзитету или

---

99 Spolsky, *Language Management*, 235. Spolsky reports that the Accademia della Crusca was founded in 1584. The Accademia itself gives 1583 as "the year of its stable constitution" (*anno della sua stabile costituzione*), see its website, accessed May 17, 2021, https://accademiadellacrusca.it/it/contenuti/storia/6981

100 B. L. Modzalevskii, *Spisok chlenov Imperatorskoi Akademii Nauk 1725–1907* (St. Petersburg: Imperatorskaia akademiia nauk, 1908), 315; Polnoe sobranie zakonov Rossiiskoi Imperii, no. 15839, accessed May 13, 2021, http://nlr.ru/e-res/law_r/search.php.

101 Ludmilla Schulze, "The Russification of the St. Petersburg Academy of Sciences and Arts in the Eighteenth Century," *The British Journal for the History of Science* 3 (1985): 307.

102 Sukhomlinov, *Materialy*, vol. 1, 14–22; Iu. Kh. Kopelevich, *Osnovanie Peterburgskoi akademii nauk* (Leningrad: Nauka, 1977); Cracraft, *The Petrine Revolution*, 240–255.

коллегіи чинитъ надлежитъ), того для, я надеюсь, что сіе зданіе удобнѣйше академіею названо быть имѣетъ.[103]

The Paris academy to which reference is made in the quotation was in all likelihood the *Académie royale des sciences*. The tsar had paid a visit to this institution in 1717.[104] He may also have been familiar with another French academy—the *Académie française*—then and now responsible for the cultivation of the French language.[105]

The newly established St. Petersburg academy was not given a role similar to that of the *Académie française*, but its founders did not ignore the issue of language. They did realize the importance of having books translated into Russian:

И понеже россійскому народу не токмо въ великую пользу, но и во славу служить будетъ, когда такія книги на россійскомъ языкѣ печатаны будутъ, того ради надлежитъ при каждомъ классѣ академическомъ одного переводчика, и при секретарѣ—одного жъ, и тако во всѣхъ четырехъ классахъ, опредѣлить.[106]

During the first decade of its existence, the St. Petersburg academy was staffed by non-Russians. The academy's first president, Laurentius Blumentrost (1692–1755), whose father had been physician to Tsar Aleksei Mikhailovich, was the exception. Despite his German-sounding name he was born in Russia, while the other academicians had been invited to Russia for the specific purpose of working in the new institution.[107]

---

103 Sukhomlinov, *Materialy*, vol. 1, 16 (Since this institution is to be an academy like that found in Paris [except for this difference and *avantazh*, that this academy is also to do what is appropriate to a university or college], therefore I hope that this institution would most conveniently be called an academy). The English translation is quoted from Cracraft, *The Petrine Revolution*, 246–247.

104 Schulze, "The Russification," 309–310.

105 *Académie française, Statuts et règlements*, 1995, 19, accessed May 13, 2021, http://www.academie-francaise.fr /sites/academie-francaise.fr/files/statuts_af_0.pdf.

106 Sukhomlinov, *Materialy*, vol. 1, 19 (And since it will be not only to a great benefit, but also to the glory of the Russian people when such books [courses written by the individual members of the academy, each in his particular subject—T.R.] are printed in the Russian language, therefore one translator shall be appointed in each of the three academic classes, and one also with the secretary, thus in all four classes).

107 Zhivov, *Istoriia*, 999.

Since, during the first decade of the academy's existence, native Russians took little part in its activities, business was conducted in Latin, German, and French. Some evidence even shows that the foreign members were reluctant to recognize the real or potential worth of Russian as an academic language.[108]

For language management in Russia during the first half of the eighteenth century, one of the academy's presidents—or commander-in-chief, as he was called—stands out: Baron Johann Albrecht von Korff (1697–1766). Born in Courland and of German ethnicity, Korff was educated in Germany and returned to the Russian Empire after graduating from the university of Jena in Thuringia "съ блѣстящимъ успѣхомъ" (with brilliant success). In 1728, he was employed as a chamber-page in the service of the future Empress Anna Ioannovna.[109] His great-nephew, and biographer, describes Korff as being endowed with "glänzende Geistesgaben" (brilliant intellectual gifts).[110]

Hermann Carl von Keyserlingk (1695/96–1764), Korff's predecessor as head of the academy, had spent most of his tenure abroad on diplomatic missions.[111] So, when Korff was appointed head of the St. Petersburg academy, some members welcomed the appointment.[112]

The public was notified of Korff's promotion through the *Sanktpeterburgskie vedomosti*:

> 18 дня сего мѣсяца изволила Ея Iмператорское Величество
> по всевысочаишеи своеи милости и особливому попеченїю
> о здѣшнеи Iмператорскои Академїи Наукъ управленїе
> оныя своему дѣиствительному Каммергеру Фонъ Корфу
> всемилостивѣише поручить, и при томъ ему обыкновенное
> Презїдентское жалованїе по 3000 рублеи въ годъ опредѣлить.
> Отъ сеи перемѣны можно заключать, что высочаишее
> намѣренїе Ея Iмператорскаго Величества, то есть чтобъ

---

108 Christopher D. Buck, "The Russian Language Question in the Imperial Academy of Sciences, 1724–1770," in *Aspects of the Slavic Language Question*, vol. 2, ed. R. Picchio and H. Goldblatt (New Haven: Yale Concilium on International and Area Studies, 1984), 192.

109 "Baron Iogann Albert Korf, 1697–1766," in *Recueil des actes de la séance publique de l'Académie Impériale des sciences de Saint-Pétersbourg* (St. Petersburg: Eggers, 1847), 76–77.

110 E. G. von Derschau, "Nekrolog: Johann Albrecht Freyherr von Korff," *Beylage zur Allgemeinen deutschen Zeitung für Rußland* 8 (1826), accessed May 13, 2021, http://dspace.ut.ee/handle/10062/44439.

111 "Baron Iogann Albert Korf, 1697–1766," 78.

112 Pekarskii, *Istoriia*, vol. 2, 520; E. S. Kuliabko, "Pervye prezidenty," *Vestnik AN SSSR* 2 (1974): 144–151.

Академія Наукъ въ возможное доброе состояніе приведена была, совершенно исполнится.[113]

From the very beginning of his term in office, Korff threw himself into his work with great energy and attention to detail:

Онъ обращалъ вниманіе даже на мелочныя подробности и давалъ приказанія: какъ вести протоколъ; какъ содержать въ порядкѣ архивъ; какъ подписывать статьи, снимать копіи и пр. Вообще онъ обходился съ академиками, какъ начальникъ съ подчиненными.[114]

Despite his great talent, Korff does not seem to have communicated officially in Russian. In a letter to the academy librarian, Johann Daniel Schumacher, dated January 9, 1735, Korff orders V. E. Adodurov to translate a text from Russian into German.[115] The letter suggests that Korff's command of Russian was insignificant. His handwriting is very untidy, yet a detailed analysis shows that he was not familiar with the spelling of the translator's name. Instead he renders Adodurov's name as ⟨Atjadurf⟩. Pekarskii, in his history of the Academy of Sciences, reports that Korff did not know Russian.[116]

The first native Russian scholar employed by the academy was the already mentioned V. E. Adodurov who served as adjunct professor of mathematics from 1733.[117] The first senior appointments of ethnic Russians were V. K. Trediakovskii

---

113 *Sanktpeterburgskie vedomosti*, September 23, 1734, accessed May 18, 2021, https://www.vedomosti1728.ru/pdf.cgi?r=99&key_pdf=XiV9nHpek5rw25MW (On the 18th day of this month, Her Imperial Majesty, by her supreme grace and special care for the Imperial Academy of Sciences in this city, condescended to bestow its leadership upon Her High Chamberlain von Korff, and to fix for him the usual Presidential salary at 3.000 roubles annually. From this change one may conclude that the supreme intention of Her Imperial Majesty will be fulfilled, that is, to improve the condition of the Academy of Sciences as much as possible).

114 Pekarskii, *Istoriia*, vol. 1, 522 (He paid attention even to petty details and gave orders: how to keep a protocol, how to keep the archive in order, how to sign articles, make copies etc. On the whole, he treated the academicians like a boss treats his subordinates).

115 SPbFARAN, F. 121, op. 2, no. 84.

116 Pekarskii, *Istoriia*, vol. 2, 68.

117 Schulze, "The Russification," 311, footnote 28. Adodurov is sometimes referred to as "the first Russian scholar to get an academic degree," S. S. Volkov, "V. E. Adodurov: neskol'ko dopolnitel'nykh zamechanii k traditsionnoi biografii," in *Vasilii Evdokimovich Adodurov: "Anfangs-Gründe der Rußischen Sprache" ili "Pervye osnovaniia rossiiskogo iazyka". Formirovanie russkoi akademicheskoi grammaticheskoi traditsii*, ed. K. A. Filippov, N. V. Kareva, and S. S. Volkov (St. Petersburg: Nauka and Nestor-Istoriia, 2014), 17, footnote 1; In the sources, Adodurov's surname is somtimes spelt Adadurov or even Ododurov, cf. O. V. Nikitin,

(1703–1768), appointed professor of Latin and Russian Eloquence, and M. V. Lomonosov (1711–1765), professor of Chemistry, both in 1745.[118] Whereas Lomonosov is undoubtedly better known to posterity than Trediakovskii, the latter was more prominent during the 1730s and 1740s. Lomonosov's star rose slightly later, in 1745, after he received his professorship, and following his appointment as editor of the newspaper *Sanktpeterburgskie vedomosti* in 1748 (cf. below, section 4.2.2). Trediakovskii had spent four years in the Netherlands and France during the late 1720s and returned to Russia in 1730.[119] Soon upon arrival in his country of origin, Trediakovskii published a translation of Abbé Tallemant's *Voyages de l'isle d'amour* (Voyage to the Isle of Love).[120] To the translation, Trediakovskii attached a preface in which he expressed his views on the Russian language. The main feature of this pioneering work is its focus on the *usus loquendi* and its denial of Church Slavicisms.[121] It has been proposed that the young Trediakovskii's thinking was influenced by the ideas of the French pedagogue and historian Charles Rollin (1661–1741), who stated that French was equal to the ancient languages.[122]

The preface to the *Voyage to the Isle of Love* has secured Trediakovskii's place in the history of the Russian language. It has also led to a widely entertained view that Trediakovskii held a leading position among the academy's translators. This idea is rejected in recent work by E. G. Pivovarov who presents evidence suggesting that the other translators were, in fact, no less prominent.[123] Trediakovskii's work on the Russian language has been researched in great detail by B. A. Uspenskii.[124]

In addition to the preface mentioned above, a few other documents involving Trediakovskii are important in the context of Russian language management: first

---

"Vasilii Evdokimovich Adodurov i ego rol' v istorii russkoi lingvisticheskoi traditsii XVIII veka: K 300-letiiu so dnia rozhdeniia," Slovo, accessed September 12, 2021, https://www.portal-slovo.ru/philology/41666.php.

118 Reyfman, *Vasilii Trediakovsky*, 28; Steven A Usitalo, *The Invention of Mikhail Lomonosov: A Russian National Myth* (Boston: Academic Studies Press, 2013), 103.

119 Reyfman, *Trediakovskii*, 24–26.

120 V. K. Tred'iakovskii, "Ezda v ostrov liubvi," in *Sochineniia Tred'iakovskogo*, ed. A. Smirdin, vol. 3 (St. Petersburg: Imperatorskaia akademiia nauk, 1849), 649–650; Zhivov, *Language and Culture*, 125.

121 Uspenskii, *Vokrug Trediakovskogo*, 90.

122 I. Z. Serman, "Trediakovskii i prosvetitel'stvo (1730-e gody)," in *XVIII vek*, vol. 5, ed. P. N. Berkov (Moscow and Leningrad: AN USSSR, 1962), 212; "Charles Rollin (1661–1741)," Bibliothèque Nationale de France, accessed May 17, 2021, https://data.bnf.fr/en/12731899/charles_rollin/.

123 Pivovarov, "K istorii sozdaniia Rossiiskogo sobraniia," 10.

124 Uspenskii, *Vokrug Trediakovskogo*.

among these is his employment contract with the Academy of Sciences from 1733, second, his inaugural speech at the Russian Conference in 1735 (cf. below, section 3.3.4), and third, his treatise on orthography from 1748.[125] By the time of the latter, Trediakovskii had radically changed his views on language, compared with the opinions expressed in the preface. He was now in favor of Church Slavic.[126]

Trediakovskii's employment contract was drawn up in French and signed by Hermann Keyserling, then President of the Imperial Academy of Sciences, on October 14, 1733. The contract clearly demonstrates that he was employed in order to carry out tasks that fell within the realm of language management:

1. Le dit Trediakoffski s'oblige de faire tout son possible pour l'interêt de Sa Majesté Impériale, et l'honneur de l'académie.
2. De perfectioner la langue russienne, soit par la prose, ou par les vers.
3. D'y donner des leçons, en cas qu'on le demandera.
4. D'achever la grammaire qu'il a commencée, et travailler conjointement avec d'autres sur le dictionnaire russien.
5. De traduire du françois et du latin en russe, tout ce qu'on lui en donnera.

Pekarskii located a Russian translation, in Trediakovskii's own handwriting:

1. Помянутой Тредіаковскій соѡбяз8ется чинить, по всей своей возможности, все то, въ чемъ состоитъ інтересъ Ея Імператорскаго Величества, и честь Академіи.
2. Вычищать язык р8ской пишучи какъ стіхами, такъ и не стіхами.
3. Давать лекціи, ежели от него потребовано будетъ.
4. Соѡкончить Грамматік8, котсоѡр8ю онъ началъ, и тр8диться совокупно съ прочіми надъ Дікціонаріемъ р8скимъ.
5. Переводить съ французскаго на р8ской языкъ все что ем8 дастся.[127]

---

125 Sukhomlinov, *Materialy*, vol. 2, 392–393; A. Kunik, *Sbornik materialov dlia istorii Imperatorskoi akademii nauk v XVIII veke*, vol. 1 (St. Petersburg: Imperatorskaia akademiia nauk, 1865), 7–16; V. K. Trediakovskii, *Razgovor mezhdu chuzhestrannym chelovekom i rossiiskim ob orfografii starinnoi i novoi i o vsëm chto prinadlezhit k sei materii* (St. Petersburg: Imperatorskaia akademiia nauk, 1748).

126 B. A.Uspenskii, *Vokrug Trediakovskogo*, chapter "Iazykovaia programma pozdnego Treiakovskogo: Trediakovskii i Shishkov," 170–171.

127 Pekarskii, *Istoriia*, vol. 2, 43 (1. The said Trediakovskii undertakes to do everything in his might for the benefit of Her Imperial Majesty, and the honor of the academy; 2. To perfect

Trediakovskii was important as an initiator of language management activities, and as a translator. In concrete terms, however, the reforms proposed by him had little or no long-term effect, as has been concluded by scholars such as Issatschenko.[128]

3.3.3 A New Function: The Founding of the Russian Conference

In his enumeration of language management agencies, Bernard Spolsky notes the importance of terminology committees.[129] In modern times, terminology committees deal with the ideological and practical elaboration of new terminologies in a language, often as parts of a language academy. The work of such committees results from the need of language management due to a changing linguistic reality and is often carried out quietly in the background, Spolsky explains. At the Imperial Academy of Sciences, its translators' assembly, the Российское собрание (Russian Conference) can, as we shall see, be said to at least partly have fulfilled the role of a terminology committee.

With no formal agency previously in existence, the prevalent image of language management in eighteenth-century Russia is that the academy translators assumed this "civilizatory task," as V. M. Zhivov has referred to it.[130] During the first two decades of its existence, the academy employed a group of about ten translators. The translators seem to have been a close-knit group of people who knew each other well: "будущие сотрудники имели большой опыт совместной деятельности." V. K. Trediakovskii and V. E. Adodurov, allegedly, even shared the same living quarters during the early 1730s.[131]

In 1727–1755, the Academy of Sciences press printed over three quarters of all books that came from secular printing houses.[132] In view of this near monopoly, the academy was the main channel by which linguistic norms could influence

---

the Russian language, either by prose or by verse; 3. To teach there, if required; 4. To complete the grammar he started, and work jointly with others on the Russian dictionary; 5. To translate from French and Latin into Russian, whatever he is given).

128 A. V. Issatschenko, "Russian," in *The Slavic Literary Languages*, ed. A. M. Schenker and E. Stankiewicz (New Haven: Yale Concilium on International and Area Studies, 1980), 132.

129 Spolsky, *Language Management*, 241.

130 Zhivov, *Ocherki*, 545.

131 E. G. Pivovarov, "Perevodchiki Akademii nauk v period ee stanovleniia," *Sotsiologiia nauki i tekhnologii* 4 (2015): 40–51; idem, "K istorii sozdaniia Rossiiskogo sobraniia," 7–20 (The future coworkers had long experience of working together).

132 Marker, *Publishing, Printing*, 45.

society.[133] The instruments used were translated books, which introduced new to the Russian, and the *Primechaniia*, which functioned as a kind of popular science journal-cum-reference dictionary for the readers of *Sanktpeterburgskie vedomosti*, explaining new and foreign terms (cf. below, section 4.2.2).

The Russian Conference was established on March 14, 1735, with the purpose of improving the Russian language.[134] The order reads:

> По указу Ея И. В. въ академіи наукъ обрѣтающій главный командиръ, дѣйствительный камергеръ баронъ фонъ Корфъ, приказалъ: Академіи наукъ переводчикамъ сходиться въ академію два раза въ недѣлю, а именно: въ среду и въ субботу, поутру и послѣ обѣда, и имѣть между собою конференцію, снося и прочитывая всё, кто что перевелъ, и имѣть тщаніе въ исправленіи россійскаго языка въ случающихся переводахъ. Чего ради въ оныхъ конференціяхъ присутствовать секретарю Тредіаковскому, адъюнкту Адодурову и ректору нѣмецкаго класса Швановичу; а о тѣхъ конференціяхъ журналъ содержать Тоуберту, и всегда въ понедѣльники оный предлагать его превосходительству господину камергеру. Korff.[135]

---

133 Zhivov, *Istoriia*, 999–1000.

134 P. P. Pekarskii, "Adodurov, Vasilii Evdokimovich, ad"iunkt matematicheskikh nauk," in *Vasilii Evdokimovich Adodurov: "Anfangs-Gründe der Rußischen Sprache" ili "Pervye osnovaniia rossiiskogo iazyka". Formirovanie russkoi akademicheskoi grammaticheskoi traditsii*, ed. K. A. Filippov, N. V. Kareva, and S. S. Volkov (St. Petersburg: Nauka and Nestor-Istoriia, 2014), 211; Pivovarov, "K istorii sozdaniia Rossiiskogo sobraniia"; Moskovkin, *Iazykovoe obrazovanie*, 10.

135 Sukhomlinov, *Materialy*, vol. 2, 633 (By orders from Her Imperial Majesty, the Commander-in-chief High Chamberlain Baron von Korff, present in the academy, ordered: The academy translators shall come together at the academy twice a week, namely: on Wednesdays and Saturdays, in the morning and after lunch, and hold a conference, bringing together and reading everything that each has translated, and they shall take care to ensure the accuracy of the Russian language in the translations that come before them. For this reason, present at these conferences shall be Secretary Trediakovskii, Adjunct Adodurov, and the director of the German class, Schwanwitz; and Taubert shall keep a journal of the proceedings, and always present this on Mondays to His Excellency the Chamberlain. Korff).

And a couple of months later, Korff wrote to the Imperial Cabinet:

> Въ Академіи наукъ воспріято сіе попеченіе, чтобы такія
> книги, которыя здѣшнему народу пользу принести могутъ, въ
> печать произведены были. ... Полѣзные оные плоды, которые
> я отъ учрежденнаго россійскаго собранія въ исправленіи и
> приведеніи въ совершенство природнаго здѣшнаго языка
> себѣ представляю, произведутъ первый свой корень въ
> обучающемся при здѣшней гимназіи юношествѣ, а отъ онаго
> потомъ и во всемъ народѣ распространится.[136]

Uspenskii finds that the initiative for the Russian Conference "undoubtedly" belonged to Trediakovskii.[137] However, as expected, the documents clearly state that the order came from Korff. This fact is recognized by Pivovarov.[138]

At the inauguration ceremony, Trediakovskii delivered a speech laying out the plans for the conference's future activities.[139] The speech has been analyzed by generations of scholars, most recently by Pivovarov who also points to his predecessors.[140] In the speech, which is written in a rich panegyric style, Trediakovskii extols the virtues of Peter the Great, Empress Anna Ioannovna, and Baron von Korff. He underscores the importance of following Latin, French, and German authors in order to create a Russian rhetoric.[141] He also points to the imperial ministers, bishops, the court, and the nobility as linguistic role models.

As positive examples, Trediakovskii refers to the Florentine Accademia della Crusca and to the Académie française. Less often discussed is his reference to the Deutsche Gesellschaft (German Association) in Leipzig:

> Не возможно, чаю, сперва казалось Лейпцигскому Со-
> обществу подражать толь благоуспѣшно вышереченнымъ

136 Quoted from Pekarskii, *Istoriia*, vol. 1, 524 (German original in Russian translation by Adodurov) (In the Academy of Sciences care is taken that such books should be produced in print as can be of use to the people of this country. ... Those useful fruits of correction and perfection of the natural local language, which I envisage as a result of the established Russian Conference, will strike their first root among the young people that are being trained at the local school, and from there it will also spread in the entire people).
137 Uspenskii, *Vokrug Trediakovskogo*, 528.
138 Pivovarov, "K istorii sozdaniia Rossiiskogo sobraniia," 8.
139 Kunik, *Sbornik materialov*, 7–16.
140 Pivovarov, "K istorii sozdaniia Rossiiskogo sobraniia," 9.
141 Uspenskii, *Vokrug Trediakovskogo*, 126.

онымъ Академіямъ, коль тѣ начавши окончали щастливо; подражаетъ, и подражала благополучно.[142]

This reference may indicate that, perhaps, the credit for having come up with the idea for the Russian Conference ought to belong to Trediakovskii and Korff collectively. They were both familiar with linguistic associations. Korff had received his education in Germany at a time when *Sprachgesellschaften* (linguistic associations) were very active in Northern Germany and along the Baltic coast. One, the Teutsche Gesellschaft, had been formed in Korff's own university town of Jena in 1728. There was even such an association in St. Petersburg from 1748.[143]

3.3.4 The Demise of the Russian Conference

Work in the Russian Conference continued throughout Korff's presidency, but it did not always run smoothly. Thus, in October of 1739, "In dato wurde resolviret, dass eine ordre an den secretair Tredjakoffsky, Wolschkoff, adjunctus Adoduroff und Taubert solle ausgefertigt werden, dass sie früher in der russischen conferentz sich einfinden und fleissiger arbeiten sollen."[144]

Korff's term in office ended abruptly in the spring of 1740, when he was dispatched as envoy to Denmark. The reason for this turn of events is said to have been that the Regent, the mighty Ernst Johann von Bühren (Biron), was looking for a pretext for removing Korff from court. A year later, following Biron's fall from power, Korff's successor, Brevern, was also dismissed, having spent very little time at the organization that he had been appointed to lead.[145] Brevern lost his position for political reasons.[146] Following Brevern's departure, the academy

---

142 Quotation follows Zhivov, *Iazyk i kul'tura*, 172 (In the beginning, it must have seemed impossible for the Leipzig association, I think, to imitate these aforementioned academies so successfully, since they ended up so lucky; it imitates, and it has imitated succesfully).

143 Dieter Cherubim and Ariane Walsdorf, "Die Tradition der Sprachgesellschaften: Leibniz—Schottelius—Gottsched," in *Sprachkritik als Aufklärung: Die Deutsche Gesellschaft in Göttingen im 18. Jahrhundert*, 2nd ed., ed. E. Mittler (Göttingen: Niedersächsische Staats-und Universitätsbibliothek, 2005), 169, accessed May 19, 2021, https://www.yumpu.com/de/document/read/5068142/sprachgesellschaften-im-18-jahrhundert.

144 Sukhomlinov, *Materialy*, vol. 4, 219 (On this day it was decided that an order should be made out to the secretaries Trediakovskii, Volchkov, Adjunct Adodurov, and Taubert, so that they show up earlier at the Russian Conference and work more diligently).

145 "Karl fon Brevern," Rossiiskaia akademiia nauk, accessed September 25, 2021, http://www.ras.ru/presidents/9a3d4acd-5c39-4fc9-a5b2-a9e8f57ecf96.aspx.

146 "Prezidenty Rossiiskoi akademii nauk za vsiu istoriiu," Rossiiskaia akademiia nauk, accessed April 9, 2021. http://www.ras.ru/about/president/allpresidents.aspx.

found itself without a president for five years, until the appointment of Count Razumovskii in 1746.[147]

At that point, the situation in the academy became critical. All the best foreign professors left Russia, and the remaining ones fought each other bitterly: "L'académie sans adacémiciens, la chancellerie sans membres, l'université sans étudiants, les règles sans autorité, et au reste une confusion jusqu'à présent sans remède."[148] Personal tragedies befell a leading member of the Russian Conference, Trediakovskii, who lost his possessions in a fire in 1736.[149] With his private economy in shambles, he was forced to leave St. Petersburg to live in the country for a year in 1738–1739. Back in the capital, he came into conflict with the nobleman A. P. Volynskii, received a beating and was forced to write and publicly declaim vulgar poems at a "fool's wedding" organized at court.[150] Later the same year, Trediakovskii was declared innocent and compensated for his suffering with the sum of 360 roubles.[151] Other linguists who had been active in the Russian Conference were called away to other duties. Thus Adodurov remained in the employment of the academy until the spring of 1741 when he was appointed Deputy Herald at the Герольдмейстерская контора (Chief Herald's Office).[152]

Even the young Lomonosov experienced promblems in the early 1740s. At the beginning of the decade, he was still a student in Germany. Upon his return to Russia he was employed by the academy, but due to "slanderous (and drunken) behavior at academy meetings" he was put under house arrest from May 1743 until January of the following year.[153]

The early 1740s was also the time of the Schumacher affair, a power struggle in the Academy of Sciences, which led to the one-year dismissal of the academy's secretary, Johann Daniel Schumacher.[154] He was later reinstated with full

147 Kopelevich, *Osnovanie Peterburgskoi akademii nauk*, 132–133; Sukhomlinov, *Materialy*, vol. 6, 528.
148 A. A. Vasil'chikov, *Semeistvo Razumovskikh*, vol. 1 (St. Petersburg: M. M. Stasiulevich, 1880), 83 (The academy [is] without academicians, the chancellery without members, the university without students, and the rules without authority, and for the rest a confusion that so far has no remedy).
149 Reyfman, *Vasilii Trediakovsky*, 27.
150 Uspenskii, *Vokrug Trediakovskogo*, 450–451.
151 Pekarskii, *Istoriia Imperatorskoi Akademii nauk*, vol. 2, 81.
152 Volkov, "V. E. Adodurov: neskol'ko dopolnitel'nykh zamechanii," 22.
153 Usitalo, *The Invention of Mikhail Lomonosov*, 223, footnote 37.
154 Simon Werrett, "The Schumacher Affair: Reconfiguring Academic Expertise across Dynasties in Eighteenth-Century Russia," *Osiris* 25 (2010): 104–125.

honors, but the difficult situation in which the academy found itself led to the cancellation of the *Primechaniia* in October 1742.[155]

The Russian Conference was dissolved by 1743, a development later deplored by Lomonosov.[156] The academy's translators no longer held official gatherings to discuss issues of language, and language management in Russia seems to have gone on hiatus.

In 1746, the academy received a new president in the person of Count K. G. Razumovskii (1728–1803). The young count's career climb was rapid. He became president of the Academy of Sciences at a time when he was still an adolescent by modern standards:

> … назначеніе молодого Разумовскаго объясняется не только исключительнымъ положеніемъ брата его при дворѣ, но еще тѣмъ полнымъ отсутствіемъ людей образованныхъ и способныкхъ, которымъ отличалось, особенно въ началѣ, царствованіе Елизаветы Петровны.[157]

Not until the end of the 1740s, the sovereign, now in the person of Empress Elizabeth, took a renewed interest in linguistic matters:

> Минувшаго генваря 27 дня сего 748 года Ея И. В. дѣйствительный камергеръ, кавалеръ и академіи наукъ господинъ президентъ, графъ Кирила Григорьевич Разумовскій объявилъ именной Ея И. В. высочайшій изо-устный указъ, которымъ повѣлено стараться при академіи наукъ переводить и печатать на русскомъ языкѣ книги гражданскія разлічнаго содержанія, въ которыхъ бы польза и забава соединена была съ пристойнымъ къ свѣтскому житію нравоученіемъ.[158]

---

155 P. N. Berkov, *Istoriia russkoi zhurnalistiki XVIII veka* (Moscow: Izdatel'stvo Akademii nauk SSSR, 1952), 69.

156 Buck, *The Russian Language Question*, 213–214.

157 Vasil'chikov, *Semeistvo Razumovskikh*, vol. 1, 82 ([T]he appointment of the young Razumovskii is explained not only by the exclusive position of his brother at Court, but also by that complete absence of educated and capable men, which characterized the reign of Elizaveta Petrovna, especially at the beginning).

158 Sukhomlinov, *Materialy*, vol. 9, 53 (On the 27th of January last of this year 1748, the High Chamberlain of Her Imperial Majesty, the Cavalier and the Lord President of the Academy of Sciences, Count Kirill Grigor'evich Razumovskii, made public Her Imperial Majesty's Supreme oral decree by which it is ordered that the Academy of Sciences should strive to translate and print in Russian language books of varied civil content, in which usefulness and amusement is combined with morals suited for a civil life).

The academy received a new charter in 1747 and new initiatives also resulted in the creation of a committee charged with the correction of translations: Историческое собрание (the Historical Conference). The members were partly the same as in the Russian Conference. Trediakovskii served as chairman of the new conference for the rest of the 1740s (until 1751), and I. I. Taubert was also a member.[159] Thus, after a five-year pause, Russia again had an agency responsible for managing the language.

3.4 Language Management in the Administration

The empire's laws prescribed that documents should be designed on the basis of templates. These template documents constitute a rather different way in which language management was performed by the Russian state. The *General'nyi reglament* (*General Regulation*), a legislative document specifying the functions of the state administration introduced by Peter the Great in 1720, states:

> Гл. XXXIV.—*О канцеляристахъ.*
>
> Канцеляристамъ надлежитъ все то, что по реэстру изъ отправляемыхъ дѣлъ отъ Секретаря повелѣно будетъ изготовлять, какъ о томъ въ 20 и 30 пунктахъ изображено, такожъ и тѣ дѣла, о которыхъ они генеральные формуляры (образцовыя письма) имѣютъ, а именно: дипломы, патенты и прочее. А что они сами сочинили, то имѣютъ прежде Секретарю для поправления подавать подъ такими же казьнми и наказаніями, какъ выше о Секретарѣ упомянуто.[160]

---

159 Moskovkin, *Iazykovoe obrazovanie*, 11.

160 Polnoe sobranie zakonov Rossiiskoi imperii, no. 3534, "General'nyi Reglament ili Ustav," 153–154, accessed October 31, 2021, http://nlr.ru/e-res/law_r/search.php (Ch. 34—*On Clerks*. The clerks are obliged to prepare all that the Secretary commands, according to the register of outgoing cases, as illustrated in points 20 and 30, likewise such cases for which they have general forms [template letters], namely: diplomas, patents, etc. And that which they themselves have composed, they must first submit to the Secretary for correction, subject to the same penalties and punishments as mentioned above about the Secretary).

Instructions concerning the layout and composition of administrative documents were issued by the central administration and sent to towns and provinces in 1738.[161]

Templates were also printed in the 1740s. Such documents regulated the form of official documents, from the highest level of government down to local administration. Below are two examples of template documents.

3.4.1 Template for the Imperial Title, 1741

The template for the imperial title[162] regulated how the imperial titles were to be written in different kinds of documents. The longest and most elaborate template states all the Emperor's titles and was intended for letters addressed abroad. For domestic use, shorter versions were prescribed.

ФОРМА

О ТІТУЛАХЪ ЕГО ІМПЕРАТОРСКАГО ВЕЛИЧЕСТВА:

I:

въ Грамотахъ, которые отправлены имѣютъ быть въ Іностранные Государства.

БОЖІЕЮ поспѣшествующею Милостію, МЫ ІОАННЪ ТРЕТІИ, ІМПЕРАТОРЪ И САМОДЕРЖЕЦЪ ВСЕРОССІИСКІИ, Московскіи, Кіевскіи, Владимерскіи, Новгородскіи, Царь Казанскіи, Царь Астраханскіи, Царь Сибирскіи, Государь Псковскіи, и Великіи Князь Смоленскіи: Князь Эстляндскіи, Ліфляндскіи, Корельскіи, Тверскіи, Югорскіи, Пермскіи, Вятскіи, Болгорскіи: И иныхъ Государь и Великіи Князь, Нова Города Низовскія Земли, Черниговскіи, Резанскіи, Ростовскіи, Ярославскіи, Бѣлозерскіи, Удорскіи, Обдорскіи, Кондіискіи, и всея сѣверныя страны Повелитель. И Государь Іверскія земли Карталинскихъ и Грузинскихъ Цареи, и Карбардинскія земли, Черкаскихъ и Горскихъ Князеи, и иныхъ Наслѣдныи Государь и Обладатель.

---

161 L. V. Cherepnin, *Russkaia paleografiia* (Moscow: Gosudarstvennoe izdatel'stvo politicheskoi literatury, 1956), 437.

162 *Forma o titulakh Ego Imperatorskago Velichestva* (St. Petersburg: Senat, October 19, 1740), accessed November 1, 2021, https://rusneb.ru/catalog/000200_000018_RU_NLR_UK_2094/.

2:

въ Грамотахъ же внутрь Государства.

БОЖІЕЮ МИЛОСТІЮ, МЫ ІОАННЪ ТРЕТІИ, ІМПЕ-
РАТОРЪ И САМОДЕРЖЕЦЪ ВСЕРОССІИСКІИ; и
протчая, и протчая, и протчая.

3:

въ указѣхъ

изъ Сената въ Колегіи и Губерніи, и изъ Колегеи въ Губерніи.
УКАЗЪ ЕГО ВЕЛИЧЕСТВА, ІМПЕРАТОРА И САМО-
ДЕРЖЦА ВСЕРОССІИСКАГО, изъ Сената или изъ
Колегеи.

4:

въ челобитныхъ и въ отпискахъ.

ВСЕПРЕСВѢТЛѢИШИ ДЕРЖАВНѢИШИ, ВЕЛ-
ИКІИ ГОСУДАРЬ ІМПЕРАТОРЪ, И САМОДЕРЖЕЦЪ
ВСЕРОССІИСКІИ, ГОСУДАРЬ ВСЕМИЛОСТИВѢИШИ.

въ челобитнои въ срединѣ передъ прошенїемъ.

ВСЕМИЛОСТИВѢИШИ ГОСУДАРЬ прошу Вашего
ІМПЕРАТОРСКАГО ВЕЛИЧЕСТВА.

во окончанїи.

Вашего ІМПЕРАТОРСКАГО ВЕЛИЧЕСТВА нижаишіи
рабъ.

въ приговорахъ.

По указу ЕГО ІМПЕРАТОРСКАГО ВЕЛИЧЕСТВА.

въ Пашпортахъ.

По указу ЕГО ВЕЛИЧЕСТВА ІОАННА ТРЕТІЯГО,
ІМПЕРАТОРА И САМОДЕРЖЦА ВСЕРОССІИСКАГО, и
протчая, и протчая, и протчая.

Подліннои за подпісанїемъ Господъ Кабінетъ Мінїстровъ,
Октября 18 дня, 1740 года.

Печатанъ въ Санктпетербургѣ при Сенатѣ Октября 19
дня, 1740 года.

3.4.2 Template for a Letter of Credit, 1744

The following document is a template for a letter of credit.[163] The text is quite detailed, and also has instructions in the margin concerning what information to include.

Формуляръ.

Противъ которого спеціальное (то есть собственное,) кредитное, (то есть вѣрющее) писмо, даемое отъ купца прикащику своему или кому нибудь другому, которои ево купцовъ не прикащикъ но только комисіонеръ, (то есть кому кто какое поручитъ свое дѣло.)

Сего 174 дня, такоита купецъ, имярекъ съ отечествомъ и прозваніемъ, объявляю что я, А: прикащику своему тако[..]та города или мѣста жителю имяреку, симъ полную мочь даю и в[.]рю въ томъ, что отпускную по выписи на мое имярекова имя и о че[.]ъ, такоита провинціи, отъ тогота города, къ томута порту [.]ли другоми городу, имянуя товары какія по выписи отпощены б[.]тъ имѣютъ, которыя по прибытіи къ помянутому порту или гор[.]ду въ цѣлости, въ тамошнеи таможнѣ на мое хозяинское имярекова [.]мя объявить, и на мои же счетъ и страхъ либо, [in margin: А: Ежели купецъ кому другому, а не прикащику своему повѣритъ, то въ вѣрющемъ писмѣ вмѣсто прикащика писать надлежитъ комисіонеръ.] б: на готовыя денги или въ мѣну на другія товары, какъ наилутче возможно продать, и заключимои въ томъ торгъ и учиненные при томъ кондиціи на м[..]жъ хозяинское имя въ таможнѣ записать, и съ купцомъ точную въ томъ роздѣлку учинить, и по удовольствованіи наличными деньгами или товарами ему въ томъ росписку дать, и взаимно отъ него купца взять 000 рублевъ. [in margin: б: Всякому купцу вольно кондиціи о продажѣ прикащику своему установить какъ хочетъ, или ему на волю дать ежели ему только вѣрятъ.]

2: Емужъ прикащику имяряку (sic!) у вышеобъявленного порта на мое хозяиское имярекова имя, и счетъ и страхъ, купить имянуя товары какіе потребно, числомъ, счетомъ, вѣсомъ, и мѣрою на готовые и на вырученные деньги или въ

---

163 *Formuliar. Protiv kotorogo spetsial'noe …* (Moscow: n. p., 1744).

долгъ, на извѣстную показавъ сумму, и въ оную сумму кто сколько (по тому кредиту) дастъ денегъ, или какихъ товаровъ, тотъ долженъ на томъ кредитивномъ писмѣ подписывать имянно, сколько далъ денегъ, или какихъ товаровъ, и на коликую сумму, а онои торгъ по силе уставу въ таможнѣ записать розделку учинить, росписатца и деньги заплатить, [...] на мои хозяискои имярекова счетъ дать отъ себя веѯель на срокъ, на вышеозначенную сумму, и что онои прикащикъ мои имярекъ вышеписаннымъ образомъ, сторгуетъ, заключитъ, и въ дѣиство произведетъ, то все я хозяинъ имярекъ совершенно и дѣиствительно приму, и во всемъ отвѣтенъ буду, власно якобы я самъ все то чинилъ. [in margin: 2: Ежели хозяинъ їностранныхъ товаровъ купїтъ не прїкажетъ, то и 2 пункта въ кредитномъ писмѣ не писать, а какїе иностранные товары купить, оные въ вѣрющемъ писмѣ и росписать надлежитъ, а буде хозяинъ прикащику своему дастъ на волю какїе товары купить онъ за благо разсудитъ, то оное тако генеральными рѣчми, и въ вѣрющее писмо внесено быть имѣетъ.]

Формуляръ.

Противъ которого генеральное кредитное, (то есть вѣрющее) писмо, даемое отъ купца прикащику своему, или кому нибудь другому, которои подлинно не ево купцовъ прикащикъ, но только комисїонеръ ево, (то есть кому кто какое поручитъ свое дѣло,) впредь засвидѣтелствомъ и печатью отъ магистрата или ратуши, (а гдѣ магистрата или ратуши нѣтъ,) то и отъ таможни дано быть имѣетъ.

Сего 174 году, дня, такогота города купецъ, имярекъ съ отечествомъ и прозванїемъ объявляю, что я прикащику своему тогота города, или мѣста жителю имяреку, симъ съ вышеписанного числа потакоето число, или на цѣлои годъ, впредь полную мочь даю и вѣрю на мое хозяиское имярекова имя и счетъ къ томуто порту торговать, внутреннїе и заморскїе товары покупать и продавать, принимать и отдавать, съ настоящею въ таможнѣ запискою, и въ тѣхъ товарѣхъ розделку чинить и росписыватца, контракты заключать, о оные въ таможнѣ записывать, денги принимать и платить, такожъ асигновать. и во оныхъ росписыватся, веѯели акseptовать, давать и брать и въ суды вступать, а

о арестованïи и о сложенïи арестовъ въ судныхъ мѣстахъ
просить, и по обстоятельству дѣла миритца, и о протчемъ по
торговому обряду во всемъ вольно поступать и дѣлать, какъ
онъ прикащикъ имярекъ за благо разсуждать будетъ, и то все
я хозяинъ имярекъ совершенно за дѣиствительно признавать
буду, власно якобы я самъ то учинилъ, и подлинно всѣ оные
дѣла самъ же производилъ, и того для наисилнѣишѣ обяюсь
во всемъ томъ отвѣтнымъ быть, что прикащикъ имярекъ
имянемъ и вмѣсто меня дѣлалъ и въ чемъ обязался.

Подлиннои за подписанïемъ Правительствующаго Сената,
Марта 14 дня, 1744 года. Печатанъ въ Москвѣ при Сенатѣ, 21
дня тогожъ года.

3.5 Conclusions

In the realm of foreign policy, the decade between 1740 and 1750 was a comparatively peaceful period for the Russian Empire, a multiethnic state that had recently established itself as one of the most powerful states in Europe. Internally, turmoil at the highest level of government characterized the beginning of the decade but did not change the structure of Russian society, and the situation quickly stabilized. The government apparatus resided in St. Petersburg, as did the central organs of the comparatively small imperial bureaucracy.

Looking at the educational system, we can conclude that only a fraction of the population received education to such an extent that they could produce texts independently. This clearly influences the number and, not least, the social distribution of documents written by people outside the nobility. For the present investigation, this has important consequences. We cannot expect to find large quantities of ego-documents, or other documents written by peasants and simpler townspeople. Since literacy education was carried out using mostly traditional textbooks and pedagogical methods, this will, in all likelihood, be reflected in the handwritten material.

The latter part of this chapter was dedicated to the study of language management in Russia during the 1740s. As seen above, the 1730s were a very active period in this respect, not least through the formation of the Russian Conference. The 1740s, on the other hand, seems to be a period of decline of existing language management institutions: the publication of the *Primechaniia* was discontinued and the Russian Conference seems to have petered out during 1742. Hopefully, the following chapters will show if any conscious efforts to manage the language can be detected in Russian documents from the period.

CHAPTER 4

Available Sources

———————

Because of the mass illiteracy that persisted for much of the history of Imperial Russia, social historians have been forced to rely on the legal-administrative records of the bureaucracy and/or the letters, memoirs, scholarship, literary works, and journalistic accounts of the educated classes.[1]

This investigation also includes a wide variety of sources, with the addition of handwritten documents, newspapers and popular prints. These sources include printed and handwritten documents found in a variety of locations and are not necessarily representative of all texts from that period. The main disadvantage of diachronic linguistics when compared to the synchronic variety is familiar: "Introspection and native-speaker competence cannot be relied on in the study of the language of previous centuries and millennia."[2] To complicate matters further, data from previous centuries are unevenly preserved. The spoken language, except for fragments, is gone forever. This makes it difficult impossible to study linguistic changes that were never written down, as modern dialectologists can do.[3] A mere fraction of all texts that once existed has survived to modern times, causing the "bad data problem" referred to above (section 1.3).

Material for this investigation comes from both handwritten and printed sources in archives, libraries and on the Internet.[4] Recreating a true image of

———————

1 Wirtschafter, "Social Categories," 232.
2 Matti Rissanen, "Corpus Linguistics and Historical Linguistics," in *Corpus Linguistics: An International Handbook*, ed. Anke Lüdeling and Merja Kytö (Berlin and New York: Walter de Gruyter, 2008), 53.
3 Michael Daniels, Ruprecht von Waldenfels, Aleksandra Ter-Avanesova, et al., "Dialect Loss in the Russian North: Modeling Change across Variables," *Language Variation and Change* 31 (2019): 353–376.
4 For terminological reference concerning documents from the eighteenth century, see A. S. Malitikov, ed., *Kratkii slovar' vidov i raznovidnostei dokumentov* (Moscow: VNIIDAD, 1974); Gregory L. Freeze, *From Supplication to Revolution: A Documentary Social History of Imperial Russia* (New York and Oxford: Oxford University Press, 1988); M. V. Babich, *Gosudarstvennye uchrezhdeniia Rossii XVIII v. Spravochnoe posobie* (Moscow: URSS, 1999); A. N. Kachalkin,

Russian in the 1740s calls for circumspection in the selection of data. This chapter describes the diverse sources used for this study.

4.1 Electronic Corpora of Eighteenth-Century Texts

The most convenient way to perform a quantitative investigation on Russian from the 1740s would be to extract data from some pre-existing, annotated, electronic corpus. In a recent book, Mikhail Kopotev, Olga Lyashevskaya, and Arto Mustajoki have presented the current state of methods for analyzing Russian linguistic data using quantitative methods. They discovered that "we have large and deeply annotated corpora available for extended quantitative research."[5] While this is an accurate assessment for contemporary Russian, the situation is not at all accurate for the mid-eighteenth century.

The corpus best suited for the purposes of this investigation is the Russian National Corpus, which is available for non-commercial scientific or educational use.[6] It has two constituent parts: contemporary texts and "mid-18th to mid-20th century texts." The texts in the latter section of the corpus "представляют также различные жанры (художественная литература, научные тексты, частная переписка, публицистика), однако по причине доступности электронных версий и современных переизданий процент художественной литературы для этого периода гораздо выше, чем для второй половины XX в."[7]

The Russian National Corpus offers the possibility of creating a searchable subcorpus. Designing one for the 1740s is relatively simple. Putting together a customized subcorpus with the variable "year of creation" (год создания) set to "1740–49" and "genre and text type" (жанр и тип текста) set to "non-imaginative texts" (нехудожественные тексты) results in a subcorpus of 137 texts with a total of 212,361 words (as of April 13, 2021). However, the

---

"Iz istorii kul'tury i pis'mennosti. Nazvaniia delovykh bumag v XVIII veke," *Russkaia rech'* 2 (2003): 79–84.

5 Mikhail Kopotev, Olga Lyashevskaya, and Arto Mustajoki, eds., *Quantitative Approaches to the Russian Language* (Abingdon: Routledge, 2018), 3.

6 "Using the Corpus," Russian National Corpus, accessed May 30, 2019, http://www.ruscorpora.ru/en/corpora-usage.html.

7 "Sostav i struktura," Russian National Corpus, accessed September 16, 2021, https://rus-corpora.ru/new/corpora-structure.html; "Content and Structure of the Corpus," Russian National Corpus, accessed April 13, 2021, http://www.ruscorpora.ru/en/corpora-structure. html (represent various genres [fiction, scientific texts, journalism, letters], but due to limited availability of such texts in electronic form or in modern reprints, the proportion of fiction for this period is much higher than for the main corpus).

number of individual authors represented in that subcorpus is limited. As many as 88 texts were written by only three authors: M. V. Lomonosov (49), V. N. Tatishchev (35), and V. K. Trediakovskii (4). Lomonosov alone is the author of more than a third of the subcorpus (35.7%). Furthermore, the corpus is exclusively written by men. Only two texts are marked as having a female author, and both are imperial decrees written *in the name of* Empress Elizabeth, that is, not personally by her.

Thus, the composition of the Russian National Corpus subcorpus for the 1740s renders it unsuitable as the only source for the present investigation. Given the high number of texts representing a small number of authors, we must take into account the possibility that the composition of the corpus may reflect the idiolects of these authors, i.e. their use of the language as individuals, rather than the mainstream written vernacular language of the period.[8] This may have implications for our knowledge of Russian in the 1740s, such as the characterization of Lomonosov as "eher ein konservativer als ein revolutionärer Autor."[9] Contemporary scholars in diachronic linguistics also voice precautions "to avoid the effects of unwanted correlations or idiolectal bias."[10] Despite the disadvantages, the 1740s subcorpus of the Russian National Corpus remains an important source. For example, it allows comparison with other texts.

Apart from the materials listed above, some additional collections of eighteenth-century texts containing material from the 1740s are available on the Internet. These include collections of imaginative literature, memoirs and diaries, and other mixed collections.[11] Some of these texts are published by official institutions, such as the Institute of Russian literature (Pushkinskii dom), while other publications are private initiatives. The orthography of such texts are typically modernized, which makes them less appropriate for the purposes of this investigation.

---

8   For the term *idiolect*, see David Crystal, *A Dictionary of Linguistics and Phonetics*, 4th ed. (Oxford: Blackwell, 1997), 189.

9   Issatschenko, *Geschichte*, 597 (rather a conservative than a revolutionary author).

10   Edgar W. Schneider, "Investigating Historical Variation and Change in Written Documents: New Perspectives," in *The Handbook of Language Variation and Change*, ed. J. K. Chambers and Natalie Schilling, 2nd ed. (Malden, MA: Wiley-Blackwell, 2013), 69.

11   "Russkaia literatura XVIII veka," Fundamental'naia élektronnaia biblioteka, accessed April 13, 2021, http://feb-web.ru/feb/feb/c18.htm; "Russkaia literatura XVIII veka," Russkaia virtual'naia biblioteka, accessed April 13, 2021, https://rvb.ru/18vek/; "Russkaia literatura, Vek XVIII," Institut russkoi literatury (Pushkinskii dom) RAN, accessed April 13, 2021, http://lib.pushkinskijdom.ru/; Korpus M.V. Lomonosova, accessed April 13, 2021, http://lomonosov.pro/; Russkie memuary, accessed April 13, 2021, http://mikv1.narod.ru/; "Rossiia—XVIII vek," Vostlit, accessed April 13, 2021, http://www.vostlit.info/Texts/Dokumenty/Russ/xviii.htm.

4.2 Printed Texts

Large numbers of printed texts from the 1740s are available today. At the time, production was strictly centralized and controlled.[12] Printed texts include books, newspapers, administrative documents, and other material. The history of printing and book production in the eighteenth century enjoys a rich scholarly literature and therefore will not be discussed here.[13]

4.2.1 Books

During the period 1740–1749, a total of 400 books were published in Russia. The annual average of books published in the civil orthography was 22.6 in 1740–1744. That number fell to 17.0 in the second half of the decade. Books printed in the old orthography represented about half the total of printed books.[14] Such books were written either in Church Slavic or—as in the case of sermons—in Russian with a strong admixture of Church Slavic (cf. above, chapter 2).

4.2.2 Newspapers

Russia's only newspaper during the 1740s was the *Sanktpeterburgskie vedomosti* (*Санктпетербургские ведомости*).[15] Chief editors during this period

---

12 K. A. Papmehl, *Freedom of Expression in Eighteenth-Century Russia* (The Hague: Martinus Nijhoff, 1971), 7–8.

13 S. P. Luppov, *Kniga v Rossii v poslepetrovskoe vremia 1725–1740* (Leningrad: Nauka, 1976); Marker, *Publishing, Printing*; P. I. Khoteev, "Biblioteka Sukhoputnogo shliakhetnogo kadetskogo korpusa v seredine XVIII v. (kolichestvennye dannye)," in *Kniga v Rossii XVI–serediny XIX v. Materialy i issledovaniia. Sbornik nauchnykh trudov*, ed. A. A. Zaitseva (Leningrad: BAN, 1990): 119–126.

14 Marker, *Publishing, Printing*, 68, especially table 2.3; A. A. Guseva, *Svod russkikh knig kirillovskoi pechati XVIII veka*; T. A. Afanas'eva, "Izdaniia kirillicheskoi pechati XVIII veka svetskogo soderzhaniia," in *Problemy istochnikovedcheskogo izucheniia rukopisnykh i staropechatnykh fondov. Sbornik nauchnykh trudov* (Leningrad: Gosudarstvennaia publichnaia biblioteka im. Saltykova-Shchedrina, 1979), 183–199; idem, "Izdaniia zakonodatel'nogo kharaktera kirillicheskoi pechati XVIII v.," in *Istochniki po istorii otechestvennoi kul'tury v sobraniiakh i arkhivakh Otdela rukopisei i redkikh knig. Sbornik nauchnykh trudov*, ed. G. P. Enin and N. A. Efimova (Leningrad: Gosudarstvennaia publichnaia biblioteka im. Saltykova-Shchedrina, 1983), 96–114.

15 Berkov, *Istoriia russkoi zhurnalistiki*, 56–64; "O gazete," *Gazeta "Sanktpeterburgskie vedomosti" XVIII veka: ukazateli k soderzhaniiu (1728–1781 gg.)*, Biblioteka Akademii nauk, accessed April 26, 2021, https://www.vedomosti1728.ru/?r=12. The English title is employed by Marker, *Publishing, Printing*, 86. It is sometimes also referred to in English as the *St. Petersburg Gazette*.

were Johann Bröme (1735–1748) and Mikhail Lomonosov (1748–1751).[16] The *Sanktpeterburgskie vedomosti* succeeded Russia's first newspaper, entitled simply *Vedomosti*. The *Vedomosti* was printed between 1702 and 1727, and the publication of the *Sanktpeterburgskie vedomosti* began in 1728.[17] Throughout the 1740s, the responsibility for newspaper production lay in the hands of the Academy of Sciences.

The process of gathering and processing the Russian materials intended for publication in *Sanktpeterburgskie vedomosti* has been described by T. Iu. Morozova. She concludes that although the Academy of Sciences was responsible for the editorship of the newspaper, the editorial work carried out by the officials of the academy was limited to the technical aspects of the publication. The state institutions that delivered information selected and organized the materials for publication.[18]

In addition, Barbara Leitner's master's thesis[19] investigates three years of the *Sanktpeterburgskie vedomosti*: 1728, 1757, and 1774. The choice of these particular years, and the long pause between them, is due to the long-lasting "linguistic chaos" of the first half of the eighteenth century and the publication of Lomonosov's *Rossiiskaia grammatika* in 1757. Leitner wanted to examine whether any reliance upon the latter can be traced in the *Sanktpeterburgskie vedomosti*.[20] Among the minor differences reported by Leitner, whose investigation deals with an intermediate period between 1728 and 1757, we find that the characters ⟨ʒ⟩, ⟨s⟩, and ⟨v⟩, present in 1728, can no longer be found in the editions from 1757.[21] Leitner also observes an increased consistency in the use of ⟨ъ⟩ in 1757, compared to the late 1720s. In the 1720s, this character was often absent in expected positions.[22] Further observations by Leitner include differences in the adjectival declension, where, in 1728, -ый is the only form

16 Unbegaun, B. O., ed., *Drei russische Grammatiken: Nachdruck der Ausgaben von 1706, 1731 und 1750* (Munich: Fink, 1969), X; Marker, *Publishing, Printing*, 48–49; T. Iu. Morozova, "Organizatsiia sbora i obrabotki original'noi informatsii v russkikh gazetakh XVIII v. (na primere izdaniia 'Sanktpeterburgskikh vedomostei')," in *Rossiia v XVIII stoletii*, vol. 1, ed. E. E. Rychalovskii (Moscow: Iazyki slavianskikh kul'tur, 2002), 28.
17 "O gazete," *Gazeta XVIII veka "Sanktpeterburgskie vedomosti*," accessed April 14, 2021, http://vedomosti.rasl.ru/?r=2.
18 Morozova, "Organizatsiia sbora i obrabotki," 35.
19 Barbara Leitner, "Die ‚Sanktpeterburgskie Vedomosti': die Entstehung der modernen russischen Standardsprache im Spiegel der frühen Presse" (Mag. phil. diss., Universität Wien, Vienna, 2010).
20 Ibid., 67.
21 Ibid., 75.
22 Ibid., 80.

encountered for masculine Nominative/Accusative, singular. The form -ой/-ей, on the other hand, was preferred in 1757.[23]

The *Sanktpeterburgskie vedomosti* remained Russia's only newspaper in this period. It was accompanied by the *Primechaniia k Vedomostiam* (*Примечания к Ведомостям*), which was published several times annually between 1728 and 1742.[24] As mentioned above (see, for example, section 3.3.4), the *Primechaniia* was Russia's first literary and popular science journal and functioned as a kind of reference dictionary for the readers of *Sanktpeterburgskie vedomosti*, explaining new and foreign terms.[25] The content of the *Sanktpeterburgskie vedomosti* was dominated by notices, announcements, and laws. Gradually private ads also appeared, as did the occasional poem.[26] Advertisements were often repeated in several successive issues. They had a fairly simple structure, such as the one promoting V. K. Trediakovskii's treatise on orthography in October, 1748:

> Въ книжной Академической лавкѣ продается нынѣ новая книга, сочиненная на Россійскомъ языкѣ господиномъ Профессоромъ Васильемъ Тредіаковскимъ, подъ титуломъ: *Разговоръ между чужестраннымъ человѣкомъ и россійскимъ о Правописаніи старинномъ и новомъ, и о всемъ, что принадлежитъ къ сей матеріи.*[27]

The news was dominated by wars, trade, and translations from Western newspapers. As of the 1740s, general information about the state of the Russian Empire began to be included on a more regular basis.[28] Foreign news articles

23 Ibid., 88.
24 A. V. Zapadov, ed., *Istoriia russkoi zhurnalistiki XVIII–XIX vekov,* 3rd ed. (Moscow: Vysshaia shkola, 1973), 22–23.
25 Berkov, *Istoriia,* 64–72; Marker, *Publishing, Printing,* 49; Alla Keuten, "K istorii russkikh i nemetskikh 'Primechanii k Vedomostiam' (1728–1742)," *Russian Literature* 75 (2014): 265–304.
26 Berkov, *Istoriia,* 63; Pavel Berkov, "Neizvestnye stikhotvoreniia Lomonosova v 'Sanktpeterburgskikh vedomostiakh' 1743 i 1748 godov," *Russkaia literatura* 4 (1961); 128–130; Marker, *Publishing, Printing,* 48.
27 *Sanktpeterburgskie vedomosti,* October 4, 1748, 6, accessed May 29, 2021, https://www.vedomosti1728.ru/pdf.cgi?r=99&key_pdf=rOSrRfF861ixiCHd (A new book in the Russian language by Professor Vasilii Trediakovskii is now for sale in the academy bookstore. It is entitled: *A conversation between a foreign person and a Russian on the old and the new Orthography and on all matters relevant to this*).
28 Alison K. Smith, "Information and Efficiency: Russian Newspapers, ca. 1700–1850," in *Information and Empire: Mechanisms of Communication in Russia, 1600-1854,* ed. S. Franklin and K. Bowers (Cambridge: Open Book Publishers, 2017), 191.

published in the *Sanktpeterburgskie vedomosti* were a translation of its German-language sister publication, the *St. Peterburgische Zeitung*.[29] Among those who translated into Russian was the mathematician and translator V. E. Adodurov.[30] While foreign news was translated into Russian, domestic news was not. As Eichhorn writes:

> Die inländischen Nachrichten waren theils direkt von den Regierungsinstitutionen zugestellt, wie den Kollegien im Jahre 1728 Allerhöchst befohlen worden war, theils Meldungen aus privater Quelle. Im ersten Falle waren sie natürlich russisch vervaßt, so daß die deutsche „St. Petersburger Zeitung," die sonst das Original der „Pet.Wed." (*Peterburgskie vedomosti*— T.R.) ist, hier zur Übersetzung wird. Die beiden Blätter sind in dieser Periode mit Ausnahme der Annoncen anfangs völlig identisch (nur der Adler ist bei den ersten Nummern des Jahres 1729 verschieden), später kommen in den „Pet. Wed." Kürzungen vor.[31]

4.2.3 Popular Prints

Popular prints, especially the so-called *lubok*, roughly the Russian equivalent of chapbooks, is another type of printed text from this period.[32] Often, such prints include short legends of only a few words and were one of few printed texts available to the illiterate majority of Russians. Because they contain short texts that were available to almost anyone in 1740s Russia, they are valuable

---

29 C. Eichhorn, *Die Geschichte der „St. Petersburger Zeitung" 1727–1902. Zum Tage der Feier des 175-jährigen Bestehens der Zeitung, dem 3. Januar 1902* (St. Petersburg: Buchdruckerei der St. Petersburger Zeitung, 1902), 8.

30 Vasilii Evdokimovich Adodurov (1709–1780), see: "Vasilii Evdokimovich Adodurov (Ododurov)," *Khronos*, accessed June 29, 2019, http://hrono.ru/biograf/bio_a/ adadurov_ve.php.

31 Eichhorn, *Die Geschichte*, 47 (Domestic news were partly delivered directly from government institutions, as the *kollegii* had been ordered by Supreme decree in 1728, partly announcements from private sources. In the first case, they were of course written in Russian, so that the German *St. Petersburger Zeitung*, otherwise the original of the *Sanktpeterburgskie vedomosti*, here becomes a translation. The two newspapers are in this period, except for the advertisements, first completely identical [only the eagle is different in the first issues from the year 1729], later, abridgements occur in the *Sanktpeterburgskie vedomosti*).

32 *Britannica Academic*, s.v. "Chapbook," accessed May 17, 2021, https://academic-eb-com. ezproxy.ub.gu.se/levels/collegiate/article/chapbook/22474.

to this investigation. A few such texts have been accessed via the web portal *Natsional'naia ėlektronnaia biblioteka*,[33] including an interesting case of a newspaper text transliterated and printed as a *lubok* (cf. below, section 6.3.1).

4.3 Archival Material

Archival materials in Russian from the 1740s are available in vast quantities. Small fractions are available in printed editions that began to appear in the nineteenth century.[34] Other resources can be found on the internet.[35] In most cases, however, archival materials are only accessible in the respective archival institutions. For this investigation material has been gathered from archives in five countries:[36]

Denmark:	Danish National Archives (Rigsarkivet), Copenhagen.
Finland:	National Archives of Finland (Kansallisarkisto), Helsinki.[37]
Russian Federation:	Archives of the Russian Academy of Sciences (SPbFARAN), St. Petersburg.
Sweden:	Swedish National Archives (Riksarkivet) and Military Archives (Krigsarkivet), Stockholm; Regional Archives (Landsarkivet), Uppsala.
Ukraine:	Central State Historical Archives of Ukraine (TsDIAK Ukraïny), Kyiv.

---

33 *Natsional'naia ėlektronnaia biblioteka*, accessed May 24, 2021, https://kp.rusneb.ru; Cf. also A. A. Pletnëva, "Russkii lubok: mezhdu Srednevekov'em i Novym vremenem," *Russkaia rech'* 6 (2014): 77–84; a nineteenth-century edition of popular prints by D. A. Rovinskii has also been consulted: *Russkie narodnye kartinki*, 5 vols. (St. Petersburg: Imperatorskaia akademiia nauk, 1881).

34 For example, Mikhail Sukhomlinov edited ten volumes of material relating to the Academy of Sciences (Sukhomlinov, *Materialy*). Business texts are available in the edition by Sumkina and Kotkov, *Pamiatniki*, to which reference has been made above, and in T. N. Mezhenina and A. P. Maiorov, eds., *Delovaia pis'mennost' Troitskogo Selenginskogo monastyria pervoi poloviny XVIII v.* (St. Petersburg: Nestor-Istoriia, 2015).

35 Cf. Arkhivnyi fond Vologodskoi oblasti, accessed October 29, 2021, https://uniqdoc.gov 35.ru/.

36 Detailed information about the individual documents is available in the list of sources at the end of this book.

37 Eljas Orrman and Jyrki Paaskoski, eds., *Vanhan Suomen arkistot. Arkiven från Gamla Finland* (Helsinki: Suomalaisen Kirjallisuuden Seura, 2012).

4.3.1 Selection of Sources

The vast majority of handwritten documents available in archives can be broadly categorized as business documents (деловые документы). However, within this macrogenre, a variety of sub-categories can be identified.[38]

In order to be suitable for analysis in this investigation, documents must fulfill certain preliminary criteria.[39] First, they must fit into the chronological framework of the investigation. This means that their date of composition must be between 1740 and 1749. Second, they must be written by individuals whose native language was Russian, or by persons of foreign extraction fluent in Russian. This is illustrated by the fluency of the writing, which demonstrates a familiarity with the use of pen and paper, Cyrillic lettering, etc.[40] Third, the documents must be representative. This means that, ideally, the documents included in the analysis represent varying social and geographic origins, male and female writers, and so forth.

4.4 Paleographic Characteristics of the Material

Eighteenth-century Russian writers had to choose between the "old" and the "civil" orthography. The civil orthography refers to Peter the Great's new, Romanized typeface, introduced from 1708 onwards, with a decreased number of characters, and a radically simplified system of diacritics, while the old orthography was a continuation of existing traditions. It was also employed for secular texts and not restricted to the religious sphere, which is a common misconception.[41] A well-known handbook on paleography sums up the developments during the eighteenth century in the following terms:

---

38 Cf. Malitikov, *Kratkii slovar'*, section 2, for a list of document types.
39 A more detailed discussion of methodological considerations is found in chapter 5.
40 In the archival material available to me, only one document shows obvious signs of having been copied by a person not previously familiar with Russian handwriting. This is a copy of a letter from the commander of Russian forces in Sweden, Patrick Stuart, dated 24 June 1744 (Swedish National Archives, Regional Archives, Uppsala, Södermanlands län, Nyköpings råd-husrätt och magistrat, Inneliggande handlingar, F VIa, 47, Stuart). As it does not fulfill the criteria, this letter was not included in the investigation.
41 Marker, *Publishing, Printing*; Daniel Bunčić, "Diachronic Observations," in *Biscriptality: A Sociolinguistic Typology*, ed. D. Bunčić, S. L. Lippert, A. Rabus (Heidelberg: Winter, 2016), 331; T. A. Afanas'eva, "Izdaniia kirillicheskoi pechati XVIII veka svetskogo soderzhaniia," 183–199.

Унификация начертания строчных букв, сокращение, а затем и полное вытеснение выносных букв, связность письма, деление текста на слова и фразы, выделение заглавных букв— наиболее характерные черты развития русского письма XVIII в.[42]

If these words are true for the eighteenth century as a whole, they apply less to handwriting from the 1740s. While printed texts from this period often appear "modern" to a twenty-first-century reader, handwritten documents—especially the more cursive forms—are an obvious continuation of earlier traditions. The difference can be seen not only in lettering, but also in the design of the entire writing system. When compared, printed and handwritten documents from the 1740s differ on many levels. This is due to the fact that typography and handwriting developed along diverging lines during the period:

Высказывавшееся в палеографии мнение, что введение гражданского типографического шрифта в России сыграло большую роль в изменении графики русского письма в начале века, надо признать необоснованным. ... В основном же графика рукописного шрифта века развивалась самостоятельно, вне зависимости от типографского.[43]

4.4.1 Developments in Printing during the 1740s

During the 1740s, books were printed in two different orthographies, the old and the civil. Whereas the old orthography continued traditions from earlier periods, the civil orthography went through a number of reforms. During the

---

42 M. N. Tikhomirov and A. V. Murav'ëv, *Russkaia paleografiia*, 2nd ext. ed. (Moscow: Vysshaia shkola, 1982), 29 (Unification in the outline of lower-case letters, reduction and later complete elimination of supralinear letters, coherence of writing, division of the text in words and phrases and marking of capital letters are the most important characteristics in the development of Russian writing during the eighteenth century).

43 A. G. Shitsgal, *Russkii grazhdanskii shrift 1708–1958* (Moscow: Iskusstvo, 1959), 76. Similarly, see P. N. Berkov, "O perekhode skoropisi XVIII v. v sovremennoe russkoe pis'mo," in *Issledovaniia po otechestvennomu istochnikovedeniiu: Sbornik statei, posviashchennykh 75-letiiu professora S. N. Valka* (Moscow and Leningrad: Nauka, 1964), 38 (The view expressed in paleography that the introduction of the civil typeface in Russia played a significant role in altering the graphics of Russian writing at the beginning of the century must be considered unfounded. ... Fundamentally, the graphics of handwriting during the century developed autonomously, without being dependent on typography).

1730s, in addition to graphemes ⟨Ѧ⟩, ⟨Ѫ⟩, ⟨ѱ⟩, ⟨ѡ⟩, already abolished through the Petrine reforms, the graphemes ⟨ӡ⟩, ⟨v⟩, and ⟨ѕ⟩ fell out of official use. In 1758, ⟨v⟩ (*izhitsa*) was reintroduced and remained in use until 1918. Also, the use of ⟨i⟩—rather than ⟨ï⟩—was regulated, at least theoretically.[44]

In 1744, the Academy of Sciences published a collection of official typefaces, twelve of which were Russian. The collection was reissued four years later. These samples reflect a new era in the development of the civil script: the form of the new typefaces differ sharply from those of the Petrine times.[45]

A typical feature of printed texts from the 1740s is the use of uppercase letters for titles denoting important people. This may vary from captalizing only the first letter, such as the word ⟨Маэоръ⟩ (major) with an upper-case ⟨М⟩, to printing entire titles in upper-case: ⟨ЕЯ ІМПЕРАТОРСКОЕ ВЕЛИЧЕСТВО⟩ (Her Imperial Majesty, cf. below, chapter 6). These examples show that, despite the academy's efforts at regulating the civil script, its usage was by no means uniform.

4.4.2 Handwritten Documents

In printed texts, uppercase and lowercase letters are differentiated, and all letters are of proportional size and homogenous design, and they rest on the same line. However, no such distinction was made in handwriting. In handwritten documents, graphemes vary greatly in size and occur in varying forms. Also, these texts teem with superscript signs, abbreviations, and a variety of accentuation marks.[46] Elements such as these are especially prominent in carefully written examples of *civil writing* (гражданское письмо), or *ceremonial cursive* (парадная скоропись), reminiscent of *semi-uncial script* (полуустав), with supralinear elements similar to those found in books printed in the old orthography.[47] In less prestigious documents, such elements are missing or occur sporadically.

---

44 Istrin, *1100 let slavianskoi azbuki*, 161; D. G. Demidov, "Dve tochki nad glasnoi bukvoi v XVII–XVIII vv. (iz istorii russkoi diakritiki)," in *Pis'mennaia kul'tura narodov Rossii. Materialy Vserossiiskoi nauchnoi konferentsii 19–20 noiabria 2008 g.* (Omsk: Omskii gosudarstvennyi universitet, 2008), 32–36.

45 A. G. Shitsgal, *Russkii tipografskii shrift: Voprosy istorii i praktika primeneniia* (Moscow: Kniga, 1985), 52–53.

46 Accents, breathings, and supralinear graphemes, see the list below and cf. illustration in Cherepnin, *Russkaia paleografiia*, 377.

47 Shitsgal, *Russkii grazhdanskii shrift*, 72–74; Berkov, "O perekhode," 43.

Sometimes they can be found at the beginning of a document, but missing in the end:

> В скорописных текстах XVIII в. в сравнении с материалами XVII в. выносные буквы менее употребительны, но возможны в тех же положениях, как и в текстах XVII в.: перед последующей согласной внутри слова и на конце слова (последние случаи более редкие). Отступления от этих норм единичны.[48]

During the 1740s, texts were separated into words according to rules that differ from modern usage. For example, prepositions are frequently adjoined to nouns, and negations to verbs.

Higly prestigeous documents were written in a clearly legible *ceremonial cursive*, in which each character was written separately and often had supralinear elements (cf. chapter 7). Scribes did not differentiate consistently between upper and lowercase characters. Titles and names were often spelled with a capital letter, and sometimes capital letters occurred randomly. The following short excerpt illustrates this:

> Бо́жїею Поспѣшеств8ющею Ми́лостїю мы А҆ННА Ї҆мператри́ца И самоде́ржица Всеросси́йская, Моско́вская, Ки́евская, Влади́мирская, Новгоро́дская, Цари́ца Каза́нская, Цари́ца Астраха́нская, Цари́ца Сиби́рская, Госуда́рыня Псковская, I Вели́кая Княги́ня Смоле́нская …[49]

Occasionally, characters are enlarged at the end of a line, in order to fill empty space.

The supralinear elements occurring in the material are:

⟨ ´ ⟩   *oksiia* (stress)
⟨ ` ⟩   *variia* (stress in absolute final position) ⟨стороны̀⟩
⟨ ’ ⟩   *paerok*

---

48 Sumkina and Kotkov, *Pamiatniki*, 7 (In cursive texts of the eighteenth century, compared to materials from the seventeenth, superscript letters are used less frequently, but permissible in the same positions as in texts from the seventeenth century: word-internally before a consonant, and in final position [the latter cases are rarer]. Deviations from this norm are infrequent).

49 Swedish National Archives, Muscovitica 623.

⟨'⟩   *psili* (breathing)

⟨"⟩   *iso*, a combination of *psili* and *oksiia*[50]

⟨◌̄⟩   *titlo*, written above abbreviations such as ⟨понн҄ѣ⟩ (until now), ⟨Бга⟩ (of God).

⟨◌̑⟩   *pokrytie*, written above superscript characters: ⟨гсдрь⟩ (sovereign).

⟨◌̆⟩   *kavyka*, employed when ⟨и⟩ functions as a consonant, most often at the end of words, is placed slightly above to the right: ⟨царе́й⟩.

The scribes behind documents in ceremonial cursive make use of both ⟨e⟩ and ⟨ѣ⟩, most often in their etymological positions, although individual variations occur.

The characters ⟨и⟩, ⟨ї⟩, ⟨i⟩, and ⟨j⟩ occur in something resembling free variation: ⟨ j" прѡчаѧ, и" про́чая, и про́чаѧ⟩.[51] The same is true for ⟨o⟩ and ⟨ѡ⟩, ⟨у⟩ and ⟨Ȣ⟩, and ⟨ю⟩ and ⟨я⟩. ⟨ѧ⟩ occurs at the end of lines. For /f/ we find ⟨ѳ⟩ alternating with ⟨ф⟩.

Compared to ceremonial cursive, documents written in *skoropis'* (скоропись), the traditional cursive of administrative documents, private letters etcetera, have their own characteristic features. Cursive characters vary greatly in size and occur in varying forms. In some documents it ⟨ь⟩ and ⟨ъ⟩ appear indistinguishable. Similarly, some superscript diacritics have been reduced to dots. In the handwritten material, numbers, especially dates, are often surrounded by ⟨„ „⟩: ⟨въ „21ом„ сего мсца⟩.[52]

4.5 The People behind the Material

Given the considerable variation found in handwriting from the 1740s, let us consider the people who wrote the documents.

---

50 This is reminiscent of the system employed in Cyrillic printed books, the старопечатная система (old printing system): A. A. Zalizniak, *Ot praslavianskoi aktsentuatsii k russkoi* (Moscow: Nauka, 1985), 200–201. The number of supralinear diacritics is considerably higher than the one employed for a short time in books printed in the civil alphabet. The latter is sometimes referred to as the новопечатная система (new printing system): I. A. Kornilaeva, "Iz istorii russkoi aktsentuatsii XVIII veka," in *Slavianskoe i balkanskoe iazykoznanie: prosodiia*, ed. A. A. Zalizniak, V. A. Dybo, and R. V. Bulatova (Moscow: Nauka, 1989), 193.

51 Swedish National Archives, Militaria 1588. Letter of safe conduct for Swedish vessels, signed by Russian General-en-Chef Count Peter de Lacy, in the camp at Helsinki, August 27, 1742.

52 Swedish National Archives, Muscovitica 623.

The age structure of the Russian population in the 1740s is not easy to calculate, even though impressive attempts have been made.[53] Infant mortality was extremely high by modern standards with 334 deaths per 1000 births. We should note, however, that these numbers are only slightly higher than those reported for France in the same period (317 per 1000). An individual in Russia who reached adulthood and was aged thirty in 1745 could expect to live another 27.2 years, while a person who had reached the age of sixty could be expected to live another 10.6 years.[54]

Although there may be exceptions, it was assumed that the authors of the majority of texts used for this investigation were between the ages of twenty and seventy.[55] An individual aged seventy in 1740 was thus born in 1670 and most probably received his/her education in the late 1670s and 1680s. On the other hand, a person aged twenty in 1740 was born in 1720 and likely educated during the late 1720s and 1730s. The rich graphic variation found in the material thus becomes more understandable when we consider this sixty-year period. We can expect to encounter writing by individuals educated before the reforms of Peter the Great, as well as writing by individuals who were educated in the post-Petrine society.

---

53 Alain Blum and Irina Troitskaya, "Mortality in Russia During the 18th and 19th Centuries: Local Assessments Based on the Revizii," *Population: An English Selection* 9 (1997): 130.
54 Blum and Troitskaya, "Mortality in Russia," 133.
55 For the sake of illustration, the ages on January 1, 1740 of a few famous individuals from the period: General Field-Marshal Peter von Lacy, born October 30/November 9, 1678: sixty-one years (cf. below, section 6.3.5); Empress Anna Ioannovna, born January 28/February 7, 1693: forty-six years; Mikhailo Lomonosov, born November 8/19, 1711: twenty-nine years.

CHAPTER 5

Methodological Considerations

The review of existing research in chapter 2 demonstrated that the Russian sociolinguistic situation of the 1740s has been insufficiently explained. In an attempt to shed more light on it, this chapter examines what research method(s) might be suitable to provide an accurate interpretation. On the following pages, a number of methodological issues will be discussed. These issues require our attention, especially since there are no immediate precursors to the present investigation.

5.1 Existing Methods

The Russian language has been recorded for many centuries using a well-known writing system, the Cyrillic alphabet. Furthermore, the structure of Russian and its vocabulary are well understood both synchronically and diachronically. With this in mind, there can be no reason why the conditions that apply to diachronic linguistics in general would not also apply to Russian in equal measure, including eighteenth-century Russian. This view is not shared by the entire scholarly community, however. For example, O. V. Nikitin expresses doubts concerning the applicability of "многочисленные зарубежные разработки" in historical sociolinguistics on Russian material.[1]

Nikitin is partly correct in stating that methods applied to other languages cannot be implemented without modifications. The application of a method to another language is dictated primarily by the nature of the sources. As discussed in chapter 3, the literacy situation in Russia during the eighteenth century was such that scholars today have little access to first-hand written

---

1   Nikitin, *Problemy ètnolingvisticheskogo izucheniia*, 77 (numerous foreign studies).

information—*ego-documents*—from broad sections of the population.[2] This problem is felt not only in linguistics, but also in social history:

> Indeed, because of the mass illiteracy that persisted for much of the history of Imperial Russia, social historians have been forced to rely on the legal-administrative records of the bureaucracy and/or the letters, memoirs, scholarship, literary works, and journalistic accounts of the educated classes.[3]

If due attention is paid to the specific conditions of the Russian material, investigations may yield new insights. However, if sources are scant, results must be interpreted cautiously.

Sociolinguistically oriented studies of eighteenth century Russian do exist, as we saw in section 2.3. Also, sociolinguistic research has been conducted on Russian material beyond the borders of Russia, namely by Anna Kretschmer, whose study of private letters from the seventeenth and early eighteenth centuries is particularly important.[4] While taking this into account, I find it necessary to include diachronic linguistics in a broader sense so as not to exclude any potential sources.

If any single method can be said to dominate research on eighteenth-century Russian, it is the quantitative. Well-known research employing primarily quantitative method includes Gerta Hüttl-Folter's syntactic investigations and V. M. Zhivov's investigation of historical morphology from 2004.[5]

In terms of orthographical and grammatical description, Michael Moser sets a high standard in his recent analysis of the language of *Юности честное зерцало* (*The Honorable Mirror for Youth*),[6] an example of Russian eighteenth-century pedagogical literature. Chapter 7 of Moser's book contains detailed analyses of orthography, morphology, syntax, and lexis. A short comparison is helpful since his work is one of the most recent, covers a period in chronological vicinity to

---

2   Concerning the term *ego-document*, cf. Rudolf Dekker, "Jacques Presser's Heritage: Ego Documents in the Study of History," *Memoria y Civilización* 5 (2002): 13–37. Having originated in the field of history, the term ego-document is now frequently employed in historical sociolinguistics.

3   Wirtschafter, "Social Categories," 232.

4   Kretschmer, *Zur Geschichte des Schriftrussischen*. Kretschmer's work includes a few texts from the 1740s.

5   Hüttl-Folter, *Syntaktische Studien*; Zhivov, *Ocherki*.

6   Michael Moser, *„Iunosti chestnoe zertsalo" 1717 g.: U istokov russkogo literaturnogo iazyka* (Vienna: LIT, 2020.).

that covered by the present investigation, and also deals with topics that are of interest for the current investigation.

While Moser's volume is impressive in many ways, there are three principal reasons why this book cannot go into a similar degree of detail. First of all, the purpose of the present investigation is to examine the function of language in society. While Moser focuses on a single text that is studied from every angle, the present investigation has a more general focus. Second, the sources analyzed here constitute a heterogeneous collection of texts of varying lengths. Elements in the long text analyzed by Moser often do not have corresponding elements in the shorter texts examined in this study. Excluding short texts in favor of longer ones would create an unwanted bias. Third, a minute analysis of the material included in the present investigation would result in a very long description without necessarily leading to new insights.

While quantitative investigations based on vast text corpora provide reliable statistical results, not all data is well suited for a quantitative analysis. As a consequence, data that fails to reach the requirements of a quantitative investigation has sometimes been discarded. This is why Zhivov chose to exclude short texts—notably business texts and private correspondence—from his investigation on methodological grounds.[7] Such a decision cannot be criticized as long as the researcher clearly states what is being done, as Zhivov did. Similarly, Alexander Issatschenko at one point discarded data from business texts, something that provoked a strong reaction from Anna Kretschmer: "[и]сключение же какого бы то ни было жанра является, на наш взгляд, принципиальной методологической ошибкой."[8]

There may be perfectly good reasons for excluding certain data. However, a decision to include or exclude data will obviously affect the outcome of any investigation. When facing the data, each researcher has two options: to exclude data that does not agree with a chosen method or to adapt the method. I argue that methodological adaptations are the way forward if we wish to attain as profound an understanding as possible of the linguistic situation in the 1740s or any other linguistic situation we investigate.

The alternative to methodological adaptation is exclusion, discarding certain varieties of language or certain text types on the grounds that they are insufficient for one reason or another. This approach has been tried many times and the result is familiar. Previously, in languages such as German and

7   Zhivov, *Ocherki*, 29–30.
8   Kretschmer, *Chelovek za pis'mom*, 284 (the exclusion of any genre whatsoever constitutes, in our opinion, a fundamental methodological error).

French, language history has often been written "from above" and viewed as "the inexorable march towards a uniform standard."[9] In French, for example, "[t]his has resulted in a sanitized version that makes the language history appear more homogeneous than it surely was."[10] Russian also has had more than its fair share of "sanitized" language history, as was explained in chapter 2.

Today, in the study of Western European languages, the situation has changed radically. Diachronic linguistics strive to include new sources: "The approach to language history that focusses on such sources [that is, sources written by women and individuals from outside the elite—T.R.] and that aims to repair the social and gender bias found in many language histories, has come to be known as language history 'from below.'"[11]

A historical sociolinguistic analysis requires methods that allow conclusions to be drawn about the linguistic realities facing the people behind the texts. In other words, the method should enable the researcher to say something about the social and educational background of the individuals and/or communities represented in the data. If this cannot be achieved, then the analysis has failed.

Since a sociolinguistic analysis must take into account information from many levels of a text, it is doubtful whether a single method is sufficient. For example, counting particular morphological elements will tell us something, but the message may be difficult to interpret out of context. This is why a combination of qualitative and quantitative methods provide a more holistic picture of a given situation. I suggest that a truly exhaustive analysis can be achieved by a combination of methods. Also, an investigation such as this may benefit by drawing on methods originally developed for other fields of linguistic inquiry beyond historical linguistics.

---

9   Stephan Elspaß, "A Twofold View 'from Below': New Perspectives on Language Histories and Language Historiographies," in *Germanic Language Histories "from Below" (1700–2000)*, ed. S. Elspaß, N. Langer, J. Scharloth, and W. Vandenbussche (Berlin and New York: De Gruyter, 2007), 4.

10   Ashby, review of *Sociolinguistic Variation in Seventeenth-Century France*, 1403.

11   Gijsbert Rutten, Rik Voster, and Wim Vandenbussche, "The Interplay of Language Norms and Usage Patterns: Comparing the History of Dutch, English, French and German," in *Norms and Usage in Language History, 1600–1900: A Sociolinguistic and Comparative Perspective*, ed. G. Rutten, R. Vosters, and W. Vandenbussche (Amsterdam and Philadelphia: John Benjamins Publishing Company, 2014), 2. See also section 5.2.3.

5.2 Methodological Renewal

As a remedy for the incomplete nature of available data (cf. above, chapters 1 and 4), it has been suggested that historical linguists should strive for *informational maximalism*—"the utilization of all reasonable means to extend our knowledge of what might have been going on in the past, even though it is not directly observable."[12]

One of the aims of the present investigation is to suggest a basic inventory of functional spheres, or *registers*, of Russian in the 1740s (section 1.1). Such an inventory can be seen as a map of sorts. *Register*, as a term, has not always been used consistently. In the Introduction, we saw that Zhivov uses this term (Ru. регистр) to refer to varieties of language used in various communicative situations.[13] I also adhere to this definition and find it similar to the definition proposed by Richard A. Hudson:

> The term R E G I S T E R is widely used in sociolinguistics to refer to "varieties according to use", in contrast with dialects, defined as "varieties according to user". ... The distinction is needed because the same person may use very different linguistic items to express more or less the same meaning on different occasions, and the concept of "dialect" cannot reasonably be extended to include such variation.[14]

Asif Agha further explains:

> From the standpoint of function, distinctive registers are associated with social practices of every kind—such as law, medicine, prayer, science, magic, prophecy, commerce, military strategy, sports commentary, the observance of respect and etiquette, the expression of civility, social status, etc.[15]

---

12 Richard D. Janda and Brian D. Joseph, "On Language, Change, and Language Change, Or, Of History, Linguistics, and Historical Linguistics," in *The Handbook of Historical Linguistics*, ed. B. D. Joseph and R. D. Janda (Oxford: Blackwell, 2003), 37; cf. also Nevalainen and Raumolin-Brunberg, "Historical Sociolinguistics," 25.

13 Zhivov, *Istoriia*, 26.

14 R. A. Hudson, *Sociolinguistics*, 2nd ed. (Cambridge: Cambridge University Press, 1996), 45 (spacing from the original—T.R.).

15 Asif Agha, "Register," *Journal of Linguistic Anthropology* 9, nos. 1–2 (2000): 216.

One way of creating a tentative set of registers for Russian of the 1740s is to apply the *uniformitarian principle*.

5.2.1 The Uniformitarian Principle

The logical basis for the *uniformitarian principle* in linguistics is that: "[i]n a fundamental sense, human beings as biological, psychological and social creatures have remained largely unchanged over time."[16] Essentially, the *uniformitarian principle* says that language in society is likely to function similarly today as it did in the past. This can be explained by the fact that modern humans are biologically more or less identical to humans that lived thousands of years ago, and thereby also have a similar capacity for human language. At the same time, many societies in which humans live have experienced radical technological developments.

5.2.2 The Uniformitarian Principle and the Registers of Eighteenth-Century Russian

In 1991, the renowned Soviet scholar Iu. N. Karaulov identified the following forms and spheres of existence of the contemporary Russian language:

- мертвый язык памятников письменности;
- устный язык русских народных говоров, диалектный язык;
- письменный язык литературы, прессы, государственной документации;
- повседневный разговорный язык и просторечие;
- научно-технический и професссиональный язык;
- русский язык в машинной (электронно-вычислительной) среде;
- неисконная русская речь;
- язык русского зарубежья.[17]

---

16 Nevalainen and Raumolin-Brunberg, "Historical Sociolinguistics," 24–25. For a history of the term and its uses, see T. Craig Christy, *Uniformitarianism in Linguistics* (Amsterdam and Philadelphia: John Benjamins Publishing Company, 1983); Janda and Joseph, "On Language, Change, and Language Change," 28–29.

17 Iu. N. Karaulov, *O sostoianii russkogo iazyka sovremennosti: doklad na konferentsii "Russkii iazyk i sovremennost'. Problemy i perspektivy razvitiia rusistiki"* (Moscow: AN SSSR. Institut russkogo iazyka, 1991), 9 (The dead language of literary monuments; the spoken language of Russian dialects, dialect language; the written language of literature, the press, and state documentation; everyday informal speech and *prostorechie*; scientific, technical, and professional language; Russian language in a machine (computer) environment; non-native Russian

Notably, Karaulov makes no mention of жаргон (jargon, slang) in his enumeration of the forms and spheres of existence of modern Russian. Why he fails to do
so is unclear. It may be an attempt to keep his classification as simple as possible;
he emphasizes that further elaboration of the list would only lead to confusion.
Another explanation is the ban on jargon studies in the Soviet Union. From the
1930s to the 1970s such studies were taboo.[18] Since the early 1990s, however,
the discipline has been fundamentally renewed by the field studies of M. A.
Grachëv, who suggests an elaborate classification of social dialects. In abbrevi-
ated form this classification includes:

> *Жаргоны:* Классово-прослоечные: дворян, мещан, крестьян,
> духовенства и т. д. Производственные. По интересам и
> увлечениям. Молодежные. Семейные (идиолекты). Арго—
> лексика деклассированных (асоциальных) элементов.[19]

If the *uniformitarian principle* is applied to Karaulov's spheres of existence (incor-
porating the sociolects identified by Grachëv), we can argue that a number of
these spheres most likely had equivalents in the 1740s. For obvious reasons,
however, the results of previous research give reason to believe that the spheres
were probably structured differently. First, beginning with the most salient difference, "Russian language in a machine (computer) environment" did not exist
during the eighteenth century. Second, it seems necessary to merge a number
of the spheres of existence identified by Karaulov in the modern language. Thus
"the spoken language of Russian dialects" and "everyday informal speech and
prostorechie" belong together since no standard language had yet developed in

speech; diaspora Russian). For further elaboration of Karaulov's classification applied to
contemporary Russian, see Arto Mustajoki, "Raznovidnosti russkogo iazyka: analiz i klassifikatsiia," *Voprosy iazykoznaniia* 5 (2013): 3–27. I am indebted to Professor Mustajoki for
providing me with a copy of Karaulov's paper. A note on *prostorechie*: Zemskaia and Shmelëv
define *prostorechie* as "the unprepared, unconstrained speech of persons who have not mas-
tered the literary language" (неподготовленная, непринужденная речь лиц, не владеющих
литературным языком), cf. E. N. Zemskaia and D. N. Shmelëv, *Gorodskoe prostorechie: problemy izucheniia* (Moscow: Nauka, 1984), 10.
18 Gutschmidt, "Die ostslawische Region," 1857.
19 M. A. Grachëv, "Sovremennaia klassifikatsiia sotsial'nykh dialektov," in *Prepodavanie i izuchenie russkogo iazyka i literatury v kontektste sovremennoi iazykovoi politiki Rossii*, ed. L. I. Ruchina
(Nizhnii Novgorod: Natsional'nyi issledovatel'skii Nizhegorodskii gosudarstvennyi universitet im. N. I. Lobachevskogo, 2002), 73 (*Jargons:* those developed by a social class: jargons
of noblemen, town-dwellers, peasants, clergy, and so forth; by people of a certain profession;
by people who share the same interests and hobbies; the language of young people; family
jargons (idiolects); and argot: the vocabulary of marginalized groups).

the 1740s. Consequently, no spoken variety of such a standard language existed. Sociolects should be added where appropriate to this sphere of informal speech and to the sphere of professional language. Third, it is doubtful whether a separate sphere of "diaspora Russian" is relevant for the 1740s. It would represent an insignificant number of people. For example, the Russian-speaking minority of the formerly Swedish province of Ingria, where St. Petersburg was founded in 1703, no longer found itself outside Russia by the early eighteenth century. Fourth, it seems necessary to split some of the spheres based on what is already known about the eighteenth-century Russian language. Research on administrative documents from the 1740s indicates that a part of the state documentation most likely belongs in a separate sphere, continuing the business language traditions from earlier periods. We may label this "traditional administrative documentation." Also, printing was under strict government control, which would require a specific sphere for the language found in printed sources. We thus end up with a hypothetical set of macro spheres looking something like this:

- traditional literature and religious language;[20]
- the language of printed texts (imaginative literature, the press, state documentation, science and technology);
- traditional administrative documentation;
- informal speech;
- professional language;
- non-native Russian speech.

5.2.3 What May Have Influenced the Registers?

For the sake of discussion, let us allow for the possibility that the varieties of Russian in the 1740s could be divided as above or in some similar way. It is likely that changes and innovations to the spheres came from different sources. William Labov explains:

> *Changes from above* are introduced by the dominant social class, often with full public awareness. Normally, they represent borrowings from other speech communities that have higher

---

20 The sphere "traditional literature and religious language" is added as a way to unite genres that had texts composed in either Church Slavic or hybrid Church Slavic, not in vernacular Russian. Cf. Zhivov, *Ocherki*, 76.

prestige in the view of the dominant class. Such borrowings do not immediately affect the vernacular patterns of the dominant class or other social classes, but appear primarily in careful speech, reflecting a superposed dialect learned after the vernacular is acquired. ... *Changes from below* are systematic changes that appear first in the vernacular, and represent the operation of internal, linguistic factors. At the outset, and through most of their development, they are completely below the level of social awareness.[21]

If we consider how the history of Russian has been written throughout the modern period, it is not unfair to conclude that the "top down" approach has been predominant.

If we wish to study the language usage of as large a portion of Russian eighteenth-century society as possible, we must take into account that the nature of the evidence is liable to fluctuate: the amount of texts, length of individual texts, and other parameters may vary. For instance, certain groups in society may have produced only short texts, while other groups are represented by long texts. I suggest that a suitable method is available in the form of *register analysis*. By applying the successive steps of register analysis (explained below), we are in a position to analyze material of every kind and are not confined by such things as quantity (a parameter that includes both length and amount of texts).

5.2.4 Register Analysis

Register analysis is the umbrella term for a set of methodological techniques to carry out analyses of text varieties.[22] It consists of three basic constituents: situational context, linguistic analysis and functional analysis. As Douglas Biber and Susan Conrad show, register analysis does not have to focus exclusively on contemporary data. It is applicable to historical material as well.[23]

The situational context can be analyzed on the basis of seven characteristics. In describing these characteristics, this investigation draws on the method described by Biber and Conrad.[24] Their model represents an "informational

---

21 Labov, *Principles of Linguistic Change*, 1, 78 (italics in the original—T.R.).
22 Biber and Conrad, *Register, Genre, and Style*.
23 Ibid., 222–253.
24 Ibid., 40–48.

maximum," and not all the features they list can be found in all texts. These features include:

(1) *Participants*. How many participants feature prominently in the text? Can we identify their social characteristics such as age, education and profession?
(2) *Relations among participants*, that is, status, personal relationship.
(3) *Channel*, or medium (speech, writing). For Russian language of the eighteenth century, writing is the only medium available, but this can be divided into print and handwriting.
(4) *Processing circumstances*, that is, the history of editing.
(5) *Setting*. Is the place of communication public or private?
(6) *Communicative purposes*. Was the document written as a report, for entertainment or in a diary? Does it summarize information from different sources? Is it factual or imaginative?
(7) *Topic*. Can the document be placed in a specific topical domain, such as domestic life, business, education, politics, and so forth?[25]

The linguistic analysis is central to a register analysis and will determine the characteristics of the text in terms of vocabulary, morphology and syntax. It generally includes a quantitative analysis of linguistic features.[26]

The final step in a register analysis is the functional interpretation, trying to answer *why* a certain text combines certain formal characteristics with a certain content.[27] While Biber and Conrad find that a register analysis typically begins with the situational context, there is also a cyclical element involved. The cyclical element may make it necessary to go over the analysis more than once.[28]

5.3 Register Analysis of Russian from the 1740s

Based on the lines of reasoning followed in this chapter, a combination of methods has been chosen for the present investigation. The basis for this combination is register analysis, but certain adaptations are necessitated by the historical material of the present investigation. The result is an analytical tool containing qualitative as well as quantitative elements. In choosing between qualitative

---

25 Ibid., 113–115.
26 Ibid., 51–69.
27 Ibid., 69–74.
28 Ibid., 39.

and quantitative approaches, it is worthwhile to consider Edgar Schneider's recommendation:

> A qualitative investigation is usually less sophisticated but more robust than a quantitative one, because some potentially distorting effects (such as overuse of a salient form) skew frequencies of occurrence but not necessarily the qualitative inventory of forms in a variety. It is possible that a written corpus allows reasonable (but isolated) observations, though not broader generalizations.[29]

In the present study, while mindful of its potential weaknesses, qualitative approach was chosen in order to allow investigation of texts regardless of length.

---

29 Schneider, "Investigating Historical Variation," 75–76.

CHAPTER 6

Situational Analysis of Registers

Since texts from the 1740s differ greatly in content and format, fitting all available data into a single, one-dimensional methodological solution may cause a methodological bias. Therefore, it was suggested in chapter 5 that the data undergo a three-pronged analysis in order to take into account as much information as possible. The goal was to allow the examination of all texts suitable for quantitative analysis, regardless of their length. The combination of methods chosen after these considerations draws on the register analysis framework, but has been adapted to suit this investigation.

The first step in a register analysis is to establish the situational context of the data. The importance of understanding the conditions in which a text has been created is emphasized in the register analysis framework as well as many other handbooks on textual analysis: "… communication does not take place in a vacuum, and texts are not constructed and interpreted in a vacuum. Therefore, to identify the meaning of a text, a careful examination of the circumstances in which the text is created and understood is always needed."[1]

To briefly summarize, a situational analysis can be achieved by studying seven features of the data: participants, relationships among participants, channel, processing circumstances, setting, communicative purpose, and topic.

6.1 Participants

In written communication, the participants are the author and the addressee. Authors are sometimes individuals or groups, sometimes institutions, and

---

1 Bodil Helder, *Textual Analysis* (Frederiksberg: Samfundslitteratur, 2011), 13.

the same is true for the addressee. We also find texts written by anonymous authors—sometimes institutions—and addressed to an anonymous recipient.

From a strictly linguistic point of view, it may be impossible to determine exactly who should be considered the author of Russian documents from the 1740s. There are several reasons for this. Sometimes, documents are entirely anonymous, leaving no clues about the identity of their creators. In other cases, as pointed out in chapter 3, the difficulties in ascribing a text to a particular author relate to the circumstances surrounding the text's production. This process may have involved template texts and/or cooperation between several individuals, including a secretary and a clerk, which makes pinpointing the author(s) essentially impossible.

6.1.1 Individuals

Beginning with printed texts, we generally find that authored and translated books from the 1740s provide the names of authors and translators on the title pages:

> *Краткое руководство къ краснорѣчію, книга перьвая, въ которой содержится Риторика показующая общія правила обоего краснорѣчія, то есть ораторіи и поезіи,* сочиненная въ пользу любящихъ словесныя науки трудами Михайла Ломоносова Императорской Академии Наукъ и Историческаго собранія Члена, Химіи Профессора. Въ Санктпетербургѣ при Императорской Академіи наукъ 1748.[2]

> *Разговоръ между Чужестраннымъ человѣкомъ і Россійскімъ объ ортографіі старінной и новой і о всемъ что пріпадлежітъ къ сей матеріі,* сочіненъ Васільемъ Тредіаковскімъ Профессоромъ елоквенціі. Въ Санктпетербургѣ прі Імператорской Академіі наукъ 1748.[3]

> *Совершенное воспитаніе дѣтей содержащее въ себѣ; молодымъ знатнаго рода, и шляхетнаго достоинства людямъ,*

---

2 Mikhailo Lomonosov, *Kratkoe rukovodstvo k krasnorechiiu* ... (St. Petersburg: Imperatorskaia Akademiia nauk, 1748).

3 Trediakovskii, *Razgovor.*

благопристойные манѣры и приличныя поведеніи. Со многими къ поспѣшествованію щастія ихъ способными правилами, и нравоучительными разсужденіями; изданное отъ Абата Белегарда. А съ францускаго на Россійской языкъ перевелъ сію книгу канцеляріи Академіи Наукъ секретарь Сергѣй Волчковъ. Печатано въ Санктпетербургѣ при Императорской Академіи Наукъ 1747 года.[4]

However, not all printed texts contain information about their authors. Authored or translated books constituted only a portion of the output from the printing shops, while the majority of printed texts were imperial edicts. For example, consider the number of imperial legislative documents compared to the total number of titles in the *Union Catalogue of Russian Eighteenth-century Secular Printed Books (1708–1800):*[5]

Year	Total number of titles	Of which edicts (указы)
1740	57	33
1741	57	37
1742	82	46
1743	52	35
1744	42	20
1745	32	13
1746	62	43
1747	60	43
1748	105	79
1749	38	23

As seen in section 3.1.3, Russia's monarch was the sole formal legislative authority. While the monarch signed the laws and may have dictated minor changes to them, the texts themselves were produced by the relevant state agencies. Thus, laws were published in the name of Emperor Ioann Antonovich, born on August 12, 1740, from the very beginning of his brief reign:

4   Abat Belegard [Jean-Baptiste Morvan de Bellegarde], *Sovershennoe vospitanie detei ...*, trans. Sergei Volchkov (St. Petersburg: Imperatorskaia Akademiia nauk, 1747).

5   *Union Catalogue of Russian Eighteenth-Century Secular Printed Book (1708–1800)*, Primo, accessed November 18, 2021, https://primo.nlr.ru/primo-explore/search?query=lsr07,ex act,1749,AND&tab=default_tab&search_scope=A1XVIII_07NLR&sortby=rank&vid= 07NLR_VU2&lang=en_US&mode=advanced&offset=0.

Божіею милостію Мы Іоаннъ третій, Императоръ и Самодержецъ Всероссійскій и протчая, и протчая, и протчая.

Имѣя всегдашнее попеченіе о своихъ вѣрныхъ подданныхъ,
кои отъ банкрутовъ въ крайнее разореніе были привожены,
и милосердуя къ нимъ указали по всеподданѣйшему Намъ,
Нашего Сената представленію съ тѣми банкрутами, кои
до сего явились, а дѣла̀ ихъ не рѣшены, и которые впредь
явятся, поступать по учиненному, и подъ симъ Нашимъ
Всемилостивѣшимъ указомъ напечатанному уставу во всемъ
непрѣменно. ... Подлинной Именемъ Его Императорскаго
Величества: отъ Ея Императорскаго Высочества Государыни
Правительницы Великія Княгини Анны Всеа россіи,
апробованъ Декабря 15 дня 1740. Печатанъ при Сенатѣ
тогожъ Декабря 17 дня.[6]

In handwritten documents, we find that various kinds of texts were written by
all literate levels of society. At the highest level, the imperial court produced
diplomatic correspondence. Letters often took the form of personal missives,
as exemplified by the following message from Empress Elisabeth to the Swedish
crown prince Adolf Fredrik, notifying him of the marriage between the future
emperor, Peter III, and the future empress, Catherine II:

[hand 1] Свѣтлѣишій кронъ принцъ; дружебно-любезный/
племянникъ./ ꙗко по ꙍсобливомъ всевышшаго бога предъ-/
усмотренію, и по моемъ соизволенію, мой/ вселюбезнѣишій
племянникъ Его jмператорское/ высочество великій князь
всероссіискій Петръ,/ наслѣдникъ норвежской, владѣющей
герцогъ/ шлезвигъ голстинской, штормарнской, и дитмар-/
ской, графъ о́лденбꙋргской и́ делменгорстской &с./ съ
ея императорскимъ высочествомъ великою княгинею
всероссіискою Екатериною, урожден-/ною княгинею
ангалтскою, герцогинею саѯонскою,/ энгернскою, и
вестфалскою, графинею асканскою, госꙋдарынею цербстскою,
бернбꙋргскою, эверскою,/ и́ книпгаузенскою &с. в̀ здѣшней
моей импера-/торской столицѣ въ „21ом„ сего мⷭ҇ца
благополꙋчно/ в̀ брачное сочетаніе встꙋпилъ. Тако я ни-/мало

---

6   *Ustav o bankrutakh* (St. Petersburg: Senat, December 17, 1740).

умедлить не хотѣла, что бъ вашемꙋ/ королевскомꙋ высочествꙋ
и́ любви, о́ такомъ/ благополꙋчномъ, и мнѣ толь радостномъ/
произшествіи, чрезъ сіе јзвѣстно не учинить,// ни како не
сꙋмнѣваясь, что ваше королевское высочество и́ любовь не
токмо мнѣ, ј моемꙋ/ јмператорскомꙋ домꙋ все то, еже ќ моемꙋ/
и́ о́ного удоволствію и благополꙋчію касается,/ о́хотно желать,
но и́ ваше в́ томъ участіе/ принять, слѣдователно же о́ семъ
счастливо/ совершившемся брачномъ сочетаніи порадоватся/
и́ вышеупомянꙋтымъ высокимъ новосочетан-/нымъ и́ с́ вашей
стороны *от* милости все-/вышшаго, всякаго благословенія
и́ благополꙋчія/ возжелать соизволите. в́прочемъ же/ с́
нео́тмѣнною благоволителною дрꙋжбою всегда/ пребываю./
вашего королевского высочества ј любви/ дрꙋжебно со́хотная
тетка./ [hand 2] Елисаветъ/ [hand 1] в санктъ петербꙋрхѣ/
„26„ авгꙋста. 1745.[7]

The Empress personally signed the letter, but the text was written by one of the administration's anonymous scribes. The original content of the letter is minimal while the majority of it consists of titles and set formulas.

Formulaic expressions are also a well-known feature of Russian private letters. However, the expressions used are characteristic to the domain of personal correspondence:

желаю вам г︷сдрямъ моим во множество летъ здра*в*ствова*ти* з
государями моими бра*т*цами.[8]

In a situational analysis, the use of formulaic expressions in a text tells us that the author wishes to situate the text within a particular social context. Purely linguistic aspects of the use of formulaic expressions will be discussed further in chapter 7.

The tradition of scribes writing private letters was not limited to the highest levels of state administration. This occurs also in other parts of society. For example, in a private letter signed by the Prince Mikhail Ukhtomskii in 1742, the Prince himself has written only the last few lines of the letter and the signature. The scribe was responsible for the rest:

---

7   Swedish National Archives, Muscovitica 623.
8   Swedish National Archives, Militaria 1588.

покорно прошу ежели возможно то пожаловать/ писа*т* ко мне о сьвоем sдор*ω*вье чег*ω̈* *ω̈*хотъ*н̈ω̈*//с радостию слышать желаю./ Так*о̇* пребуду вашъ моег*ω̈*/ г͡сдря добр*ω̈*желателны слуга/ к͡нзъ михал*ω* ухтомскои.⁹

Finally, the following description of individuals involved in the production of documents would not be complete unless we acknowledge a formulaic expression that is very common throughout the period under investigation: the tradition of vouching for the content of a document written by another by "laying one's hand" to it:

> … к се*ï* скаске попъ Михаи*л*/ ј*г*на*т*евъ р8к8 приложи*л*.¹⁰

> … ксем8 допросу вм*е̑*сто гранодера василя *ѳ*едорова по ево прошению кабар*д*инскои гранодерскои роты ротнои писа*р* никиѳо*р* рябовъ р8к8 приложилъ.¹¹

As seen in the last example, a soldier asked the company scribe to vouch for his information. Considering that historian Boris Mironov calculated the literacy among army recruits to be about 0.5 percent (section 3.2.2), it is highly like that Vasilii Fëdorov was unable to sign his own name.

What do we know about the authors? Well-known historical individuals such as the Empress Elisabeth, Mikhailo Lomonosov, or Vasilii Trediakovskii have been thoroughly studied. The majority of authors, however, remain largely anonymous. Some have indicated their name and professional title, but still they remain anonymous in the sense that we know nothing about them other than their name. We have the documents that they left behind and, based on the content, we can determine some information about the author's educational background.

---

9   Ibid.

10 *Skazka prikhodskogo sviashchennika tserkvi Nikolaia Chudotvortsa, chto na Konanove Vologodskogo uezda, Mikhaila Ignat'eva o rodivshikhsia, brakosochetavshikhsia i umershikh v prikhode za 1740 god,* KAU VO "GAVO," f. 496, op. 1, d. 10251, l. 713, accessed November 4, 2021, https://uniqdoc.gov35.ru/docs/view/532.

11 Swedish National Archives, Extranea Ryssland 157.4. It should be noted that "laying hand" does not imply putting one's fingerprint on a document. This idea, which is sometimes found in popular descriptions, is erroneous. In eighteenth-century Europe, fingerprints were not used as means of identification, cf. "Fingerprinting History," accessed May 26, 2021, https://tri-statefingerprinting.com/fingerprinting-history/.

Peter the Great, in his *General'nyi reglament* of 1720, established the rules for training young men as administrators. In order to be hired, the candidates were to be trained in copying text and in arithmetic. Once hired, they were to receive further training under the guidance of a secretary. Both noblemen and commoners could be trained and later employed.[12]

A tentative conclusion is that junior clerks whose names appear in documents were, by twenty-first-century standards, young men in their twenties and thirties and thus born and educated in the 1710s to 1730s. Only a handful of people mentioned in the material can be positively identified as being older than sixty. Two such individuals are Field-Marshal Peter de Lacy (born 1678) and the diplomat and military leader, Count A. I. Rumiantsev (born 1680). Unfortunately, neither wrote more than his signature.

6.1.2 Institutions

In many cases, printed texts originate from institutions, notably the state. In such cases, the institution appears as the author and no mention is made of the individuals behind the text:

> *Описаніе обоихъ тріумфальныхъ воро́тъ поставленныхъ въ честь Всепресвѣтлѣйшей Державнѣйшей Великой Государынѣ Императрицѣ Елисаветѣ Первой Самодержицѣ Всероссійской по воспріятіи въ Москвѣ короны Шведовъ побѣдившей всю Финландію державѣ своей покорившей и торжественно въ Санктпетербургъ возвратившейся для засвидѣтельствованія всеподданнѣйшія ревности и всеусерднѣйшихъ желаній Ея Императорскому Величеству съ глубочайшимъ благоговѣніемъ отъ Сенатской канторы поднесенное.* В Санктпетербургѣ декабря 22 дня 1742 года.[13]

The *Sanktpeterburgskie vedomosti*, Russia's newspaper during the 1740s, belongs to the category of institutional texts. Articles in the newspaper were not signed, and as discussed in section 4.2.2, Russian-language content was delivered to the

---

12 *Ego Tsarskogo Velichestva general'nyi reglament ili ustav* (St. Petersburg, February 27, 1720), 27, accessed November 5, 2021, https://raritety.rusarchives.ru/dokumenty/generalnyy-reglament.

13 *Opisanie oboikh triumfal'nykh vorot …* (St. Petersburg: n. p., 1742).

editorial office from various state agencies. Although not named, the author of the *Vedomosti* is the state. Focusing exclusively on the Russian content of the *Vedomosti*, that is, excluding the translated foreign news, we find that much of the domestic reporting consists of matters concerning the state, such as court festivities and government matters. This is true also for the advertisements, although private initiatives also occur. The domestic content below is from a single issue of the *Vedomosti*, no. 1 (1741) and serves as an illustration.

Отъ города Архангельскаго 12 декабря.

Ея императорскаго высочества нашей пресвѣтлѣйшей великой княгини и государыни правительницы всеа Россіи Анны высокій день рожденія 7 числа, а высокое тезоименитство Ея же императорскаго высочества 9 дня сего мѣсяца, съ великою радостію и всенароднымъ восклицаніемъ здѣсь праздновано. При отправленія божія службы въ россійской соборной церкви была съ крѣпости пушечная пальба, а отъ поставленныхъ въ параду полковъ трикратняя пальба изъ мѣлкаго ружья учинена. О полудни Его превосходительство господинъ вице-губернаторъ и обер-комендантъ фонъ Лицкинъ, всѣхъ присутствующихъ здѣсь знатнѣйшихъ, военныхъ, статскихъ, и лучшее купечество, богато у себя трактовалъ; а какъ при столѣ за высокія здравіи пили, въ то время происходила изъ поставленныхъ передъ оберъ-комендантскимъ домомъ пушекъ пальба. При наступленіи вечера всѣ домы здѣшняго города были илюминованы, а притомъ всякъ ревностно старался, дабы искренную свою радость для сихъ высокоторжественныхъ дней, разными образы публично засвидѣтельствовать.

Въ Санктпетербургѣ 2 генваря.

Вчерашняго утра то есть въ день новаго года; бывшіе у двора здѣшніе и чужестранные господа министры, и прочіе обоего пола знатнѣйшіе персоны Еѣ императорскому высочеству государыни великой княгини и правительницѣ всея Россіи Аннѣ, симъ торжественнымъ праздникомъ всенижайше поздравляли.

Для извѣстія.

О поставкѣ въ Кронштатскую и Оранїенбомскую морскія гошпитали, на дачу больящимъ генваря съ перьваго сего 1741 года чрезъ цѣлой годъ свѣжаго говяжья мяса многократно уже публиковано; а буде кто оное мясо ставить пожелаетъ, тѣ бъ заблаговременно являлись въ здѣшней Адмиралитействъ коллегїи по экспедїцїи комисарїатской.

Въ гварнизонномъ зейггаузѣ находящїяся, ямбургскїя чистыя стекла числомъ двести девяносто девять, да пять зеркалъ стѣнныхъ, велѣно по опредѣленїю здѣшней гварнизонной канцелярїи продать съ публичнаго торгу; а ежели кто оныя купить желаетъ тѣ бъ являлись въ упомянутой гварнизонной канцелярїи заблаговременно.

О перевозѣ нынѣшнею зимою съ Нарвской ломки казенной ординарной плиты, тысяча семи сотъ тритцети восьми кубическихъ сажень, такожъ и изъ находящеися въ Крон- /штатѣ/ штатѣ на тѣхъ мѣстахъ гдѣ по привозѣ выгружена была, ординарной штуковой и тесаной плиты, до тысячи кубическихъ и квадратныхъ сажень, неоднократно уже публиковано, только еще и по нынѣ охотниковъ къ тому не явилось, ежели же кто означенную плиту; а именно Нарвскую съ ломки на судовую въ Нарвѣ же пристань, а изъ находящейся въ Кронштатѣ съ мѣстъ внутрь заворотовъ, въ каналѣ и въ другїя показанныя мѣста нынѣшнимъ зимнимъ временемъ перевозить, и ставить пожелаетъ, тѣ бъ для торгу и договору въ (sic!—T. R.) цѣнѣ являлись въ канторѣ кронштатскихъ строеней недмедлѣнно.

Сего генваря седьмаго, восьмаго и девятаго числа во второмъ часу по полудни будетъ продавать, на Адмиралитейскомъ острову у Галерной верьфи, во второмъ домѣ отъ Крюкова канала указомъ опредѣленной аукцїонистъ Сутовъ, серебреной сервисъ, а притомъ мѣдную и оловяную посуду, аглинскїя кабинеты, зерькалы, столы, стулья, хрустальныя паникадилы, и подсвѣшники стѣнныя, галанскїе полотна, корѣты каляски, и другїя вещи а буде кто изъ оныхъ купить что пожелаетъ, тѣ бъ являлись въ вышеозначенной домъ по вышеписаннымъ днямъ въ уреченные часы.

> У торговаго иноземца Ивана Брунланта продаются свѣжїе устерсы повольною цѣною, о чемъ чрезъ сїе объявляется.[14]

As the text demonstrates, domestic newspaper articles and advertisements are all preoccupied with the state's affairs. The domestic news report begins with a piece on the celebrations of the birthday and name day in the northern town of Arkhangelsk. This is followed by a short notice, a court circular of sorts, that describes how foreign ambassadors and other dignitaries paid their respects by personally bringing their New Year's wishes to the Empress. Following the news, we find a section devoted to the state, which includes a government invitation for tenders for the delivery of beef to military hospitals. The text reveals that the invitation has already been published several times. Then there is an advertisement for glass and mirrors to be sold at a state auction organized by the garrison office. This section of the newspaper, focused on the state and its needs, ends with another invitation of tenders, this time for transport. Only at the very end of the newspaper do we find advertisements for private enterprises: Sutov's auction house has placed an advertisement, and Ivan Brunlant, a "foreign merchant," is selling moderately priced fresh oysters.

Comparing the texts found in the *Vedomosti* in 1741 and 1748, we find texts that are very similar in structure. Two advertisements—one by the state and one private—serve as evidence:

> О поставкѣ въ морскїя Санктпетербургскую и Кронштатскую гошпитали хмелю Клязмы 200. пудъ хотъ двоекратно и публиковано, токмо охотниковъ никого не явилось: чего ради чрезъ сїе третично объявляется, чтобъ желающїе тотъ хмель поставить немѣдленно явились въ Адмиралтейскомъ комисарïатѣ.[15]

> Въ Милïонной улицѣ въ домѣ господина Генерала Ушакова живеть мастерица, которая умѣетъ всякїя богатыя матерïи, золотыя и серебреныя позументы, такожъ шелковыя кружива и сицъ весьма чисто мыть, о чемъ чрезъ сïе охотникамъ объявляется.[16]

---

14 *Sanktpeterburgskie vedomosti* 1 (1741).
15 *Sanktpeterburgskie vedomosti*, January 1, 1748, 8, accessed November 17, 2021, https://www.vedomosti1728.ru/pdf.cgi?r=99&key_pdf=75ixo0KdKmmbRhtz.
16 *Sanktpeterburgskie vedomosti*, January 1, 1748, 8.

The advertisements from the beginning and end of the 1740s contain closely related patterns. This can be explained in two possible ways. First, by assuming that the Russian economy—state and private—worked in similar ways in the beginning and the end of the decade: state infrastructure projects were conducted according to similar principles, as was privately organized trade. Second, by assuming that the *Vedomosti* editorial office maintained essentially the same organization throughout the 1740s. Johann Bröme (cf. section 4.2.2) edited the newspaper in both 1741 and 1748.

Similar to newspapers, the author of administrative documents also appears to be an institution. The composition of texts involved a team of individuals, as the following example shows:

[hand 1] Промемория/ Канцеляріи Главнои артилеріи j
ѳортификаціи/ гсдрьственнои каморъ коллеги в кантору
лифлянских/ и эстълянскихъ делъ: понеже в силе
гсдрьственнои/ военнои коллегіï и канцеляріи главнои
артиллеріи/ и ѳортификаціи указовъ для некоторого секре/
тного исправления; посылается в выборхъ jнже/нерного
корпᲂса прапорщики иванъ меншеи/ лукомскои и симонъ
лаптевъ. и надлежитъ ехать в скорости: с ними ж посылается
нужнеишие чертежи/ j инструменты. того ради по Ея/
Імператорскаго Величества указᲂ/ канцеляріи главнои
артилеріи и фортификаціи/ кантора приказали во оную
гсдрьственнои/ каморъ коллегіи в канторᲂ лифлянских j
эстлянских делъ послать промеморию и требовать чтоб/
оным прапорщикам для проездᲂ до выборха гдѣ/ ямовъ
не имеется даны для каждомᲂ по три/ уездныя подводы за
ᲂказныя прогоны и гсдрьстве/ннои камор коллеги кантора
лифлянских j эстъ/лянских дел да благоволитъ ᲂчинить о
тᲂм/ по ея jмператорскаго величества/ указу [hand 2] S.
Schultz./ [hand 3] секретарь гавріил міхаилов/ [hand 1]
канцеляристъ степан ивановъ/ маия 2 дня/ 1749 году/ о даче
инженерам прапорщикам по три подводы каждому.[17]

Judging by the handwriting and Ivanov's signature, we can see that the clerk Stepan Ivanov was the individual holding the quill. The text, however, hardly

17 National Archives of Finland, Vanhan Suomen tilejä, 10034 Kamarikonttorin käsittelemiä ja ratkaisemia asioita, jotka koskevat Viipurin provinssia (1749).

reflects his individual linguistic choices. The text is a memorandum and closely follows the typical sequence for that particular type of text: author and addressee, description of the matter at hand introduced by понеже, and instructions concerning the desired action introduced by того ради. At the end of the document, the officials involved have signed their names. While the document contains examples of spelling emanating from the scribe, it may in equal measure contain input from the other members of the team, in this case Schultz and Mikhailov.

6.2 Relationships among Participants

The relationships among participants can be grouped into three categories: superior, equal, and inferior.

In the third category is included the relationship between the imperial power and its subjects. In the style of the times and similar to forms of address employed elsewhere in Europe, official documents prescribed that Russian subjects should refer to themselves as "the lowest slaves" when contacting the authorities in supplications:

> Вашего Імператорскаго Величества нижаишїи рабъ.[18]

The deep respect was typical of correspondence with the government, as well as in traditional epistolary style between family members:

> покорно ва̃с г̃сдръ батюшка/ прошу пожаловать отдать/ мой
> нижаиши поклонъ г̃сдрю/ моему и затю петру гаврилеви/
> чу и г̃сдрыне моей сестрице/ лукере гересимовне и въсем/
> нашим приятелям/ присем писав[ъ] вашъ/ государей мой
> покорны/ слуга и сынъ миха/ила турчениковъ/ земны свои
> поклон/ отдаю и благословения вашего/ прошу.[19]

Minimizing self-importance was the rule in correspondence between perceived social equals. Thus, a Russian major general—writing from a position of power—would conclude a letter to a Swedish count with the formula:

---

18 *Forma o titulakh Ego Imperatorskago Velichestva.*
19 National Archives of Sweden, Militaria 1588.

вашего сиятелства/ милостиваго гсдря моегѡ/ покорныи сл8га.[20]

The first category—a superior ordering an inferior—is found in countless orders from the Empress, the state, and its agencies to subordinate levels. For example:

.... сия вѣдомость поб8ждаетъ насъ исполняя Ея императорского величества повелениѧ преодолѣть всѣ тр8дности возпослѣдовавшияся ѿ оттепели, которая близь трехъ недел продолжалась, и спѣшим какъ найболше возможнѡ с вашими превосходителствами увидится и тр8дится ѿ мирномъ делѣ. ...[21]

6.3 Channel

In the register analysis framework, *channel* is used to refer to the medium of the information, that is, speech or writing. Fragments of spoken language can be preserved in writing, although, for the most part, Russian language of the eighteenth century is accessible to us only in written form. This written language, in turn, can be divided into printed, engraved, and handwritten texts.

Handwritten documents are quite heterogeneous: some texts are the result of meticulous preparation while others represent little more than scribbling.[22] Rather than dividing handwritten documents according to genre or text type, I suggest dividing them into three groups labeled *elaborate*, *intermediate*, and *basic*, based on how carefully they have been prepared.

Documents in the *elaborate* group show evidence of meticulous preparation. Evidence of such preparation exists in the form of drafts archived along with a fair copy, or documents carefully penned in ceremonial cursive (парадная скоропись). This group includes official documents originating in the central Imperial administration or in close proximity to it. Such texts were produced by professional scribes. The *intermediate* group is by far the largest and consists of

---

20 Swedish National Archives, Regional Archives, Uppsala, Södermanland, Landskontoret, D VI 17 (Your Highness, [I am] Your Lordship's humble servant).

21 National Archives of Sweden, Muscovitica 664.

22 Cf. Chloé Ragazzoli, Ömür Harmanşah, Chiara Salvador, and Elizabeth Frood, eds., *Scribbling through History: Graffiti, Places and People from Antiquity to Modernity* (London: Bloomsbury Academic, 2018).

civil and military administrative documents and correspondence. Such documents are often written by professionals but display fewer features of careful editing than the documents in the *elaborate* group. Finally, the *basic* group includes texts that show little or no signs of having been edited. They may or may not be written by a professional scribe and may represent a draft or a simple note.

6.3.1 Change of Printed Medium: A Weather Phenomenon in Spain

In late December of 1743, a curious phenomenon was observed and heard in Cartagena, Spain. The incident was so remarkable that it sparked an interest across Europe. Exactly what caused the incident is difficult to say. Perhaps it was an electrical discharge or parts of a meteorite breaking up in Earth's atmosphere.

In Russia, an article about the event was published in the *Vedomosti*. Later, this *Vedomosti* text was transliterated from the civil typeface and its modern orthography to a more traditional one, engraved, and printed in the form of a popular print. The Russian text was a translation from a source in some other language. Although not identical, the Russian and English texts contain significant similarities:

the *Vedomosti* version[23]	the *lubok* version[24]	the *Scots Magazine*[25]
Въ четвертокъ февраля 16. дня 1744. года.	Вчетвертокъ февралѧ 16 днѧ 1744.	
Изъ Мадрита отъ 6. января	измандрита ѿтъ 6: генварѧ.	
Изъ Картагены уведомляютъ, что декабря 28. дня поутру въ началѣ 6. часа	Изъ Картагены 8вѣдомлѧютъ что декабрѧ 28 днѧ по8тр8 в началѣ 6 часа	A surprising *Phænomenon* was observed at Carthagena in Old Spain on the 17th of December. About five in the evening there appeared, on the side of the mountain of Roland, situate some leagues to the West of that city,
усмотрѣно на воздухѣ весьма чрезвычайное явленïе	8смотрѣно на воздухъ весьма чрезвычаиное ѧвление	
	кроландовои горѣ. которѧ лѣжитъ на нѣсколько миль отъ помѧн8таго города къ запад8	

23 *Gazeta "Sanktpeterburgskie Vedomosti" XVIII veka: Ukazateli k soderzhaniiu*, accessed 26 April, 2021, https://www.vedomosti1728.ru/card.cgi?r=60&d=1744-02-16.

24 "Iavlenie, vidennoe v Karfagene 6 ianvaria 1744 goda," NĖB Knizhnye pamiatniki, accessed October 14, 2021, https://kp.rusneb.ru/item/reader/yavlenie-vidennoe-v-karfagene-6-yan-varya-1744-goda. The text was also edited in the nineteenth century, but the edition contains errors and must be considered obsolete: Rovinskii, *Russkie narodnye kartinki*, vol. 2, 59.

25 *The Scots Magazine* 6, accessed November 17, 2021, https://babel.hathitrust.org/cgi/pt?id=nyp.33433076839087&view=1up&seq=61 (italics from the original).

the *Vedomosti* version[23]	the *lubok* version[24]	the *Scots Magazine*[25]
къ Роландовой горѣ, которая лежитъ на нѣсколько миль отъ помянутого гóрода къ зáпаду.	оно представляло огонь на подобие рѣки в немалои широтѣ разливающеисѧ. кото/рои распространялсѧ къ восток8. и производилъ так8ю ѧсность. что глаза едва того терпѣть могли.	a vast stream of light, resembling a river of fire, with a kind of fall or cascade; which afterwards formed a sort of sheet of fire, extending several leagues to the East, affording so bright a light, that the eye could scarce endure it.
Оно представляло огонь на подобіе рѣкй въ немалой широтѣ разливающейся, которой распространялся къ востоку, и производилъ такую ясность, что глазà едва того терпѣть могли.		
Пóслѣ сего перемѣнилась оная рѣка въ горящей шаръ, которой на нѣкоторое разстояніе по воздуху катавшись, вдругъ раздѣлился на 4. разныя огня, изъ которыхъ одинъ съ великою силою обратился къ сѣверу, другой къ югу, третій къ востоку, а четвертой къ зáпаду,	послѣ сего перемѣнилась онаѧ рѣка в горѧщеи шаръ. которои на нѣкоторое расстоѧніе по возд8х8 катавшіісь. вдр8гъ раздѣліѧсѧ на 4 разныѧ огнѧ из которыхъ юдинъ с великою силою обратилсѧ къ сѣвѣр8 ар8гои къ юг8 третеи къ восток8. а четвертой к запад8.	There afterwards appeared a great globe of fire beneath it, which, in the space of some minutes, broke into four lesser balls, that flew off to the North, South, East, and West.
и притомъ здѣлался такой жестокой громъ, что всѣ жители на нѣсколько миль вкругъ оной услывавши, устрашились.	и притомъ здѣлалсѧ такои жестокои громь. что всѣ жители на нѣсколко миль вкр8гъ юнои 8слышавши 8страшились.	This irruption (*sic!*—T.R.) was attended with a clap of thunder, so loud, that it wakened, and even stunned, the inhabitants for several leagues around.
Пóслѣ сего слышны были еще 4. другіе такіе удара, но не такъ сильны какъ первой,	послѣ сего слышни былї еще 4 др8гие такие 8дара. но не такъ сïлны какъ первои.	The four lesser balls broke each with a thunder-clap, but nothing near so loud as the first.
а чрезъ все сïе время небо было весьма ясно, также и звѣзды сильно свѣтили.	и чрезъ все сие времѧ небо было весма ѧ (*sic!*—T.R.) ѧсно. таже и звезды силно свѣтили	During the whole time, the sky was perfectly serene, and the stars shone very bright.

From a business perspective, the easiest thing for the producer of the *lubok* version would have been to simply copy the civil typeface text of the *Vedomosti* version without alterations. The transliteration of the entire text to a more traditional graphic style and orthography was a labor-intensive process and occurred for a reason. In all probability, the producer of the *lubok* version was aware of the reading habits of his intended audience and knew that it was unfamiliar with text printed in the civil typeface. This, in turn, supports the idea that during the

1740s, texts printed in the civil typeface were not very common among ordinary people.

6.3.2 Speech to Writing: Witness Statements

Fragments of spoken language from the eighteenth century are scarce. However, legal documents, such as witness statements may contain short passages of spoken language. The following example, taken from a witness statement, tells the story of a conflict between a landlady and a group of soldiers living in her house. A fight breaks out when the landlady tears the sheet from one of the beds:

> … j в то время/ пришла квартиры моеи хозяика j схватила/ прастыню с постѣли котор8ю товарищь мои/ гранодеръ василѣи ѳедоров вырвал 8 нѣи обратно/ j за то сержантъ шиповаловъ ево ѳедорова/ 8дарил вщок8 и обявленно (*sic!*—T.R.) м8жикъ нилсъ/ юнъ сонъ схватя ево зсади за волосы j повалил/ промеж к8ля м8ки и шкапа j селъ коленками/ на гр8ди и билъ к8лакомъ по голове j бранил/ р8синъ каналия шелма а потомъ схва/тя стоящѣе близ шкап8 р8же j бил прик/ладомъ в гр8дь и и (*sic!*—T.R.) сорвал на немъ р8ба/шк8 тогда онои ѳедоров схватил за при/клад одною р8кою и закричал мнѣ jзо *все* (*sic!*—T.R.) силы чтоб ево отнял ибо тотъ м8жикъ/ *бьет* ево смѣртѣлно а мѣня сержантъ/ шиповалов тогда тоскал за волосы/ а квартиры моеи хозяинъ работник j *девка*/ 8хватя меня поперекъ и за р8ки держали/ чтоб ево ѳедорова *от* побоеи я нѣ отнелъ однакож/ 8слыша тотъ ево ѳедорова крикъ прибѣжал/ еще гранодеръ быковъ и какъ прибѣжалъ// то оне j спужали битъ меня j ѳедорова/ покин8ли j покин8вши пошли вонъ *от* насъ/ то я вк8пѣ з гранодеромъ ѳедоровымъ/ о *тех* своих побоях на обявленного м8жика/ нил*с*она пришедъ 8 гсдна подпор8тчика/ ѳонамѣрса просили гдѣ и онои м8жикъ пришед на дворъ к подпор8тчик8 почем8 онои гсдинъ под/пор8тчикъ ѳон амѣрсъ призвал к себѣ лѣцмана[26]/ и говорил ем8 чтоб sато м8жика штраѳо/вал и дал бы сати свакцыю то онои лецманъ/ штраѳъ ем8 никакова нѣ 8чинил за что/

---

26 Sw. *länsman* (county sheriff).

гсднъ подпор8тчикъ приказал капрал8/ т8т же штрафовать того м8жика/ палкою а сержанта поставил под восемь р8жеи которои и стоял три часа/ в чемъ и подпис8юсь; ксем8 допросу/ вмѣсто гранодера аѳонася щербакова/ по ево прошению кабардинскои гранодер/скои роты ротнои писарь никиѳоръ/ рябов р8ку прилажил [hand 2] читал сержантъ александръ старковъ.[27]

The witness statement is taken from a group of documents containing a statement by the grenadier Afanasii Shcherbakov, a statement by his fellow soldier Vasilii Fëdorov, and a statement by an officer, Lieutenant Andreian von Amers. The different versions tell the same story in almost identical words. While it is tempting to consider Shcherbakov's statement as a case of spoken language transferred to writing, we must apply caution. It may well be that the language of the statements has been edited by the scribe, Nikifor Riabov, the sergeant Aleksandr Starkov, who signed the documents, or by some unnamed commanding officer. This example illustrates that it is indeed very difficult to access the spoken language of the 1740s.

6.4 Processing Circumstances

Processing circumstances differ widely between the various parts of the material. Printed texts and the *elaborate* group of handwritten texts are the result of careful editing.

In one case, we have access to a draft as well as the finished product. The document in question is a manifesto published in the name of the infant Emperor, Ioann Antonovich. In reaction to the declaration of war by Sweden in late July, 1741, the Russian government published a manifesto in mid-August. The printed version was signed by the young tsar's mother, the regent Anna Leopoldovna.[28]

---

27 Swedish National Archives, Extranea Ryssland 157.4.

28 *Ihro königlichen Majestät in Schweden* Publication *Den Krieg wider den Czaarn in Rußland betreffende* (Stockholm: Königl. Buchdruckerey, July 24, 1741), War Manifestos Database, accessed May, 28, 2021, https://documents.law.yale.edu/publication-his-royal-majesty-sweden-relating-war-against-czars-russia-given-council-stockholm-24th; Swedish National Archives, microfilm F035.31094: *Manifest. Bozhieiu milostiiu My Ioann tretii, imperator i samoderzhets vserossiiskii . . .* (St. Petersburg: Senat, August 14, 1741).

There is also a German version translated from Russian.[29] What is most important for the present investigation is the preservation of the handwritten draft of the text, entitled *Formuliar manifesta* (Форм8ляръ манифеста). This document allows us to follow the changes that were introduced when a handwritten text was typeset.[30] The printed version appears in the left column below and the handwritten draft in the right. In the handwritten draft, some words have been crossed out and others have been added. The additions appear in bold:

Манифестъ	Формуляръ манифеста
Божіею милостію Мы Іоаннъ третій, императоръ и самодержецъ всероссійскій. И прочая, и прочая, и прочая. Объявляемъ чрезъ сіе.	Бжіею млⷭ҇тію мы їоа҃ннъ третіи/ їмператоръ и самѡдержецъ всероссійскіи/ и протчая и протчая и протчаѧ./ сѡбъявляемъ чрезъ сіе./ хотя ѡт коро́ны шведскѡй ~~какъ/ при нашемъ гⷭ҇дрствѡваніи~~ **с того времяни что мы/ на самодержавнои и на/слѣднои н҃шъ всерорⷭ҇сіис/кои императорскои пре/стол вступили** такъ/
Хотя отъ короны Шведской как съ того времяни что Мы на Самодержавной и наслѣдной Нашъ Всероссійской Императорской престолъ вступили,	и прежде тогѡ при предкахъ/ нашихъ, бл҃женныя и́ вѣчнѡ/дѡстои́ныя памяти їмператор/скихъ величествъ, по заклю-/ченіи со всероссійскѡю їмперіею/ въ 1721„ом гѡд8 вечного мира/ трактата, и потѡмъ поста/нѡвленныхъ и со обоихъ сторо́н/ подтвержденныхъ союзѡвъ/ къ
такъ и прежде того при предкахъ Нашихъ Блаженныя и Вѣчнодостойныя памяти ИМПЕРАТОРСКИХЪ ВЕЛИЧЕСТВЪ, по заключенïи со Всероссійскою имперïею съ 1721 году вѣчнаго мира трактата,	нашей їмперïи въ разны́хъ/ сл8чаяхъ ~~многіе~~ **множественные** предосудите[л]/ные и нар8шительные// ѡном8 блаженнѡм8 мир8 по-/ст8пки происхѡдили, ~~къ нема/лѡм8 намъ возчювствѡванію и́ о́скорбленію,~~
и потомъ постановленныхъ и съ обоихъ сторонъ подтвержденныхъ союзовъ, къ Нашей имперïи въ разныхъ случаяхъ множественные предосудительные и нарушительные оному блаженному миру поступки происходили,	

29 *Rußisches Manifest wieder Schweden*, War Manifestos Database, accessed May 28, 2021, https://documents.law.yale.edu/generic-title-printed-version-russian-manifesto-against-sweden-actual-title-within-document.

30 Comparisons of printed texts with their handwritten drafts have been undertaken before by Zhivov, who analyzed the *Geometria*, printed in 1708, with its draft, cf. Zhivov, *Ocherki*, 186.

Манифестъ	Формуляръ манифеста
и особливо отъ нѣкоторыхъ лѣтъ къ наичувственнѣйшему Намъ оскорбленїю и поврежденїю Нашихъ интересовъ и государства Нашего благополучїя, отъ оной короны такимъ недружескимъ и злобнымъ образомъ къ Намъ поступлено, что отъ явно декляpованнаго непрїятеля вящше и горше того ожидать было невозможно, какъ весь беспристрастной свѣтъ, предъ очьми котораго все то происходило, праведное свидѣтельство тому подать не отречется.	и особливо ѿ некоторыхъ /лѣтъ к̃ на́йчювствен/нѣишему нам оскорбле/нию и повреждению/ н̃шихъ интересовъ и г̃рства н̃шего / бл̃гопол8чия ѿ со̃нои/ короны таким недр8/жеским и злобным соб̃ра/зом, к̃ нам пост8плено/ что ѿ ю̃вно деклаpован/наго неприятеля вящ/ще и горше того со̃жидат было невозможно/ какъ вес̃ бе́зпристрастнои/ свѣтъ пред̃ очми кото/раго все то происходило/ праведное свидѣте́льство/ тому подат может, и/ подат не ѿречет̃ся./ со̃днакож
Однако жъ Мы желая оной вѣчнаго мира трактатъ и союзъ съ своей сторонъ свято и ненарушимо содержать, и дабы Наши вѣрныя подданныя плодами мира и благословеннымъ отъ Всевышшаго Бога покоемъ въ совершенной тишинѣ пользоваться могли,	однакож/ мы желая ѿнсо̃й вѣчнсо̃гсо/ мира трактатъ и союзъ с̃ свсо̃ей/ стороны свято̃ и ненар8/шимсо̃ ссодержать, и дабы наши вѣрные подданные/ плодами того мира и благсо-/слсо̃вен̃нымъ ѿ всевышшагсо̃/ бг̃а поксо̃ем в совершеннсо̃и/ тишинѣ, ползсо̃ватся могли;
все то съ терпѣливостїю сносили, уповая что при усмотрѣнїи такой Нашей великодушной неотмѣняемой умѣренности напослѣди съ Шведской стороны всѣ противные мирному трактату поступки дружескимъ образомъ къ пользѣ и благополучїю обоихъ странъ подданныхъ поправлены и пресѣчены будутъ,	все то съ терпеливсо̃стїю сноси́ли,/ уповая чтсо̃ при усмотрении такои/ нашеи великод8шнои/ нес̃оменяемои 8мѣрен/ности напослѣди/ с швецксо̃й сто/роны всѣ противные мир/нсо̃м8 трактат8 пост8пки/ др8жеским со̃бразсо̃м/ къ ползѣ и благсо̃псол8чию// обоихъ стран̃ псо̃дданныхъ/ поправлены и пресѣчены б8д8т,/
къ чему съ Нашей сторонъ съ вѣрнаго желанїя къ непоколебимому содержанїю мира и покоя, ко убѣжанїю Богу противнои войны и напраснаго человѣческаго кровопролитїя не оставлены, всякїе пристойные и съ Императорскимъ достоинствомъ Нашимъ сходные пути употреблять.	къ сем8 с̃ нашеи стороны/ с̃ вѣ́р/нсо̃гсо желанїя къ непоколебимо́му/ содержанїю вѣчнсо̃гсо̃ мира и̃/ покоя ко убѣжанїю бо́г8 против̃/нсо̃й всо̃йны и̃ напраснсо̃гсо -лю/дем̃ человеческаго кровсо̃пролитїю, не остав/лены всякіе пристоиные и с̃ императорским достоинством нашим сходные ревнсо̃стные спо-/собы и п8ти употреблять;/
Однако жъ всѣ тѣ Наши миролюбительные поступки, вмѣсто желаемаго добраго успѣха только къ тому служили, что сїя корона зло злымъ умножать продолжала, и ужѐ давно предвоспрїятое свое намѣренїе, къ начатїю явной неправедной войнъ толь скорѣе въ дѣйство произвесть поспѣшила, понеже получена нынѣ изъ Стокголма вѣдомость, что помянутая корона Шведская наруша явно имѣющей съ Нами вѣчнаго мира трактатъ и союзъ минувшаго Iюля 24 числа противъ Насъ и Нашей Всероссїйской имперїи войну дѣйствительно объявила, и о томъ въ Стокголмѣ въ народъ публиковано, якоже межъ тѣмъ и Шведскїе войска и карабли и другїе военные суда къ дѣйствамъ воинскимъ ужѐ въ готовности находятся.	однакож всѣ тѣ н̃ши миро/любите́льные пост8пки с̃ нашеи стсо̃-/роны добрсо̃желателные ста-ранїи, у онсо̃й швецксо̃й ко-/рсо̃ны никакого̃ вмѣсто желаемаго добраго успѣха не возимѣли, и не токмсо̃ со̃т ѿнсо̃й/ къ поправлению и прекраще/нїю, продолающихъ от нѣе/ къ нашеи стороны против/ных и прелосудителныхъ то́лко к̃ тому служили что сия корона/ sло sлым 8множат продо́лжала и 8/же давно предвозприя/тое свое намѣрение/ к̃ начатию ю̃внои/ неправеднои воины/ то́л скорѣе в̃ дѣист/во произвесть поспѣшила // вѣчном8 ми́ру пост8покъ, не/воспослѣдсо̃вало, понеже нсо̃ вмѣстсо̃/ тогсо̃ пол8чена нн̃ѣ из стсо̃к/холма подлинная вѣдомость что помян8тая корона

Манифестъ	Формуляръ манифеста
	швед/ская ~~безъ всякосои ипо́данной/с~~ ~~нашей стороны притчины/~~ нар8ша я᷉ вно̃ имѣющей/ съ нами вѣчнсого мира/ тракта́тъ **и союзъ**,/ минувшаго jюля/ 24г числа противъ насъ/ и на́шей всеросси́ской jмъ/ пери́и воин8 дѣ́иствител-/нсо обявила, и о то́мъ въ сток̂/голмѣ в нарсодъ публиксова/нсо, я᷉коже межъ тѣмъ и/ шведскія войска, и карабли и другие военные с8да/ къ дѣ́иствамъ воинским/ у᷉же в готовности находя́тся.// jс чего каждо́й разв8дить можетъ/ что такого̃ страннаго поступк8/ какъ н̃нѣ от швеци́и чинится, ме/жд8 христианскими державами еще **между невѣрными и/ дикими бг̃а неиспо/вѣдающими паганами не токмо/ между хртиянскими державами еще** не слыхано было̃, чтобъ необъявя напередъ о̃ причи́нахъ неудоволства своегсо, jли не учиня по послѣднеи мѣрѣ ~~справедливыхъ jа́вной~~ ~~воины достоиных жалоб~~, воину начать **хотя мало основанны̂х жалоб и не треб8 ю со пристоином испра/влении соныхъ вои/ну начат какъ то дѣсиствите́лно н̃нѣ ō швеци́и чинится.**/
Между невѣрными и дикими Бога неисповѣдающими поганами, не токмо между Христіанскими державами еще не слыхано было, чтобъ не объявя напередъ о причинахъ неудовольства своего, или не учиня по послѣдней мѣрѣ хотя мало основанныхъ жалобъ, и не требуя о пристойномъ поправленіи оныхъ войну́ начать, какъ то дѣйствительно нынѣ отъ Швеціи чинится.	
При такомъ оной короны мира нарушеніи и объявленной противъ Насъ, и Нашего имперія войны́, Мы по положенному на Насъ отъ Бога о безопасности Нашихъ государствъ попеченію необходимо принуждены, для обороны и защищенія государствъ, и вѣрныхъ Нашихъ подданныхъ призвавъ въ помощь всеправеднаго и всемогущаго Бога, отъ негоже Намъ дарованные силы употребить, и чрезъ оружіе государство и подданныхъ Нашихъ отъ сего мира нарушитеьнаго и злостнаго непріятеля, надлежаще защищать и оборонять.	при такомъ сонои с короны швецко́й/ мира нар8шени́й, j объявленны̂й/ проти́в насъ j нашего jмперія воины,/ мы̀ по положенном8 на насъ от бг̃а/ о безопасности нашихъ гс̃дрствъ/ попеченію, необходи́мо принн8жде/ны, для обороны й защищениа̃ гс̃дрствъ j вѣрныхъ нашихъ под/данныхъ, призвавъ в помощь все/праведного j всемог8щаго бг̃а от негоже/ на́мъ дарованные силы у᷉потребить/ j чрезъ о̃р8жие jмперíй **гс̃дсрство** j подданныхъ/ нашихъ от сего мира нар8шитель/ного й злост̂ного неприятеля над/лежаще тверд[8ю] безопасность/ на н̃нѣшние j предбудущие [. . . . . .] доставить **защищат и сооронят** // Того ради мы̀ о том̂/ чрезъ сíе ко всенародном8/ jзвѣстию п8бликовать по/велѣли, дабы всѣ наши вѣрные/ подданные о семъ вѣдали, j все/вышшем8 бг̃8 о благословении/ къ (sic! — T. R.) ихъ собственнои ползе j обо/ронѣ у᷉потребляемыхъ наши̂х противъ шведовъ **праведныхъ** ор8жей усер/дно j со всякимъ благоговѣнíем̃ молились, j от него юко от истсо/чника всѣхъ благъ, счастли/вого благоповедѣня сихъ спра/вѣдливыхъ нашихъ намерений/ просили **в чем и тол̂ нај͞крѣп/чаиш8ю тверд8ю j бес8мнен/н8ю надежд8 на всемог8щество ево имѣем, юко сонои есть ōмсти/тел неправды и да вержет/ враговъ и супостатовъ/ нашихъ в юму юже/ нам искапываютъ.**
Того ради Мы о томъ чрезъ сíе ко всенародному извѣстíю публиковать повелѣли, дабы всѣ Наши вѣрные подданные о семъ вѣдали, и всевышнему Богу о благословеніи къ ихъ собственной польѣ и оборонѣ употребляемыхъ Нашихъ противъ Шведовъ праведныхъ оружей, усердно и со всякимъ благоговѣнíемъ молились, и отъ него яко отъ источника всѣхъ благъ щастливаго благоповеденія сихъ справедливыхъ Нашихъ намѣреній просили, въ чемъ и толь наикрѣпчайшую твердую и бессумнѣнную надежду на всемогущество его имѣемъ, яко оной есть отмститель неправды, и да ввержетъ враговъ и супостатовъ Нашихъ въ яму, юже Намъ искапываютъ.	

Манифестъ	Формуляръ манифеста
Впрочемъ чрезъ сíе какъ подданнымъ такъ и всѣмъ прочимъ службою и присягами Намъ обязаннымъ Всемилостивѣйше повелѣвается,	впортчемже вѣсмъ нашимъ/ подданнымъ j особливо в погра/ничныхъ с швециею городахъ, и мѣ/стахъ находящимся, надлѣжит/ вездѣ какъ от всякого с швецкой/ стороны непрiятелского предвоспрi/ятiя j незапныхъ нападенеи/ такъ j от всѣхъ протчих слꙋчаевъ/ яко шпионовъ j дрꙋгихъ подобныхъ// томꙋ людей всегда во всякои твердой осторожности быть/притомъ же
отъ сего времяни съ подданными Швецкой короны никакой коммуникацíи, пересылокъ, комерцíи и корреспонденцíи всякаго званíя не имѣть, и отъ всякаго непрíятельскаго нападенíя, отъ шпíоновъ и другихъ подобныхъ непрíятельскихъ людей и предвоспрíятíй быть всегда во всякой твердой осторожности, и при всѣхъ случаяхъ за Насъ, государство и отечество Наше стоять и защищать не щадя жизни своей, какъ вѣрнымъ подданнымъ по присяжной своей должности принадлежитъ и достойно, подъ опасенíемъ за неисполненíе сего тяжчайшаго отвѣта и жестокаго наказанíя,	Впротчемже чрез сие/ какъ подданнымъ нашимъ такъ j всѣмъ протчим слꙋжбои j при/сягами намъ ѡбязаннымъ с под/данными швецкой короны ника/ чрез сие всемлⷭтивѣише повелѣвается; ѿ сего времяни с подданными швецкои короны никакои комꙋникацíи, пересылокъ,/ комерцíи, и кореспонденцíи вся/кого званiя не jметь најкрѣ/пчаише запрещается и ѿ всякого неприя/телⷭкаго нападения и шпи/ѡновъ и дрꙋгих по/добныхъ неприятелⷭких людеи и предвоз/приятiи быт всегда во всякои твердои ѡ/ сторожности и при всѣхъ слꙋчаяхъ за насгⷭⷣрство/ и ѡтечество наше стоят и защищат не щадя/ жизни своеи какъ вѣр/нымъ подданнымъ по при/сяжнои своеи долⷤ/ности прjнадлежит и достоино подъ ѡпасенiемъ за неисполненiе/ сего тяжчаишаго отвѣта j же/стокого наказанiя, для/ вящего увѣренiя всѣмъ мы/
для вящшаго увѣренíя всѣмъ мы сей Нашъ манифестъ во всей Нашей имперíи публиковать повелѣли. Данъ въ Санктпетербургѣ Августа 13 дня 1741 года.	сеи нашъ маниѳестъ во всеи/ нашеи jмперíи пꙋбликовать/ повелѣли. данъ в санктъ петер/бꙋрке, авгꙋста „13ⷢ„ дня 1741ⷢ/ годъ./ jмянем
Подлинной подписанъ именемъ ЕГО ИМПЕРАТОРСКАГО ВЕЛИЧЕСТВА Ея Императорскаго Высочества Государыни Великой Княгини и Правительници всея Россíи собственною рукою, тако: АННА.	его jмператорского велⷯичества/ на подлинном подписано ея jмператорⷪского величества гⷭⷣрни великои кнⷢгини j правителницы
МП	[всероссíискои], тако: Анна
Печатанъ въ Санктпетербургѣ при Сенатѣ Августа 14 дня 1741 года.	

Comparing the printed text to its handwritten draft, we find many alterations. The number of characters has been reduced, excluding variation such as ⟨y/8⟩. The orthography and punctuation has been modified to correspond to the practices of the Senate printing office. The character ⟨ѣ⟩ is found in both the draft and printed text. In the draft it is not used in all etymologically correct positions. This error is corrected in the printed version. In the spelling of case forms of the adjectives, occasional differences are found in the Genetive singular, such as ⟨-ѡгѡ⟩ (draft) vs. ⟨-аго⟩ (print) but this is not systematic. In the morphology, the draft we find a Genetive singular годъ where the printed version has года. Both the draft and printed version contain one example of an aorist (наруша), which was most likely chosen in order to add to the solemnity and gravity (cf. below, section 8.1). In almost all cases, the differences between the draft and the printed version of the manifesto are of a graphic and orthographic nature. A plausible interpretation is that such alterations were made routinely by those involved in the typesetting process. At the same time, other elements have not been corrected, not even the obviously faulty interpretation of империя (empire) as a masculine noun: ⟨Насъ, и Нашего имперїя⟩ (printed version). Elsewhere in the manifesto the word is treated correctly as a feminine noun.

6.5 Setting

Most of the texts available for this investigation were produced in and for the public sphere. The printed texts were, of course, produced in order to be read by an audience, and the purpose of administrative documents was to convey public information or to request such information. There is one source that represents the private sphere: personal correspondence. We can assume that private letters and personal notes were produced in great quantities during the 1740s but, unfortunately, have been poorly preserved.

6.6 Communicative Purpose

In the corpus of texts gathered for the present investigation, many different communicative purposes can be identified: information, family matters etc. Other purposes are less frequent, such as entertainment. At the high end of the social spectrum, we find that by the 1740s opera librettos were being translated into Russian and printed by the Academy of Sciences. One such work was the opera *Seleuco* with its libretto by Giuseppe Bonecchi. The Russian translation is anonymous but associated with the names of A. V. Olsuf'ev and A. P. Sumarokov.[31] For the majority, written texts intended for entertainment took the form of traditional novels and chapbooks, so-called *lubok*. Sometimes, a text could "migrate" functionally, as in the case of the newspaper article on the meteorological phenomenon in Cartagena, taken over from *Vedomosti*. This was transliterated and

---

31 *Selevk opera* …, trans. Iozef Bonekki (Moscow: Imperatorskaia Akademiia nauk, April 25, 1744); Zarina Akhmetshina, "'Selevk' F. Araii: opera i ee rukopisi v biblioteke Peterburgskoi konservatorii," *Opera musicologica* 3.

printed with an illustration, likely meant to arouse people's imagination, it would enjoy a long afterlife.

6.7 Topics

The data in the present investigation was gathered from texts dealing with a wide range of topics, including science, news, diplomacy, information, administration, and more. Only a small portion of the material concerns the private sphere.

6.8 Conclusions

This chapter has presented a situational analysis of texts in Russian from the 1740s. The analysis has resulted in several important points that must be considered when conclusions are made about the Russian language of the 1740s.

The first and most important observation is that men produced the entire corpus of texts. Although women are referred to in the texts, and some of the texts have been signed by women, no single text can be positively identified as written by a woman. The age of the men behind the texts cannot be precisely determined. However, since so much of the material was written by professional scribes, it is reasonable to conclude that the writers were adult men, probably aged between twenty and fifty. No texts written by children have been identified in the material.

Some texts were written by highly educated men although the majority of texts appear to have been written by individuals who had an intermediate educational background, that is, professional scribes who were part of the official administration. Even in texts whose contents can be classified as private, the author's involvement is often limited to a greeting and a signature. Since the production of the texts often involved more than one person, conclusions regarding the personal linguistic habits of individuals require great caution.

Finally, any comments concerning the social background of authors must also be made with great care. In most cases, professional scribes were young men from outside the nobility. Because many documents were produced jointly by several people, they contain little linguistic evidence of their social background.

When examining texts in Russian from the 1740s, we must realize that they come nowhere near to showing us the true picture of the Russian linguistic situation. They do, however, provide glimpses into parts of the linguistic reality.

CHAPTER 7

Linguistic Analysis

———————

From a linguistic point of view, using written sources to learn about language is riddled with problems because "a written record of a speech event stands like a filter between the words as spoken and the analyst."[1] Like any other investigation of the distant past, written records is our only option when investigating the registers of Russian in the 1740s. So far, in the previous chapters, we have investigated the circumstances under which texts were created, and we have drawn some tentative conclusion about the people who created them. In chapter 6, we saw that the majority of sources available were written by professional scribes. The number of *bona fide* autographs, also known as holographs, that is, documents written in the author's own hand and linked to an identified individual, is minimal. In the present chapter, the focus of attention will shift to the linguistic evidence offered by the sources. The goal of this linguistic analysis is to investigate orthography, morphology, syntax, and vocabulary, and how these can be linked to various registers of the language.

The general development of Russian morphology during the eighteenth century, as it is reflected in printed sources, is comparatively well known thanks to research performed during recent decades (cf. chapter 2). The same is true for the vocabulary found in printed texts (cf. section 4.1.2).

7.1 Autographs

In an attempt to get a glimpse of the living Russian language of the 1740s, a natural starting point is to examine autographs. As already stated, such sources are scarce in the corpus gathered for the present investigation. Another obvious weakness of the corpus is its glaring gender bias. Considerable efforts to locate sources written by women have yielded no results.

———————

1   Cf. Schneider, "Investigating Historical Variation," 58.

7.1.1 Mate Filipp Lanikin's Receipt

The first autograph to be examined is a short receipt. It is written and signed in the same hand. Judging by the signature, the signature belonged to First Mate Filipp Lanikin of the Russian imperial navy. A brief explanation of the document's context will assist in its interpretation.

While maneuvering in Stockholm Harbor during the summer of 1748, a Swedish merchant vessel collided with the Russian ship *Shturman*. The *Shturman* was a small ship, known as a *galiot*, propelled by sail and oars. Memory of the collision would have faded quickly were it not for the fact that the it resulted in minor damage to the rigging of the Russian ship. The parties involved did not agree on the issue of compensation, and the authorities were notified. From the Russian side, the case was handled by the ambassador to Stockholm, later the famous foreign minister of Catherine the Great, Nikita Ivanovich Panin (1718–1783). In the end, Peter Brauer, the captain of the Swedish merchantman, agreed to pay three Dutch ducats for the damages sustained by the Russian ship, and its first mate gave him a receipt.

> 1748 год8 авг8ста 7. дня принелъ я *от* шхипера/ швецкои наци [*sic*!—T.R.] местечка висмеръ которои/ на галете бреиде ѳритъ питеръ брогора/ за запорченые на россиском военном галете/ имянн8емом штюрмане вещи а и-/мянно боумъ кливеръ шпjрта гюисъ ѳла/штока съ ево шпирои и кеизерсъ ѳлага/ и протчее денегъ затолою [*sic*!—T.R.] манетою/ три червонца которыя червонцы/ галландския. штюрма*н* россискаго/ ѳлота филипъ ланикинъ.[2]

The receipt is written in an untidy cursive. The shaping of the characters ⟨л⟩, ⟨ш⟩, ⟨ѳ⟩, and ⟨ъ⟩ support the idea that the document was written and signed by the same person, first mate Filip Lanikin. The document gives the impression that it was written in a hurry. Also, the form ⟨затолою⟩ is an obvious error for an intended ⟨золотою⟩ and may also support this interpretation. The character variants in the document include ⟨у/8⟩ and ⟨ф/ѳ⟩. The character ⟨ѣ⟩ is entirely absent. The text contains relatively few superscripts and among those included, ⟨и⟩ and ⟨м⟩ are reduced to slanting lines.[3]

---

2 Swedish National Archives, Muscovitica 628, Ryska beskickningar, memorial och noter 1744–58, Panin 1748–58.
3 Cf. the illustration in Cherepnin, *Russkaia paleografiia*, 444.

Among noteworthy examples of spelling, we find the form ⟨принелъ⟩, modern принял (accepted), and the forms ⟨наци⟩ and ⟨россискаго⟩ for нации (nation) and российского (Russian). In both these cases, we would have expected a double ⟨ии⟩. Lanikin's spelling ⟨россискаго⟩ shows that he had been taught a spelling, which deviates from the pronunciation [-əvə]. Michael Groening, in his grammar from 1750, lists two possible spellings of the Genetive singular of adjectives in the masculine: добраго and доброва.[4] Lomonosov allows only -aro.[5] The adjectival endings in Nominative/Accusative plural appear to be gender-neutral: ⟨запорченые … вещи⟩ (referring to feminine noun) and ⟨которыя червонцы⟩ (referring to a masculine noun).

The text contains a syntactically interesting clause: a relative clause with a repeated antecedent,

… три червонца которыя червонцы/ галландския …

Zhivov claims that this construction disappears forever from the new linguistic standard during the second half of the 1730s.[6] In business texts such as Lanikin's receipt, however, the construction obviously remains.

Despite being very short, the text of the receipt contains a number of nautical terms of Dutch and German origin:

боумъ кливеръ шпјрта (a triangular sail on the bowsprit, from Dutch *kluiver*),
гюисъ (jack, from Dutch *geus*),
флашток (jackstaf, from Dutch *vlaggenstok, vlagstok*), and
кеизерсъ флаг (imperial flag, from German *Kaiserflagge*)

The meaning of ⟨шпира⟩ is unclear but might be "finial." It is obviously related to Dutch *spire* (point, summit).

The composition of the receipt follows a clear pattern: date, payer, specification, amount paid, and signature. A similar structure is found in other receipts from the period, written by professional scribes and signed by military officers:

---

4   Michael Groening, *Rossiiskaia grammatika Thet är Grammatica Russica, Eller Grundelig Handledning till Ryska Språket*, intro. B. O. Unbegaun (Munich: Fink, 1969, original ed. Stockholm: Hos Directeuren Pet. Momma, 1750), 109.

5   Lomonosov, *Rossiiskaia grammatika*, 77.

6   Zhivov, "Literaturnyi iazyk i iazyk literatury," 18.

[hand 1] 1744 го*ду* ѳевраля 6 дня дана̀ сия кви/та̑нцыя в том что҃ взято҃ ѿ города̀/ ли́нкипинга д҃ со норкопинга̀ лꙺшадеи ше̑сть/ па*р* кеӡ'гꙺлм́ского по́лку по*д* денежную казну/ а *от* норкопинга̀ до мызи не̑с разстоянием/ ѿ норкопинга̀ до сꙺноӥ мызы две мили/ оныеж вышепоказа̑нные по*д*воды ше̑сть/ па*р* по҃д сꙺною денежною казною ѿ норкопинга̀/ д҃ со сꙺноӥ мызы были в том сия им и̑ к̑ви/та̑нцыя дана̀/ [hand 2] прапо*р*щикъ к: шахо*в*скои[7]

And in the following:

[hand 1] Квитанцыя/ 1744г҃ год𐌖 июля .3г҃. дня да̀на сия квитан/цыя с𐌖ркипинскому обыва̀телю ма̀гн𐌖с𐌖/ 𐌖люѳъ сон𐌖 в том что҃ имелся он на̀ да̀нной/ из норкопинга швецкой яхте шхӥпором на̀/ кото̀роӥ поса̀жены были нӥсовскаго пехо*т*ного/ по́лку салда̀ты и протчи́я чи́ны та̀кож и пол/ковыя тягости погр𐌖жены на котороӥ/ яхте он шхӥпо*р* от норкопинга̀ д҃ со острова̀/ романсꙺ прӥбылъ бл҃гопол𐌖ченꙺ котꙺроӥ/ и отпущен о̀братнꙺ в норкопингъ в чем и по*д*пис[ую]сь/ [hand 2] A.S. von Brevern[8]

Similarly structured receipts were produced all over the Russian Empire at the time.[9]

Lanikin's adherence to the structure suggests different possibilities: that he was previously familiar with the structure of receipts, that he had a written template, or that the structure was dictated to him. Either way, his short text is a witness to the central role played by templates in Russian eighteenth-century writing.

From the perspective of registers, Lanikin's receipt can be associated with two of the hypothetical registers suggested in section 5.2.2: traditional administrative language and professional language. The receipt format clearly belongs in the traditional administrative language, while the use of nautical terminology

---

7 Swedish National Archives, Military Archives, 1742-58 års krigsrustningshandlingar, Div. krigsrustningshandlingar 1744–46, vol. 10. A photographic reproduction of the text is available in Thomas Rosén, "Fragmenty odnoi voiny. Russkoiazychnye materialy russko-shvedskoi voiny 1741–1743 godov v arkhivakh Shvetsii," *Slovo* 51, accessed October 10, 2021, https://www.diva-portal.org/smash/get/diva2:392119/FULLTEXT01.pdf.

8 Swedish National Archives, Military Archives, 1742–58, års krigsrustningshandlingar, Div. krigsrustningshandlingar 1744-46, vol. 10; Rosén, "Fragmenty odnoi voiny," 64.

9 Cf. Mezhenina and Maiorov, *Delovaia pis'mennost' Troitskogo Selenginskogo monastyria*, 114.

suggests that a new register had developed in Russian at this point: it was now possible to discuss nautical matters in Russian.

7.1.2 Mikhail Turchenikov's Letter and Its Cultural Context

In the summer of 1742, in the second year of war between Russia and Sweden, a merchant vessel, the *fluyt Somers*, captained by one Cornelius Kurt, was boarded and captured by units of the Royal Swedish Navy.[10] The incident took place off the island of Hogland (Ru: Гогланд, Fi: Suursaari) in the Gulf of Finland. The thirty-six-member Russian crew, under the command of its captain, Cornelius Kurt, and a commissar of the fleet, Prince Mikhail Petrovich Ukhtomskii, was brought to Stockholm as prisoners of war.

Mikhail Turchenikov was one of the navy cadets on board the *Somers* en route to various other ships of the Imperial navy where they were to receive training by serving as second mates. Since Turchenikov held this junior training position, it can be assumed that he was a very young person, perhaps in his mid- to late teens. Most likely, he was educated during the late 1730s and early 1740s.

A letter from Turchenikov to his parents is preserved in the National archives of Sweden. The letter was never sent, most likely because there was an armistice, and the prisoners of war were released. Turchenikov writes in his own hand:

> милостивы мои гсдръ/ батюшка герасимъ jванови/чъ и
> милостивая моя/ гсдрыня матушка матрена/ степановна
> желаю вам/ гсдрямъ мои (sic!—T.R.) во множество/ летъ
> здравствоват и з госуда/рями моими братцами/ а о себе
> доношу ежели изъволите/ милостию своею напаметоват/
> и я по нещастию своему взят/ в полонъ в ыюне мсце въ 23
> числе/ при гогланъте острове въ шве/цкои флотъ ѳъ полонъ и
> по/ ныне обретаюсъ при стекголме/ за помощию божескою
> живъ хотя/ и содежржусъ пот кара8лом токмо/ в пропитани
> по милости// королевскаго величества/ я нужды не имею
> и для нашей/ краинои нужды выданъ нам и му/ндеръ/
> покорно вас гсдрь батюшка/ прошу пожаловать отдать/ мои
> нижаиши поклонъ гсдрю/ моему и затю петру гаврилеви/чу и
> гсдрыне моей сестрице/ лукере гересимовне и въсем/ нашим

10 The Dutch *fluyt* was a three-masted, long, relatively narrow ship designed to carry as much cargo as possible. *Britannica Academic*, s.v. "Ship," accessed May 28, 2021, https://academic-eb-com.ezproxy.ub.gu.se/levels/collegiate/article/ship/110744#259195.toc.

приятелям/ присем писав[ъ] вашъ/ государей мой покорны/ слуга и сынъ мйха/ила турчеников/ земны свои поклон/ отдаю и благословения вашего/ прошу ... // а кто изъ наших 8чениковъ/ со мною обретаютъца о том/ явъствуетъ ниже сего/ гаврила богомоловъ/ jванъ канъдратевъ/ семенъ никиθоровъ/ дмитре серебрековъ/ василеи дунаевъ 8мре при сътек/голме/ мца ноября дня/ 1742 году/

On the reverse side:

пожаловатъ ѿдать сие/ писмо в санктъ питер/бурхе во адмиралтеистве/ чесоваго дела мастеру/ герасиму ивановичу турче/никову/ истекголма[11]

Mikhail Turchenikov probably did not spend his days writing letters. His hand-writing is unwieldy, he sometimes corrects himself, and his orthography reflects his pronunciation: ⟨θъ полонъ⟩, ⟨мундеръ⟩. Turchenikov's addressee, his father, the clockmaker Gerasim Ivanovich, whose name and title are found on the back of the letter, offers an interesting example of pronunciation and spelling norms: ⟨чесоваго дела мастеру герасиму ивановичу турченикову⟩. The word ⟨чесоваго⟩ may suggest that the writer pronounced the reduced /a/ of the first syllable as [e], an example of *ekan'e* (еканье).[12] The form ⟨-аго⟩ of the Genetive singular of the adjective is a spelling rule, most probably learned at school.

Although Turchenikov's letter is an autograph, it is a poor witness to the writer's personal linguistic habits apart from the information offered by the spelling. This is partly because of its brevity, partly also because the entire content, with the exception of personal names, are formulaic expressions typical of the traditional epistolary style, or information borrowed from another source. The reason why Turchenikov's letter has been chosen as an example is that it forms part of a group of closely related texts. The documents, which are held at the National Archives of Sweden, consist of an official report and three personal letters. Apart from Turchennikov's text, the other two letters were, for the most part, written by an anonymous scribe who left no clues as to his identity. He was, presumably, one of the persons listed in the report to the Admiralty. The second

---

11 National Archives of Sweden, Militaria 1588.

12 L. L. Kasatkin, "Ekan'e," in *Russkii iazyk: Ėntsiklopediia*, ed. F. P. Filin (Moscow: Sovetskaia ėntsiklopediia, 1979), 81. Today, *ekan'e* is found in central and northern dialects of Russian and was considered the normative pronunciation during the nineteenth century.

hand in these letters belongs to Prince Ukthomskii, also added short sentences at the end of the letters.

The official report belongs to a genre known as *donoshenie* (доношение), a message from a subordinate official to a higher-level authority.[13] It was also written by a scribe and signed by Prince Mikhail Petrovich Ukhtomskii.

Mikhail Petrovich was a progeny of the Tver′ branch of the Ukhtomskii family of nobles, as far as can be established.[14] He survived his time as a prisoner of war, was repatriated and went on to pursue his military career. He retired in 1771 as a lieutenant colonel and *krigs-komisar*.[15] Based on this genealogical data, Mikhail Petrovich Ukhtomskii was a young man during his time as a prisoner of war, probably in his twenties. If this assumption is correct, he was most likely educated during the 1730s.

a) *The Report*

The report was prepared by Prince Mikhail Ukhtomskii for his superiors at the Admiralty explaining the circumstances surrounding the capture and imprisonment:

> В гос8дарственн8ю Адмиралтѣиствъ коллегию/ Покорнеишѣе доношение/ В нынешнем год8 въ июне мⷭ це в .19./ чиⷭ ле командированы мы із глав/ной кронштатской канторы/ над портом во флотъ на флеите/ сомерсе с шхипером корнили8съ к8/ртом которой флеитъ нагруженъ/ был пивом при оном же флеите и ко/мандир был помян8той шхиперъ/ я и академи 8ченики в должности/ подштюрманской „6„ члвⷦ ъ поса/жены на оной флеитъ для отво/з8 на разные карабли ϳ во ѡном же/ мⷭ це а „23„м чиⷭ ле взяты мы при/ ѡстрове гогланте в полонъ в шве/цкой флотъ и содержалиⷭ при оном/ флоте сентебря по „28„ чиⷭ лѡ а во ѡ/ном чиⷭ ле изо флот8 отосланы// в стекголмъ где и по ныне о"бретаемса/ и по высокой егѡ кѡролевскаго велⷯ ичества милоⷭ ти ϳ высокопревоⷭ сходителныⷯ гⷭ дъ/ сенаторовъ ученена с нами милость/ и для нашеи краинеи н8жды какъ мне/ такъ и академи 8ченикам „5„ челвⷦ комъ/ выданъ м8ндир о взпрозбѣ

13 Malitikov, *Kratkii slovar′*, 60.
14 "Ukhtomskie kniaz′ia," *Istoriia russkikh rodov*, accessed February 5, 2021, https://russianfamily.ru/uhtom.
15 *Sanktpeterburgskie vedomosti* 20 (1771): 2, accessed May 6, 2021, https://www.vedomosti1728.ru/card.cgi?r=60&d=1771-03-11.

нашеи҆ а г̃сднъ/ сия́телны графъ и сенатоⷬ Юлинъбурхъ/ мило́стию своею мне отдалъ взятыя/ отⷮ меня „12„ червонцоⷡ притом же обявил что/ досталное платье и денги отобранное/ от меня и отⷮ протчих сл8жителеи возвратно/ нам отдано б8детъ да и матросам же на́/шим м8ндир выдан б8детъ же притоⷨ/ же изволилъ приказать мне чтоб jмеⷮ/ над вышереченными учениками j матрω/зами́ каманⷣ8 и обо всем обстоятелнω/ писать в санктъ питерб8рхъ в камаⷨⷣ8 а в пропитани и в содержани́ на̑с явяⷮ/ к нам всяк8ю высок8ю свою милость а содеⷬ/жимся под кара8лом токмо для н8жды/ выходом свободно а шхиперъ куртъ умре/ въ иⷯ швецком ѳлоте авг8ста́ „22„ дня а скоⷭ/лкω j каких чинов взеты в полонъ j с того/ чи̑сла помре и ныне на лицо явств8етъ/ ниже сего имянно́и списокъ всепокорно/ прош8 г̃сⷣⷬⷬⷬⷬⷬⷬ государственн8ю адмиралтеиствъ/ коллегию явиⷮ к нам высокою свою милость// и” пожаловать прикаꙃать пи̑сать/ о” удоволстви̑ на̑с в пище в Стекголмъ/ ж высоки́ иⷯ сенатъ чтоб мы j впреⷮ/ в пропитани не оставлены были́ j содеⷬ/жаны б были въ иⷯ ми̑лости или съ/ отп8ском в Росию ѻ̑свобождены были хотя/ на размен8. [hand 2] Ѳлота” ка”мисаⷬ кн̃ꙃь Миха”илω/ 8хтωⷨ́скωи/[16]

Ноября „17„ дня/ 1742 гωⷣ8
”Имя̑ⷩнои списокъ морским и адмиралтеиском сл8жителям бывшим на ѳлеите сомерсе

Полки	Роты	Раⷩги и і́мяна	сⷨтбытие
2	8	Шхиперъ Корнили8съ К8ртъ	Умре 22 дня авг8ста
		Камисаръ Кнꙃь Михаила Петровъ снъ Ухтомскои	
		в должности подштюрманскои академи 8ченики	
		Дмитреи Ѳедоровъ снъ Серебряковъ	
		Гаврила Семеновъ снъ Багамоловъ	
		Семенъ Никифороⷡ снъ Никифоровъ	
		Іванъ Ѳедоровъ снъ Кандратьеⷡ	
		Михаила́ Герасимовъ снъ т8рчениковъ	
		Василеи Фаминъ снъ Д8наевъ	Умре 17 дня октября

16 In Ukhtomskii's signature the character ⟨a⟩ has a diacritic that is difficult to interpret. It is rendered here as ⟨ ̋ ⟩.

Полки	Роты	Ранги и імяна	ѿбытие
		Боцманъ матъ	
1	8	Карпъ Івановъ снъ Сысоевъ	
		За квартермеистера матрозы 1 статьи	
1	6	Семенъ Івановъ снъ Киселевъ	Умре при Стекголме 23 дня октября
		Матрозы 1 стати	
1	14	Василеи Василевъ снъ Патакин	
1	14	Іванъ Даниловъ снъ Ляп8новъ	Умре при флоте
	14	Сергей Ѳоминъ снъ Ѳоминъ	
		Данила Елизаровъ снъ Елизаровъ	
	15	Сидоръ Петровъ снъ Петровъ	
		Степанъ Прокофьев снъ Б8ркав	
		Тиханъ Василевъ снъ Болшей	
		Титъ Ѳедоровъ снъ Истошинъ	
		2 стати	
1	4	Василеи Ѳедоровъ снъ Кокилевъ	
	8	Еремеи Ѳадеѣвъ снъ Шепенковъ	
	14	Михаило Денисовъ снъ Денисовъ	
	10	Юрья Артюшнинъ	
	14	Ѳирсъ Трофимовъ снъ 38евъ	
		Афонасеи Гордѣевъ снъ Митков	
		Егор Ильинъ снъ Бреневъ	
		Ѳедоръ Архиповъ снъ Кляповъ	
		Григореи Івановъ снъ Попковъ	Умре при флоте
	12	М8рза Ижб8латов	
		Имсеи Бекеѣвъ	
		К8лдяшъ Долгуткинъ	
	17	Ларионъ Андрѣевъ снъ Козминъ	
2	17	Григореи Івановъ снъ Івановъ	Умре при Стекголмѣ
	18	Павелъ Петровъ снъ Лесѣдевъ	Умре при флоте
		Тимоѳеи Нефедовъ снъ Нефедовъ	Умре при флоте
		Конопатчикъ	
2	5	Игнатеи Іванов снъ Івановъ	
		да собственнои мои члвкъ	
		Емельянъ Григорьев снъ Кривоновов	
		И того всех чиновъ взятые в полонъ „36„ члвкъ	

We shall have reason to return to the report below.

b) The Letters

The description of events found in the report are retold, sometimes verbatim, in the three letters:

Letter A	Letter B	Turchenikov's letter
милостивоj г͠сдрь мои̓ jванъ ивановичъ	милостивои̓ г͠сдрь мои василеи павловичъ/	милостивы мои г͠сдръ/ батюшка герасимъ jванови̓/ чъ и милостивая моя̓/ г͠сдрыня матушка ма͠трена̓/ степановна̓ желаю вам/ г͠сдрямъ мои̓ (sic!—T.R.)
во мно/жество летъ желаю здравствовать купъно/ j с любящими вашими/	во множество летъ желаю вамъ здра͠вство/вать купно j с любящими вашими:/	во множество/ летъ здравствоват и з госуда̓/ рями моими братцами/
а про меня ежели jзволишъ напаметова͠т	а про меня ежели jзволишъ напаметова͠т/	а о себе доношу ежели изъволите/ милостию своею напаметова͠т/
и я в ны/нешнемъ году в маие м͠сце из кронштатцкоj кан/торы над портом командирован бы̓л во θлотъ на/ карабль сантъ андреи при том же j академи̓ учени̓кi/ в должности подштюрмонскаи (sic!— T.R.) „6„ ч͠лвкъ и поса/ жены для отвозу во онои θлотъ на θлеитъ соммер͠с/ на которомъ командиръ бы̓л шхипе͠р куртъ/		
j по несчастию нашему в вышереченном м͠сце въ/ „23м„ числе взяты мы при острове гогланте/ в швецкои θлотъ в полонъ всех чино͠в служителеи̓/ взято „36„ ч͠лвкъ и были при оном θлоте сентебря/ по „28„ чи͠сло	j я по несчастию моему в нынешнем год8 въ/ jюне м͠сце „23м„ числе взятъ вполонъ в швец/кои θлотъ	и я по нещастию своему взят/ в полон в ыюне м͠сце въ 23 числе/ при го̓гланъте острове въ шве/цкои θлотъ θъ полонъ
а во оном чи͠сле изо θлоту свезены в сте/кголмъ где и поныне обретаемся за помощию/ божиею я и с хлопцам своим живъ а шхипе͠р и с͠лужи/телеи „7„ ч͠лвкъ умре досталные	jзо оного θлоту въ сентябре м͠сце/ отосланы в стекголмъ где и поныне обре/таю͠с за помощию бжиею j с человеком своим/ живъ/	и по/ ныне обретаюсъ при стектолме/ за помощию божескою живъ хотя/

Letter A	Letter B	Turchenikov's letter
служители/ обретаютца при стекголмеж благополучно:/ токмо содержимся под караулом а для наших нуждъ/ выпуском под карауломже свободны а по высоко коро/левскаго величества милости и гсдъ сенаторов/ для нашеи краинеи нужды какъ мне такъ j уче/никам выданъ мундиръ а и матрозам же обещанно мундир/ выдат же а и пропитание нам определено а сиятелны// гсднъ графъ, j сенаторъ юлинбурхъ по высокоj своеи/ милости отдал мне „12„ червонцовъ которые при в/зятье нас в полонъ от меня отобраны былй/ при том же обьявилъ что j досталное денги j плате/ отобранное от меня отдано мне возвратно буде же/ j изволил приказать мне над вышереченными/ ученикиами j маторзами команду и обо всем писать/ в санктъ питербурх. в команд8		и содежржусъ пот кара8лом токмо/ в пропитани по милости// королевскаго величества/ я нужды не имею и для нашей/ краинои нужды выданъ нам и му/ндеръ/
и для того от меня/ обо всем ко известию в государственную адмиралттеjс/твъ коллегию доношение послано при том же доно/шениj и к вам и къ гсдину мастеру василю павловичу/ шершавину от меня писма посланы пожалуj гсдрь мои/ зделаи мне одолжение отдаи моj нижаиши поклон мило/ стивым моим гсдрямъ флоцким высокородным гасподам/ капитаном макару jвановичу баракову кнзь петру/ андреевичу барятинскому высокоблагородным гсдамъ/ леитенантам якову василичу лвову jвану	при сем писме послал я къ гсдину сьянов8/ писмо жъ прошу оное разсмотрить какие/ мои нужды и писать о том же прошу обо мне/ к гсдрю моему батюшку и къ братьям а оное/ писмо не удержавъ прошу к нему сьянов8/ сотослать а братьямъ я за тем непи/ салъ что не надеюс jмъ быть при пите/рбурхе прошу отдать мои поклон высоко/ благородному гсдину маиору федору jвановичу/ окулову благородным господам камисар8/ федору богдановичу деревецкому j секретарю/ ма3иму лаврентьевичу казакову и гсдну/ клерку андрею	

Letter A	Letter B	Turchenikov's letter
алеѯандровичу/ нащокину семену јвановичу лыкову никиѳору јвано/вичу сьянову антону еремеевичу валуеву благород/ным гⷭдамъ мичманом андреяну андреевичу левашеву/ евстигнею ѳедоровичу лаптеву морских салдац/ких полковъ высокородному гⷭдину подполковнику/ николаю ѳедоровичу языкову благородному гⷭдину ка/питану ѳедору яковлевичу јевлеву спокорностию/ моею ваⷭ гⷭдрь прошу пожалуи отпиши обо мне к ми/лостивому гⷭдрю моему батюшку и к гⷭдрям моимъ/ братьям где они обретаютця что я вполон8// пристекголме живъ и прошу иⷯ чтобъ они меня мило/стию своею неоставили и ежели будетъ им позволено/ тобъ комне пожаловали писали к тому жъ ј ваⷭ ј брата/ вашего никиѳора јвановича покорно прошу гⷭдри мој/ ежели будетъ возможно писаⷮ же ко мне о своем здоровье/ такожъ прошу писат же о здаровье гⷭдря моего батю/шка и о братьяⷯ чего усердно слышеⷮ о вашем здравиі/ желаю а ежели я о братьяхъ уведаю где они обрета/ются то долженъ к ним писать чтобъ пожалова/ли они прислали комне [.ак...]нибуть меры денегъ/ для моиⷯ нуждъ и содержания к тому жъ я обьявляю/ что по прозбе моеи дано мне взамимно подросписⷭ/ку иⷭ казенныⷯ денегъ „20„ рублевъ в тои надежде/ я заплатил оные денги какъ взятые оⷮ меня денги/ мне отданы будутъ	дмитревичу еремеев8/ а еже/ли кто из братеи моиⷯ при санктъпитербурхе/ то гⷭдна сьянова писмо вручи[ⷮ] из ниⷯ кому:/ [hand 2] покорно прошу ежели возможно то пожаловать/ писаⷮ ко мне о сьвоем ꙃдорѡвье чегѡ ѡхотнѡ//с радостию слышать желаю./	покорно ваⷭ гⷭдрь батюшка/ прошу пожаловать отдать/ мои нижаиши поклонъ гⷭдрю/ моему и затю петру гаврилевӥ/чу и гⷭдрыне моеи сестрице/ лукере гересимовне и въсем/ нашим приятелям/ присем писав[ъ] вашъ/ государеи мои покорны/ слуга и сынъ мӥха/ила турчеников/ земны свои поклон/ отдаю и благословения вашего/ прошу … // а кто изъ нашиⷯ 8чениковъ/ со мною обретаютъца о том/ явъствуетъ ниже сего/ гаврила богомоловъ/ јванъ канъдратевъ/ семенъ никиѳоровъ/ дмитре серебрековъ/ василеи дунаевъ 8мре при сътек/голме/ мца ноября дня/ 1742 году/

Letter A	Letter B	Turchenikov's letter
возвратно еще жъ вас гсдрь про/шу отдать мои поклонъ обретаящемуся у прави/антских дел јвану гавриловичу головину и потребовал/ от него замоею рукою регестръ и потому от него/ взать мои богажъ которои я у него оставил/ ј[з]о взятья оного богажу хотя дал ему и росписку/ а тотъ багажъ прошу пожаловать соотдать/ братьямъ моимъ пожалуи гсдрь не отставь/ меня в своеи приязне в чемъ на вас имею надежд8/		
[hand 2] Такѡ пребуду вашъ гсдря/ моегѡ добърсожелателны слуга/ камисар кнзъ михалѡ (sic!— T.R.) 8хтомскѡои/ Ноябьря .17г. дня:·/ .1742 га. гсоду/ из стекьголма://	Такѡ пребуду вашъ моегѡ/ гсдря добрсожелателны слуга/ кнзъ михалсо ухтомскои	
On the reverse side:		On the reverse side:
пожаловать вручить сие писмѡ/ всанктъ питербурьхе морьскихъ полковъ/ ѳендрику ивану ивановичю сьянову или/ брату евѡ ѳлота леитенанту выссоко/благородному гсдину никиѳору ивано/ вичю сьяновуж:/ изтекгсольма [a corrected from 8]		пожаловатъ соотдать сие/ писмо в санктъ питер/ бурхе во адмиралтеистве/ чесоваго дела мастеру/ герасиму ивановичю турче/ никову/ истекголма

The secretary's writing is an easily legible, rounded cursive with comparatively few supralinear elements. The most frequently occuring element is a dot placed over vowels, especially over ⟨й⟩. During the eighteenth century, the supralinear over the last open syllable of a word often has the form of a dot.[17] It is possible that this dot fulfilled more than one role. Here, however, it is uniformely

---

17 Ol'ga Trofimova, "Russkii dokument XVIII veka: punktuatsiia rukopisnogo originala i transliterirovannoi ego publikatsii," *Annales Universitatis Paedagogicae Cracoviensis. Studia Russologica* 7.

rendered by ⟨ ' ⟩. Other supralinears include the *titlo* of abbreviations ⟨ ͡ ⟩ *iso* over vowels ⟨о̆бретаемса⟩.

Prince Ukthomskii's handwriting suggests that he was used to writing by hand. His style is readable and distinctly separate from that of the scribe. This distinction is indicated by the use of dots above vowel characters, as well as by the form and the character ⟨ж⟩ that appears as two overlapping ⟨х⟩.

In terms of morphology, the language of the documents contains little that cannot be expected in a text from the 1740s. An exception is the verb "to die," which occurs in the aorist tense in both Ukhtomskii's and Turchenikov's texts:

… василеи дунаевъ 8мре при сътекголме.

The letters share several formulaic elements at the beginning and end of the letters. These elements are reminiscent of formulas found in letters from the beginning of the eighteenth century, investigated by Kretschmer.[18] She distinguishes between *opening forumlae* (*Anfangsformel*) and *closing forumulae* (*Schlußformel*), and the letters concerned in the present investigations display obvious similarities with the structure described by her.[19] The presence of such formulae indicate that there was considerable continuity in the general composition of private letters throughout the first half of the eighteenth century.

Unnamed scribe, signed by Mikhail Ukhtomskii, letter A	Unnamed scribe, signed by Mikhail Ukhtomskii, letter B	Mikhailo Turchenikov
Opening forumulae:		
милостивоj г͡сдрь мои jванъ ивановичъ	милостивои г͡сдрь мои василеи павловичъ	милостивы мои г͡сдръ батюшка герасимъ jвановичъ и милостивая моя г͡сдрыня матушка матрена степановна
во множество летъ желаю здравствовать купъно j с любящими вашими	вомножество летъ желаю вамъ здравствовать купно j с любящими вашими:	желаю вам г͡сдрямъ моим во множество летъ здравствовати з государями моими братцами
а про меня ежели jзволишъ напаметоват	а про меня ежели jзволишъ напаметоват	а о себе доношу ежели изъволите милостию своею напаметоват

18 Kretschmer, *Zur Geschichte des Schriftrussischen*, 115–125.
19 Ibid., 74.

Unnamed scribe, signed by Mikhail Ukhtomskii, letter A	Unnamed scribe, signed by Mikhail Ukhtomskii, letter B	Mikhailo Turchenikov
Closing formulae:		
Такѡ пребуду вашъ гсдря моегѡ добърѡжелателны слуга камисар кнзъ михаило 8хтомскѡи	Такѡ́ пребуду вашъ моегѡ гсдря добрѡжелателны слуга кнзъ михалѡ ухтомскои	вашъ государеи мои покорны слугаи сынъ михаила турчеников земны свои поклон отдаю и благословения вашего прошу

The formulaic elements are not restricted to the text or the letters. They can be found also in the address: "пожаловатъ ѡтдать сие писмо …" (Turchenikov). The "пожаловатъ ѡтдать" is also found in seventeenth-century letters.[20] As Anna Kretschmer points out, even during the late eighteenth century the language found in Russian letters is in many ways the same as at the beginning of the seventeenth century.[21]

Reading Turchenikov's letter and comparing it to what Kretschmer terms *parental letters* (*Elternbriefe*), it becomes clear that Turchenikov forms part of a long tradition:

> … государеи мои́ покорны слуга и сынъ ми́хаила турчеников земны свои поклон отдаю и благословения вашего прошу.

Although the phrase "отдать нижаиший поклон" is encountered also in Ukthomskii's letter, the final salutations in Letters A and B form part of a different tradition, one with Western origins:

> Такѡ пребуду вашъ гсдря моегѡ добърѡжелателны слуга́.[22]

It is not surprising that the language found in the report and in letters A and B should contain parallels since they were written by the same scribe and associated with Prince Ukhtomskii. It may be more surprising that Turchenikov's letter echoes the same phrases. Thus, the episodes of the capture, present

---

20 Ibid., 289.
21 Ibid., 246.
22 Cf. D. A. Sdvizhkov, *Pis'ma s prusskoi voiny: liudi rossiisko-imperatorskoi armii v 1758 godu* (Moscow: Novoe literaturnoe obozrenie, 2019).

whereabouts, material needs, and the benevolence of the king all reflect the corresponding passages in the report and in letters A and B.

The private letters borrow much of the information and formulations from the report. This is not surprising. As Kretschmer points out, there are great similarities of expression between private letters and other text types of the business language.[23]

Due to the generous use of formulaic language in private letters, some might consider them to be weak representatives of ego-documents. Why, it may be asked, should we study them? The primary reason is to come closer to the language used by individuals outside the elite, and private letters offer one of very few possibilities to do this. Due to the literacy situation in eighteenth-century Russia, and the traditions prevalent in letter-writing, we do not have access to vast quantities of ego-documents, as is the case in some other European countries.

The situation characterizing mid-eighteenth-century Russia, with few sources written by non-elite authors, has parallels in other European cultures. Pál Nagy, a Hungarian scholar who has studied Roma people in eighteenth-century Hungary, uses the term "semi-ego-document" when referring documents focused on individuals, such as court cases and petitions.[24] Nagy writes: "There is not a single documentary source that conveys the words of a Roma person directly. We can only obtain information indirectly through partial and fragmented evidence."[25] While the situation is different in the case of Russian from the 1740s—private letters exist in which the voices of individuals can be heard—they are far from plentiful. However, large quantities of documents containing "ego-elements" are available.

While Russian private letters of the eighteenth century continue the tradition of formulaic expressions originating in earlier periods, they do not provide a complete picture. During the post-Petrine period, new kinds of formulas appeared in Russian letters.[26] In contrast to the traditional letters exemplified above, the new expressions came from abroad, notably from the French-speaking area.[27]

The following example contains a request by a Russian military commander, Patrick Stuart, to a Swedish government administrator, Count Bonde. Neither man is Russian, but the letter is composed in the Russian military headquarters

23 Kretschmer, *Zur Geschichte des Schriftrussisichen*, 73.
24 Pál Nagy, "Roma in semi-ego documents in 18th century Hungary," *Frühneuzeit-Info*.
25 Ibid., 96.
26 Kretschmer, *Zur Geschichte des Schriftrussischen*, 233.
27 Offord, Rjéoutski, and Argent, *The French Language in Russia*, 332.

in the Swedish town of Nyköping in early 1744.[28] As the letter shows, the formulas are more similar to Western European letters of the eighteenth century than to Russian private letters of the period:

> [hand 1] Сиятелныи граѳъ/ милостивыи гсдрь мои/ присланнымъ ко мне от его высокопревосхо/дителства гсдина генерала аншеѳа и кова/лера кеита ордеромъ, имеющеися на прибы/вших сюда галиотах росіискои правиантъ в ма/газеины выгр8зить определено, и в выгр8ске/ оного по требованию находящагося здесь об[еръ]/правиантъ меистера павлова надлещажѣ[е]/ вспомоществование учинить велено, а нне/ онои оберъ правиантъ меистеръ павлов[.]/ поданным ко мне доношениемъ обявляет[ъ]/ что означенные галиоты не дошед до неи[ки]/пинга пяти верстъ обмерзли, и требует/ чтоб для перевоски с них в неикипингъ в ма/газеинъ правианта, определено было сто/ подводъ, вследствие сего вашего сия/телства прош8 для помян8тых/ потребностеи вышепи/санное// число подводъ приказа/ть определить,/ вашего сиятелства/ милостиваго гсдря моегw/ покорныи сл8га/ [hand 2] *Patrike Stuart*/ [hand 1] генваря 12 дня/ 1744 году/ неикипингъ

As this letter, and many others like it, show, the inspiration for the closing salutation is not to be sought in traditional Russian letter-writing, but in the French *Votre humble serviteur* (your humble servant). In circles familiar with western practices during the 1740s, the private letter became a ground for competition between old traditions and new impulses from abroad.

7.2 The Language of Regional Administration

Above (sections 6.1.2 and 7.1.2a), we saw examples of administrative documents from the 1740s. One document was sent from the Artillery and Fortifications Office of the Kamer-kollegiia to the Office of Livonian and Estonian Affairs.[29] In other words, this document represents a unit of the central administration

---

28 Regional Archives, Uppsala, Södermanland, Landskontoret, D VI 17.
29 The Kamer-kollegiia was later replaced by the Ministry of Finance, cf. Amburger, *Geschichte der Behördenorganisation*, 119.

writing to an administrative unit at the provincial level. The document in question is a *promemoriia*, that is, a memorandum. Prince Ukhtomskii's report, as was stated above, represents the opposite direction, that is, a subordinate reporting to a senior officer.

In the Russian Federation, and in other countries, archival institutions hold administrative documents like *promemorii, donosheniia*, and other administrative documents whose structure was regulated. Such documents originate from all corners of the empire: from the center, from the Baikal area, and from the Russian North.[30]

Regional business documents from the middle and second half of the eighteenth century, are characterized by a tendency towards standardization of the formulaic language.[31] In specific documents, the boundaries between formulaic language and original content can sometimes be observed on the basis of the frequency of the letter *iat'* ⟨ѣ⟩. The character is sometimes found in formulae, such as the heading of reports: ⟨В госꙋдарственнꙋю Адмиралтѣиствъ коллегию, покорнеишѣе доношение⟩, but diminishes or disappears in the informational portion of texts.[32]

Thanks to scholars like Kotkov, Maiorov, Nikitin and many others, the traditional administrative register belongs to the most well-known spheres of Russian eighteenth-century language. In view of this, the topic will not be pursued further. Our attention will turn to other, less well-known topics.

7.3 The Language of Diplomacy

Among the most prestigious forms of Russian eighteenth-century language belong international treaties and correspondence with foreign rulers. For the purposes of the present investigation, Russia's diplomatic correspondence with two neighboring states has been investigated: Sweden (a traditional rival of Russia) and Denmark (a traditional ally). By the 1740s, a number of terms of French origin had entered Russian diplomatic correspondence, and later in the century, Russian diplomats even used French to communicate among

---

30 Sumkina and Kotkov, *Pamiatniki moskovskoi delovoi pis'mennosti*; Mezhenina and Maiorov, *Delovaia pis'mennost' Troitskogo Selenginskogo monastyria*; Arkhivnyi fond Vologodskoi oblasti, accessed November 16, 2021, https://uniqdoc.gov35.ru/docs/.

31 Nikitin, *Delovaia pis'mennost'*, 215.

32 Cf. Sumkina and Kotkov, *Pamiatniki moskovskoi delovoi pis'mennosti*, 3.

themselves.[33] With its Baltic Sea neighbors, however, Russia still undertook much of its correspondence in Russian.

The texts examined were:

- An assurance by the Empress concerning subsidies to Sweden.[34]
- Letters to the Swedish royal family, 1740–1748.[35]
- Letters to the Danish royal family, 1740–1749.[36]
- A diplomatic letter from Russian Plenipotentiary, Count A. I. Rumiantsev to the Swedish Chancellery president (Prime Minister), Count Carl Gyllenborg, November 29, 1742.[37]

7.3.1 The Treaty on Subsidies

Бо́жїею поспѣшеств́ующею ми́лостїю,/ мы елисаве́тъ пе́рвая јмператри́ца/ и́ самоде́ржица всеро́ссїйская, московская,/ ки́евская, влади́мерская, новгородская, цари́ца/ каза́нская, цари́ца астраха́нская, цари́ца си/би́рская, гос8да́рыня псковска́я, и́ вели́кая княги́ня смоле́нская, княги́ня эстля́ндская,/ лифля́ндская, каре́лская, тверская, ю́горская,/ пе́рмская͂, вя́тская, бо́лгорская ј і́ныхъ гсдрня,/ и великая княги́ня нова̀ города низовския зем-/ли, черниговская, рязанская, ростовская, ю́росла̄в-/ская, бѣлоозерская, удорская, обдорская, конди́и-/ская, и́ всея̀ сѣверныя страны̀ повели́телни-/ца, и́ гос8да́рыня и́верския земли́, карталинъ-/скихъ и гр8зинскихъ царей, и кабардинския зем-/ли́, черкаскихъ, и горскихъ князей, ј і́ныхъ на-/слѣдная гос8да́рыня и облада́телница./ Божіею ми́лостию пресвѣтлѣйшем8 и́-/ державнѣйшем8 кня́зю и гос8да́рю гсдрю фри-/дрих8 королю свѣйском8, го́тском8, и вень-/

---

33 Offord, Rjéoutski, and Argent, *The French Language in Russia*, 287–291.

34 Assurance of subsidies, June 22, 1745. RA, Originaltraktater med främmande makter (traktater), 25 juni 1745, SE/RA/25.3/2/28/E (1745)

35 Swedish National Archives, Muscovitica 623.

36 Danish National Archives, 301 Tyske Kancelli, Udenrigske Afdeling, 1516–1769, Rusland: Breve fra russiske kejsere og kejserinder. Kejserinde Anna Ivanovna Romanov 1730–1740 m.m.; Danish National Archives, Copenhagen, Denmark, 301 Tyske Kancelli, Udenrigske Afdeling, 1516–1769, Rusland: Breve fra russiske kejser og kejserinder, Kejserinde Anna Ivanovna Romanov 1730–1740 m.m.

37 Swedish National Archives, Kabinettet UD E1 A2.

денском8, и́ протчая, и́ протчая, и́ протчая, ландъ/граф8
ге́ссенском8, князю в гиршфелде, граф8/ в кацен эл̃ленбогене,
дице, цыгенгейне, ни́дде,/ и ша8мб8рхе, и про́тчая, вашем8
величеств8 [in bottom margin: его́ вели́честву королю
шве́цком8] // на́ше др8жебно сосе́дское поздравление. на́ши/
упователно уже доволно изве́стные к̓ вашем8/ величеств8,
отличные сентимены, к с8мне̃нію/ ме̃ста не оставляютъ, о
томъ удоволствіи, с ка-/ковымъ мы̀ пол8чили грамот8 вашего
величества,/ о те̃хъ четырехъ стахъ тысячахъ р8бляхъ, кой от
на́съ/ его королевском8 высточеств8 прошлого 1743г̃: год8
по-/ притчие̃ тогда́шнихъ обстоятелствъ были обе-/щаны.
и хотя̀ по отме́не бывшихъ в̓ то̀ вре́мя/ де̃лъ и минованию
всякой, для̀ шведской коро́ны/ опасности, и̓ помян8тое на́ше
обеща́ніе нат8рал̃-/но состоятелнымъ признаваемо быть
не мо́жетъ,/ о боле̃е в̓ себѐ не настои́тъ, однако мы̀ јстинно
же-/лая во всякихъ сл8чаяхъ, какъ наш8 к угодностямъ
ва-/шего величества особлив8ю атенцию не лицеме̃рно/
засвиде̃телствовать, такъ и́ короне̃ шведской/ действително
удостоверителные о́пыты и томъ/ пода́ть, колико мы̀ хоти́мъ,
даже до наимне̃йшаго/ л8ча́, какой либо по притчине̃
постановленныхъ/ в союзномъ тракта́те̃ секретныхъ
арти́к8ловъ/ касающихся до гара́нтіи голштинского
владе́ния/ нашего вселюбезне̃йшаго племянника великагѡ/
кня́зя всеро́ссіиского, и̓ содержаниъ в̓ полше̃ тишины̀/
тягости преду́преждать, и̓ он8ю по возможности объ-/
легчать. то с8мм8 четыре́х̑ сотъ тысяч р8бле́въ/ для̓ того
определили, кото́рая в̓ четыре одинъ за-/ др8гимъ сле̃дующие
года̀, с̑читая от ратификаціи// союзного тракта́та, а јмянно
по прошествіи кажъ-/дыхъ шестѝ ме̃́сяцовъ по пятидестъ
ты́сячъ р8блевъ/ и справно шведской короне̃ платима
быть јме̃етъ,/ а при најсилне̃йшемъ о томъ обнадеживаніи
совершенно/ уве̃рены̀ находимся, что̀ ва́ше величество,
и корона/ шве́дская по счастливо пребывающем8 межд8
наш-/ми обоюдными двора́ми узл8 кре̃пкого соедине́ния,/
какъ нашем8 наме̃рению, в непреме̃нномъ додержаніи/
постановленныхъ обязателствъ совзаимствовать,/ та"къ
особливо во всякомъ благосостояніи и защищеніи/
герцокско-голшти́нского владе̃дниія нашем8 вселюбезне̃й-/
шем8 племянник8 јскренно усердствовать сојзволите./

впрочемъ мы̀ ваше величество милостивомꙋ защи-/щенїю всевышшаго бóга, ко всякомꙋ постоянно сча-/стливомꙋ благополꙋ́чїю препорꙋчаемъ. данъ в санктъ/ петербꙋрге јюня .22. днѧ̀ 1745: гóда./ вашего величества/ вѣ́рная сестра и прїятелница./ [hand 2] Елисаветъ/ [hand 3] граѳъ Алеѯѣй Бестужевъ Рюминъ

The first impression of the text is its strong emphasis on formal, symbolic expressions. The text, which has much in common with private letters, begins by stating the full title of the Empress of Russia, followed by titles of the King of Sweden.

The business part of the text is signaled by a greeting:

вашемꙋ величествꙋ нáше дрꙋжебно сосѣдское поздравление.

This is followed by another formulaic expression, expressing the satisfaction experienced by the Empress upon receiving a letter from the King, for whom she has warm feelings:

... нáши упователно уже доволно извѣстные к̕ вашемꙋ величествꙋ, отличные сентимены, к сꙋмнѣнїю мѣста не оставляютъ, о томъ удоволствїи, с ка-/ковымъ мы̀ полꙋчили грамотꙋ вашего величества.

Only following this greeting does the letter go on to discuss specific issues.

7.3.2 Letters to the Royal Families

The majority of letters in this group are addressed to the kings, but there are also examples of letters to other members of the royal families, such as the queen and crown prince.

During the 1740s, the Russian Empire and the Kingdom of Sweden found themselves at war for two years, August 1741–August 1743. The war caused a certain coolness in the salutations. Thus, a letter written before the war, on October 18, 1740, from the infant Emperor Ioann Antonovich to the King of Sweden includes the salutation

Вашего величества/вѣрныи братъ другъ ј сосѣдъ.

During the war, on July 30, 1742, the new Empress, Elisabeth, instead chose to restrict herself to expressing a desire for friendship:

Вашего величества др૪жебносⱳхотная сестра …

The Empress expressed herself in more affectionate terms to the King of Denmark, a traditional ally of Russia:

Ва́шего короле́вского вели́чества ј любви̏ ве̏рная сестра̀ и̏ прия́телница … [38]

As in the assurance of subsidies, letters to the monarch begin with the formulaic titles of the Russian and Swedish rulers, occupying approximately the first 200 words.[39] Letters to the Danish court have exactly the same structure, although, of course, with a different set of titles for the Danish monarch.[40]

The letters' statement of purpose follows the titles and greetings. This statement, or explanation, is often marked by an initial понеже (since, because), familiar from administrative documents. Following the statement of purpose an account of measures taken or decisions made is often marked by того ради (for that sake) or something similar. The letters generally end with a lengthy formula requesting the blessing of the Almighty upon the recipient and declaring the writer's general benevolence.

The final element reports the place and date of issue, and an indication of the regnal year of the sender.

The corpus also contains examples of shorter, somewhat more informal greetings. Although the titles of the recipient may be somewhat short, long enumerations of titles may occur also in the business part of the letter if the matter treated

---

38 Letter to Christian VI, May 25, 1744, Danish National Archives, Copenhagen, Denmark, 301 Tyske Kancelli, Udenrigske Afdeling, 1516–1769, Rusland: Breve fra russiske kejser og kejserinder, Kejserinde Anna Ivanovna Romanov 1730–1740 m.m.

39 The presence of such lengthy titles in eighteenth-century diplomacy was motivated by the importance of these titles as symbols of power and influence. In Russo-Swedish relations, royal titles had been a sensitive issue for generations, cf. Jan Hennings, "The Semiotics of Diplomatic Dialogue: Pomp and Circumstance in Tsar Peter I's Visit to Vienna in 1698," *The International History Review* 3 (2008): 515–544; Ulla Birgegård, "En ständig huvudvärk i relationerna mellan Sverige och Ryssland: Tsarens och kungens titlar," *Slovo* 55 (2014): 34–46.

40 Cf., for example, Empress Elisabeth, letter of condolence to Frederik V, August 31, 1747, Danish National Archives, Copenhagen, Denmark, 301 Tyske Kancelli, Udenrigske Afdeling, 1516–1769, Rusland: Breve fra russiske kejser og kejserinder, Kejserinde Anna Ivanovna Romanov 1730–1740 m.m.

happens to concern people in high places. Such an example is illustrated in the letter announcing the marriage between the future Tsar Peter III and the future Empress Catherine II:

Свѣтлѣишїй Кронъ принцъ; Дружебно-любезный/ племянникъ./ юко по ѡсобливомъ всевышшаго бога предъ-/ усмотренїю, и по моемъ соизволенїю, мой/ вселюбезнѣишїй племянникъ Его jмператорское/ высочество великїй князь всероссїискїй Петръ,/ наслѣдникъ норвежской, владѣющей герцогъ/ шлезвигъ голстинской, штормарнской, и дитмар-/ ской, графъ ѻлденбъргской и делменгорстской &с./ сь ея императорскимъ высочествомъ великою княгинею всероссїискою Екатериною, урожден-/ною княгинею ангалтскою, герцогинею саѯонскою,/энгернскою, и вестфалскою, графинею асканскою, госъдарынею цербстскою, бернбъргскою, эверскою,/ и книпгаузенскою &с. в здѣшней моей импера-/торской столицѣ въ „21де„сего мⷭца благополъчно/ в брачное сочетанїе встъпилъ. Тако я ни-/мало умедлить не хотѣла, чтобъ вашемъ/ королевскомъ Высочествъ и любви, о такомъ/ благополъчномъ, и мнѣ толь радостномъ/ произшествїи, чрезъ сїе jзвѣстно не учинить,// ни како не съмнѣваясь, что ваше королевское высочество и любовь не токмо мнѣ, j моемъ/ jмператорскомъ домъ все то, еже к моемъ/ и о"ного удоволствїю и благополъчїю касается,/ ѻхотно желать, но и ваше в томъ участїе/ принять, слѣдователно же о" семъ счастливо/ совершившемся брачномъ сочетанїи порадоватся/ и вышеупмянътымъ высокимъ новосочетан-/нымъ и с вашей стороны от милости все-/вышшаго, всякаго благословенїя и благополъчїя/ возжелать соизволите. в прочемъ же/ с неотмѣнною благоволителною дръжбою всегда/ пребываю./ вашего королевского высочества j любви/ дръжебно сѡхотная тетка./ [hand 2] Елисаветъ/ [hand 1]в санктъ петербърхѣ/ „26„/ авгъста. 1745.[41]

---

41 Empress Elisabeth to Adolf Fredrik, Heir Apparent of Sweden, February 12, 1745, Swedish National Archives, Muscovitica 623.

From the point of view of morphology, the imperial letters are reminiscent of administrative documents and contain few surprises. The titles have examples of archaic forms, such as the Genetive singular of adjectives ⟨кабардинския⟩.

The most characteristic traits of this group of documents are found in their highly formulaic language, expressed through a long-winded syntax, teeming with subordinate clauses. There is a strong tendency towards placing the verb at the end of sentences.

7.3.3 A Letter by A. I. Rumiantsev

Although Russia and Sweden were at war during the first half of the 1740s, there was no change in the level of diplomatic courtesy. In the following example, the Russian diplomat A. I. Rumiantsev writes to a leading politician. Sweden has been soundly beaten, and the Russian delegate will conduct the negotiations from a position of strength. Nonetheless, he adheres to the formal demands of letter-writing.

> Мой гсднъ/ отвѣты высо́кого министе́рства ея jмператор/ скаго вели́чества всероссїиской моей всеавг8/стейшей j всемлⷭтивѣйшей гсдрни привезе́нные ка/питаномъ дре́нтелемъ к гсдну барон8 нолкин8 вⷲе/ превосходи́телство 8вѣдомили что я снабде́нъ над/лежащими полномо́чьями тр8ди́тся о возстановленїи/ доброго согла́сия межд8 соⷦбоими дворами, и что по/р8чено мнѣ доста́вить в стокголмъ обьяви́телн8ю/ гсдрни jмератрицы гра́мот8 о счастли́вомъ/ ея возшествїи на родителской престо́лъ к̕ его вели/честв8 королю швецком8 гсдрю ва́шем8./ я бъ 8же давно сие повеле́ние jсполни́лъ/ ежели б̕ перемена обстоя́телствъ воспослѣдовшаяся в̕ финля́ндїи не возрепя́тствовала и всякой/ сл8чайктом8не отняла но баронъ нолкинъ писмомъ/ своимъ к покойном8 великом8 каⷩцлер8 черка́ском8 [in bottom margin: его п: г: графу фоⷩ гиллембурху]// отъ 5г. октября́ подавъ внᲈвь к том8 поводъ и показа́в̕/ что сие предвари́телное предше́ствие к негоциа́цїи/ жела́ется да́лѣе не отлага́ю отправля́я гсдина подполко/вника м8рзина коего приемлю сме́лость адресовать/ к ва́шем8 превосходи́телств8 яко первом8 департа/мента иностра́нныхъ дѣлъ мини́стр8

с проше́ниемъ/ что б под приказа́ниямъ ва́шимъ оной
мꙋрзинъ мо́гъ/ имѣть честь королю самомꙋ пода́ть онꙋю
обьяви/телнꙋю гра́мотꙋ, кото́рꙋю буде в томъ какое за/
трꙋдне́ние найдется врꙋчить и вашемꙋ превосходи/телствꙋ,/
в̾ ꙋчиняемомъ {: на онꙋю грамотꙋ} отвѣте я лшꙋ/ себя что
возимѣется старание внести ꙋпотребляемые/ предкамъ
ея вели́чества титꙋлы и без которыхъ/ всеавгꙋстейшая
моя г҃сдрня јмператрица ни/какой грамоты приня́ть не
соизволитъ, о чемъ јмѣю/ честь вш҃емꙋ превосходителствꙋ
дать зна́ть ꙋпо/вая что вы не захоти́те за си́мъ неспоримымъ/
напреd сего дѣломъ и должнымъ высокомꙋ достои́нству/ ея
јмпера́торскаго вели́чества остановить/ и вновь отдали́ть
то́ль кра́тно повторе́нные к мирꙋ/ добрые склонности./
Его превосходителство вицеканцлеръ графъ/ бестꙋжевъ
рюминъ в отвѣте своемъ г҃сднꙋ баронꙋ нол/кинꙋ обещая
скорое назна́чение втораго еѧ/ величества пономочного
я не хотѣлъ без ꙋвѣдомле/ния ва́мъ моемꙋ г҃сднꙋ соста́вить
чтѡ// г҃сдрня јмператри́ца его превосходителствѡ/ г҃сдна
генера́ла анше́фа барона фонлюбраса вместе/ со мною к
семꙋ полезномꙋ дѣлꙋ определить соизволила/ сие известие
мнѣ наипаче нꙋ́жно показа́лось, понеже/ в слꙋ́чае что б
его короле́вское вели́чество изволилъ/ переменить ꙋже
назна́ченныхъ к томꙋ жъ с швецкой/ стороны или пожела́л
бы обьяви́ть {: еже однако в̾ его/ соизволенïи состоитъ} кого
свои́мъ вторымъ мини/стромъ кто б соѡтветственъ былъ
ра́нгꙋ г҃сдна любраса/ и слѣдственно посланные с капита́номъ
дрентелемъ/ пашпо́рты недѣйствителны были, то я по
первому/ о томъ от ва́шего превосходи́телства јли вашихъ/
полномоченыхъ ꙋвѣдомлению в состоянïи нахожусь/
новые присла́ть и о все́мъ томъ еже до конгреса/ каса́ется
с ни́ми постановить./ јного мнѣ ничего не остается какъ/ в
благосклонность вш҃его превосходителства/ г҃сдна мꙋрзина
рекомендовать с прошенимъ оного/ безпродолжи́телно
отправить с такою безопаснѡ/стию какову имѣли у насъ
присыла́емые из швецïи/ јмѣю честь быть спочтителною
обяза̑н/ностию./ вашего превосходителства/ всепослушныи
ј нижаишïи слꙋга/ [hand 2] а румя́нцевъ/ [hand 1] ноября 20г҃
дня/ 1742 году/ из выборха

As the letter clearly shows, the characteristics of Russian diplomatic language were not restricted to imperial letters. The syntax and wording of Rumiantsev's letter, which is written by a professional scribe, suggests that the Russian foreign administration possessed a staff of highly trained secretaries and scribes. The orthography maintains ⟨ѣ⟩ in its etymological places with occasional deviations: ⟨в отвѣте⟩.

The examples of diplomatic language shown above support the idea of a specific register for state documentation, separate from that of traditional administrative documents, although elements of the administrative registers are found also in the diplomatic correspondence.

7.4 The Life of Printed Texts

When a text is copied by hand, minor errors and changes inevitably occur. This fact forms the basis of *textual criticism*, a branch of scholarship that explores the history and development of textual traditions.[42] Greatly simplified we can say that textual traditions contain patterns of changes that we can follow, like rings of a tree.

Printed texts behave altogether differently. Since printed texts can be mass produced, there is no longer any need to copy them by hand, and all copies turn out identical. Changes between versions of a printed text can occur between editions but not between individual copies. When studying printed text from a limited time span—a single decade, as in the case of the present investigation—it is of interest to note whether the text represents a first edition, or if it is a second or later edition. This is significant because in second and later editions, traces may be left behind from one or more of the earlier editions. If we are analyzing an edition from 1745 of a text first published in 1720, can we be sure that the language represents that of the 1740s, or does it represent the language used in the 1720s?

7.4.1 Printing and Obsolete Characters

In the 1730s, two reforms of the civil alphabet were introduced. Prior to 1735, the characters representing /i/ were not used consistently. In theory, ⟨ï⟩ was employed in positions before vowels, ⟨i⟩ was used in foreign words, ⟨и⟩ in most

---

42 M. L. West, *Textual Criticism and Editorial Technique Applicable to Greek and Latin Texts* (Stuttgart: Teubner, 1973); D. S. Likhachëv, *Tekstologiia*, 2nd ed. (Leningrad: Nauka, 1983).

other cases, and ⟨v⟩, *izhitsa*, in a handful of words. In 1735, the Academy of Sciences introduced ⟨й⟩ while abolishing ⟨ѯ⟩ (*ksi*) and ⟨v⟩. In 1738, a new reform abolished the use of ⟨ï⟩ while reserving ⟨i⟩ for use before vowels, and ⟨и⟩ in other positions.[43]

Examining the set of characters in printed texts from the 1740s, and the rules for their combination, we sometimes find that the rule explained above is not without exception, and that printed texts from the 1740s contain traits from an earlier period. As an example, in the margin of a template text for a letter of credit printed in 1744 (section 3.4.2), we find evidence that this particular template is based on an earlier text because the editor/typesetter has neglected to bring the use of ⟨ï⟩ up to date:

Ежели хозяинъ їностранныхъ товаровъ купїть не прїкажетъ.[44]

During the decades following the introduction of the civil typeface, the character ⟨ï⟩ representing /i/, occurred initially, between consonants, as well as before vowels and /j/ in ⟨-їя⟩, ⟨-їе⟩ and other endings. In 1744, however, this was no longer the case. By the mid-1740s, the use of ⟨ï⟩ in printed texts had been limited. It was usually no longer found in initial position or between consonants.

The use of obsolete characters or outdated orthographic rules in a text cannot always be explained as a consequence of second editions. Sometimes, a deviation may simply be result of the work of an individual typesetter, as the following example suggests.

In a series of reports from the front in Finland, in 1742, Field-Marshal Peter de Lacy sent a number of reports to the government that were deemed interesting enough to merit printing. The printing was carried out in the civil typeface at the Senate printing shop in Moscow. The present investigation has had access to a collection of front reports comprising approximately 21,120 words. For the most part, the texts adhere to the character sets and orthographic rules current at the time, but there are also seemingly inexplicable deviations. The word экстрактъ (extract, résumé) occurs fifteen times in the corpus. In twelve of these cases, the spelling is the expected ⟨экстрактъ⟩ spelled with ⟨кс⟩. In three cases, however, all from the same issue, printed on October 17, 1742, the form ⟨эѯтрактъ⟩ is used despite the fact that the character ⟨ѯ⟩ was abolished in the 1730s (section 4.4.1). Why does this character suddenly reemerge in

---

43 Shitsgal, *Russkii grazhdanskii shrift*, 81–82.
44 *Formuliar. Protiv kotorogo spetsial'noe. …*

print? The front reports were written just a few weeks prior to being printed, so this is clearly not a case of second edition. Instead, it most likely did so due to the habits of an individual typesetter. Perhaps he adhered too closely to the handwritten draft, or maybe he received his training during earlier decades, when the character ⟨ѯ⟩ was still being used in text printed in the civil typeface.

There is additional evidence suggesting that the use of characters formally abolished by the Academy of Sciences continued to be used throughout the 1740s. Thus in the printed announcement of the marriage between the future Peter III and Catherine II, the patronymic of the bride uses ⟨ѯ⟩:

> Понеже Мы съ помощію и благословенїемъ божїимъ Всемилостивѣишее намѣренїе воспрїяли, благопостановленное ихъ Императорскихъ Высочествъ, Нашего Вселюбезнѣишаго Племянника, Великаго Князя Всероссїискаго владѣющаго Герцога Шлезвихъ Голстинского ПЕТРА ѲЕОДОРОВИЧА, и обрученнои невѣсты Его Великои Княжны ЕКАТЕРИНЫ АЛЕѮѢЕВНЫ сочетанїе бракомъ совершить, …[45]

The situation concerning *izhitsa* ⟨v⟩ is similar. In an imperial edict from the very end of the decade, printed at the Senate printing office in Moscow and concerning forbidden books, the words ⟨сѵнодъ⟩ and ⟨Іеромонахъ⟩ use characters that appear archaic. ⟨ѯ⟩ also occurs in the text, as does the Locative plural ⟨городѣхъ⟩ featuring an obsolete case ending.[46] This, however, may depend on the nature of the topic.

7.4.2 The Development of Printed Texts

How did texts printed in successive editions during the first half of the eighteenth century develop over time? A practical way of illustrating this is to present parallel texts of three editions. The text chosen for this purpose is the *Artikul voinskii* (*Articles of War*) in the editions from 1715, 1735, and 1744.

---

45 *Ponezhe My s pomoshchiiu i blagosloveniem bozhiim* (St. Petersburg: Senat, March 17, 1745).
46 *Ukaz eia imperatorskago velichestva* (Moscow: Senat, June 3, 1749).

The *Artikul* is a collection of military laws and regulations that first appeared in 1714,[47] and the Russian collection was modeled on international prototypes.[48] For the purposes of this investigation, a portion of the text, found in three successive editions (1715, 1735, and 1744) has been analyzed.[49] The full text, in its 1744 edition, comprises 255 printed pages.

The text of the *Articles of War* was intended for public use and represents legal language. The portion of the text analyzed here consists of two parts: a declaration and an oath. It is written in the name of the Tsar and directed to officers and soldiers of the armed forces. There is a clearly defined relationship among the participants: they take the oath owe their allegiance to the sovereign. On the whole, the situational context does not change between the three editions examined here. The institution of the monarchy remains the same, as does the relationship between the monarch and the individuals taking the oath. The only element that changes is the person of the ruler. When the text was originally composed, Russia was ruled by Peter the Great (1672–1725). By the time of the second edition, his niece, Anna (1693–1740), had acceded to the throne. In 1744, when the last of the three editions was printed, Peter's daughter, Elisabeth (1709–1761), was in power.[50]

---

47 *Artikul voinskii*, NĖB Knizhnye pamiatniki, accessed May 5, 2021, https://kp.rusneb.ru/item/material/artikul-voinskii-2. The title of the Russiian text is in the singular—Артикулъ—while in the German parallel text, it is in the plural—*Articuln*. Here and below, the title in English is in the plural, as is traditional in the English-speaking world.

48 Eugene O. Porter, "The Articles of War," *The Historian* 2 (1946): 77–102; Per-Edvin Wallén, review of *Den karolinska militärstraffrätten och Peter den stores krigsartiklar* by Erik Anners, *Svensk juristtidning* 573 (1962), accessed May 5, 2021, https://svjt.se/svjt/1962/573.

49 *Artikul voinskii kupno s protsesom nadlezhashchii sudiashchim. Napechatasia poveleniem tsar-skago velichestva* (St. Petersburg, 1715), accessed May 3, 2021, https://kp.rusneb.ru/item/material/artikul-voinskii-1; *Artikul voinskii s kratkim tolkovaniem*, 2nd ed. (St. Petersburg: Imperatorskaia akademiia nauk, 1735); *Artikul voinskii s kratkim tolkovaniem*, 3rd ed. (St. Petersburg: Imperatorskaia akademiia nauk, 1744).

50 Porter, "The Articles of War"; Wallén, review of *Den karolinska militärstraffrätten*.

1715	1735	1744
БОЖІЕЮ МІЛОСТІЮ МЫ ПЕТРЪ ПЕРВЫИ,	БОЖІЕЮ МИЛОСТІЮ МЫ ПЕТРЪ ПЕРВЫИ,	БОЖІЕЮ МИЛОСТІЮ МЫ ПЕТРЪ ПЕРВЫЙ,
ЦАРЬ И САМОДЕРЖЕЦЪ ВСЕРОССІИСКІИ. и протчая, и протчая, и протчая	ЦАРЬ И САМОДЕРЖЕЦЪ ВСЕРОССІИСКИ. и протчая, и протчая, и протчая	ЦАРЬ И САМОДЕРЖЕЦЪ ВСЕРОССІЙСКІЙ. и прочая, и прочая, и прочая
Повелѣваемъ всѣмъ обще нашімъ генераломъ, штапъ оборъ и ундеръ офіцерамъ, и салдатамъ, какъ подданнымъ, такъ и чужестраннымъ, въ службѣ нашеи пребывающімъ, покорнымъ и послушнымъ быть по своеи должности. и всѣ пункты сего артікула право исполнять, и всякому особо высокого и нѣского чіна, безъ всякаго изъятія	Повелѣваемъ всѣмъ обще нашимъ Генераломъ, штапъ оборъ и ундеръ офіцерамъ, исалдатамъ, какъ подданнымъ, такъ и чужестраннымъ, въ службѣ нашеи пребывающымъ, покорнымъ и послушнымъ быть по своеи должности. и всѣ пункты сего артікула право исполнять, и всякому особо высокого и низкого чина, безъ всякаго изъятія,	Повелѣваемъ всѣмъ обще нашимъ Генераламъ, Штабъ Оберъ и ундеръ Офицерамъ и салдатамъ, какъ подданнымъ, такъ и чужестраннымъ, въ службѣ нашей пребывающимъ, покорнымъ и послушнымъ быть по своей должности. и всѣ пункты сего артикула право исполнять, и всякому особо высокаго и низкаго чина, безъ всякаго изъятія,
намъ яко государю своему прісягу чінѣть:	Намъ яко Государю своему присягу чинить:	Намъ яко Государю своему присягу чинить:
въ томъ да бы имъ вѣрно честно съ доброю охотою себя содержать, и какъ сіи послѣдствующіе пункты въ себѣ содержать. какъ честнымъ воїнскімъ людемъ благопрістоїно, протівъ всѣхъ нашіхъ и государствъ нашіхъ непріятелеи, тѣломъ и кровію хотя въ полѣ во осадахъ сухімъ и водянымъ путемъ прілучітца, служіть, и по крайнѣи возможности тщателно радѣть,	въ томъ дабы имъ вѣрно честно съ доброю охотою себя содержать, и какъ сіи послѣдствующіе пункты въ себѣ содержать. какъ честнымъ воинскимъ людемъ благопристоино, противъ всѣхъ нашихъ и государствъ нашихъ непріятелеи, тѣломъ и кровію хотя въ полѣ во осадахъ сухимъ и водянымъ путемъ прилучитца, служитъ, и по крайнѣи возможности тщателно радѣть,	въ томъ дабы имъ вѣрно, честно съ доброю охотою себя содержать, и какъ сіи послѣдствующіе пункты въ себѣ содержать. какъ честнымъ воинскимъ людемъ благопристойно, противъ всѣхъ нашихъ и государствъ нашихъ непріятелей, тѣломъ и кровію хотя въ полѣ во осадахъ, сухимъ и водянымъ путемъ прилучится, служить, и по крайнѣй возможности тщателно радѣть,
и чтобъ имъ нашъ и государствъ нашіхъ подданныхъ убытокъ отвращати, протівъ тогоже прібытокъ и лутчую пользу знати и вспомогати, и въ томъ нікакова ради страха не отбѣгать, ніже трудовъ жалѣти толь долго пока Богъ всякому животъ продолжітъ,	и чтобъ имъ Нашъ и государствъ нашихъ подданныхъ убытокъ отвращати, Противъ тогоже прибытокъ и лутчую пользу знати и вспомогати, и въ томъ никакова ради страха не отбѣгать, ниже трудовъ жалѣти толь долго пока Богъ всякому животъ продолжитъ,	и чтобъ имъ Нашъ и государствъ нашихъ подданныхъ убытокъ отвращати, Противъ тогоже прибытокъ и лутчую пользу знати и вспомогати, и въ томъ никакова ради страха не отбѣгать, нижѐ трудовъ жалѣти толь долго пока Богъ всякому животъ продолжитъ,

1715	1735	1744
и да бы невѣдѣнїемъ нїкто не отговарївался,	и да бы невѣдѣнїемъ никто не отговаривался,	и дабы невѣдѣнїемъ никто не отговаривался,
надлежїтъ сеи артїкулъ на смотрѣхъ, а особлїво про всякомъ полку по едїножды прочїтать въ недѣлю, чтобъ всякъ своего стыда наказанїя и безчестїя удалялся и бѣгалъ, протївъ тогожъ о благодѣянїи храбрости и повышенїи прїлѣжанїе имѣлъ.	надлежитъ сеи артїкулъ на смотрѣхъ, а особливо при всякомъ полку по единожды прочитать въ недѣлю, чтобъ всякъ своего стыда наказанїя и безчестїя удалялся и бѣгалъ, противъ тогожъ о благодѣянїи храбрости и повышенїи прилѣжанїе имѣлъ.	надлежитъ сей артїкулъ на смотрахъ, а особливо при всякомъ полку по единожды прочитать въ недѣлю, чтобъ всякъ своего стыда наказанїя и безчестїя удалялся и бѣгалъ, противъ тогожъ о благодѣянїи храбрости и повышенїи прилѣжанїе имѣлъ.
О ПРИСЯГѢ.	О ПРИСЯГѢ.	О ПРИСЯГѢ.
какїмъ образомъ прїсягу или обѣщанїе чїнїть.	какимъ образомъ присягу или обѣщанїе чинить.	какимъ образомъ присягу или обѣщанїе чинить.
Отъ ГЕНЕРАЛОВЪ и до ФЕНДРЇХА.	Отъ ГЕНЕРАЛОВЪ и до ФЕНДРІХА.	Отъ ГЕНЕРАЛОВЪ и до ФЕНДРИХА.
Положїть лѣвую руку на евангелїе, а правую руку поднять въ верхъ съ простертыми двѣма болшїми персты.	Положить лѣвую руку на Еѵангелїе, а правую руку поднять вверхъ съ простертыми двѣма большїми персты.	Положить лѣвую руку на Еѵангелїе, а правую руку поднять вверхъ съ простертыми двѣма большими персты.
А салдатамъ {понеже ихъ множество} правую толко руку поднять предъ предлежащїмъ евангелїемъ, и говорїть за чїтающїмъ прїсягу, и по прочтенїи цѣловать еванлегїе.	А салдатамъ {понеже ихъ множество} правую только руку поднять предъ предлежащимъ Еѵангелїемъ, и говорить за читающимъ присягу, и по прочтенїи цѣловать Еѵангелїе.	А салдатамъ, {понеже ихъ множество} правую только руку поднять предъ предлежащимъ Еѵангелїемъ, и говорить за читающимъ присягу, и по прочтенїи цѣловать Еѵангелїе.
Сїя прїсяга бываетъ генералїтету въ воїнскои консїлїи, а штапъ, оборъ и ундеръ офїцерамъ, и салдатамъ при полку или ротѣ, при распущеномъ знамени.	Сїя присяга бываетъ Генералїтету въ воинскои консїлїи, а штапъ, оборъ и ундеръ офїцерамъ, и салдатамъ при полку или ротѣ, при распущеномъ знамени.	Сїя присяга бываетъ Генералитету въ воинской консилїи, а Штабъ, Оберъ и ундеръ офицерамъ, и салдатамъ при полку или ротѣ, при распущеномъ знамени.
ПРИСЯГА,	ПРИСЯГА,	ПРИСЯГА,
или обѣщанїе всякаго воїнскаго чїна людемъ.	или обѣщанїе всякаго воинскаго чина людемъ.	или обѣщанїе всякаго воинскаго чина людемъ.
Я {имерекъ} обѣщаюсь всемогущїмъ Богомъ служїть, всепресвѣтлѣишему нашему Царю Государю вѣрно и послушно что въ сїхъ постановленныхъ такожъ и въ предъ поставляемыхъ воїнскїхъ артїкулахъ, что оные въ себѣ содержати будутъ,	Я {имярекъ} обѣщаюсь всемогущимъ Богомъ, служить всепресвѣтлѣишему нашему Царю Государю вѣрно и послушно что въ сихъ постановленныхъ такожъ и впредъ поставляемыхъ воинскихъ артїкулахъ, что оные въ себѣ содержати будутъ,	Я {Имя рекъ} обѣщаюсь всемогущимъ богомъ, служить всепресвѣтлѣйшему нашему Царю Государю вѣрно и послушно что въ сихъ постановленныхъ такожъ и впредъ поставляемыхъ воинскихъ артїкулахъ, что оные въ себѣ содержати будутъ,

1715	1735	1744
все исполнять исправно. Его Царскаго велічества, государства и земель его врагамъ тѣломъ и кровїю въ полѣ и въ крѣпостяхъ, водою, и сухїмъ путемъ, въ баталіяхъ, партіяхъ, осадахъ, и штурмахъ, и въ протчїхъ воїнскїхъ случаяхъ.	все исполнять исправно. Его Царскаго Величества, государства и земель его врагамъ, тѣломъ и кровїю въ полѣ и въ крѣпостяхъ, водою, и сухимъ путемъ, въ баталіяхъ, партіяхъ, осадахъ, и штурмахъ, и въ протчихъ воинскихъ случаяхъ.	все исполнять исправно. Его Царскаго Величества, государства и земель его врагамъ, тѣломъ и кровїю въ полѣ и въ крѣпостяхъ, водою, и сухимъ путемъ, въ баталіяхъ, партіяхъ, осадалъ (*sic*!—T.R.), и штурмахъ, и въ протчихъ воинскихъ случаяхъ,
какова оныя званія ні есть храброе и сїлное чїнїть протївленїе, и всякїми образы оныхъ повреждать потщусь,	Какова оныя званія ні есть храброе и силное чинить противленїе, и всякими образы оныхъ повреждать потщусь.	какова оныя званія ні есть, храброе и силное чинить противленїе, и всякими образы оныхъ повреждать потщусь.
и ежели что вражеское и предъосудїтелное протївъ персоны Его Велїчества, или его воїскъ, такожде его государства людеи, їлї	И ежели что вражеское ипредосудительное противъ персоны Его Величества, или его воискъ, такожде его государства людеи, или	И ежели что вражеское и предосудителное противъ персоны Его Величества, или его войскъ, такожде его государства людей, или
їнтересу государственного что услышу, или увїжу, то обѣщаюсь объ ономъ по лутчеи моеи совѣсти, и сколко мнѣ извѣстно будетъ, извѣщать и нїчего не утаїть,	їнтересу государственного, что услышу, или увижу, то обѣщаюсь объ ономъ по лутчеи моеи совѣсти, и сколко мнѣ извѣстно будетъ, извѣщать и ничего не утаить.	интересу государственнаго, что услышу, или увижу, то обѣщаюсь объ ономъ по лутчей моей совѣсти, и сколко мнѣ извѣстно будетъ, извѣщать и ничего не утаить.
но толь паче во всемъ, ползу его и лутчее охранять и исполнять.	Но толь паче во всемъ, пользу его и лутчее охранять и исполнять.	Но толь паче во всемъ, пользу его и лутчее охранять и исполнять.
а командїрамъ моїмъ поставленнымъ надомною, во всемъ, гдѣ Его Царского Велїчества воїскъ Государства и людеи благополучїю и прїращенїю касаетца. въ караулахъ въ работахъ и въ протчїхъ случаяхъ, должное чїнїть послушанїе и весма повеленїю ихъ непротївїтца.	А командирамъ моимъ поставленнымъ надомною, во всемъ, гдѣ Его Царского Величества воискъ Государства и людеи благополучїю и приращенїю касаетца. въ караулахъ въ работахъ и въ протчихъ случаяхъ, должное чинить послушанїе и весма повеленїю ихъ не противитися.	А командирамъ моимъ поставленнымъ надомною, во всемъ, гдѣ Его Царскаго Величества войскъ Государства и людей благополучїю и приращенїю касается, въ караулахъ, въ работахъ и въ протчихъ случаяхъ, должное чинить послушанїе, и весма повеленїю ихъ не противитися.
отъ роты и знамя гдѣ надлежу, хотя въ полѣ обозѣ или гварнїзонѣ нікогда не отлучатца, но за онымъ пока жївъ непремѣнно, добоволно и вѣрно такъ какъ мнѣ прїятна честь моя, и жївотъ мои, слѣдовать буду,	Отъ роты и знамя гдѣ надлежу, хотя въ полѣ обозѣ или гварнїзонѣ никогда не отлучатца, но за онымъ, пока живъ, непремѣнно, доброволно, и вѣрно такъ, какъ мнѣ прїятна честь моя, и животъ мои, слѣдовать буду.	Отъ роты и знамя, гдѣ надлежу, хотя въ полѣ обозѣ или гварнизонѣ, никогда не отлучатся, но за онымъ, пока живъ, непремѣнно, добровольно, и вѣрно такъ, какъ мнѣ прїятна честь моя, и животъ мой, слѣдовать буду.

1715	1735	1744
и во всемъ такъ поступать какъ честному вѣрному послушному, храброму и не тороплïвому салдату надлежïтъ.	И во всемъ такъ поступать, какъ честному вѣрному. послушному, храброму и не торопливому Салдату надлежитъ.	И вовсемъ такъ поступать, какъ честному вѣрному. послушному, храброму и неторопливому Салдату надлежитъ.
Въ чемъ да поможетъ мнѣ господь богъ всемогущïи.	Въ чемъ да поможетъ мнѣ господь Богъ всемогущïи.	Въ **чемъ** да поможетъ мнѣ Господь Богъ всемогущïй.
Понеже сïя прïсяга въ обще всякому чïну положена, того ради надлежïтъ тому, кто къ прïсягѣ прïводïтъ, выпïсывать, которому чïну что принадлежïтъ, а ундеръ офïцерамъ и салдатамъ все.	Понеже сïя присяга въ обще всякому чину положена, того ради надлежитъ тому, кто къ присягѣ приводитъ, выписывать, которому чину что принадлежитъ, а ундеръ Офïцерамъ и Салдатамъ все.	Понеже сïя присяга въ обще всякому чину положена, того ради надлежитъ тому, кто къ присягѣ приводитъ, выписывать, которому чину что принадлежитъ, а ундеръ Офицерамъ и Салдатамъ все.

Comparing the three versions, we see that the texts remains identical in terms of vocabulary and syntax. The only changes observable are found in orthography and morphology.

The most salient change in the orthography concerns the use of the charachter ⟨ï⟩. In the 1715 edition, it occurs initially, medially between consonants, and in final position. All these usages were later abandoned in favor of ⟨и⟩:

> … и ежели что вражеское и предъосудïтелное протïвъ персоны Его Велïчества, или его воïскъ, такожде его государства людеи, ïлï ïнтересу государственного что услышу, или увïжу … (1715).

> И ежели что вражеское и предосудителное противъ персоны Его Велїчества, или его войскъ, такожде его государства людей, или интересу государственнаго, что услышу, или увижу (1744).

In the 1735 edition, the use of ⟨ï⟩ seems to follow a different rule, although not entirely consistently. For example, ⟨ï⟩ is admissible in words of foreign origin: ⟨ïнтересу⟩, ⟨гварнïзонѣ⟩, ⟨Офïцерамъ⟩, and so forth. The soft sign ⟨ь⟩ is not used consistently in the 1715 edition, but greater consistency exists in the 1735 edition. In the edition from 1744, the distribution of ⟨ь⟩ almost coincides with the situation found in modern texts, with a few exceptions: ⟨силное⟩. A peculiar use of the hard sign ⟨ъ⟩ is found in the 1715 edition: ⟨предъосудïтелное⟩. This is abandoned already in the 1735 version.

According to Shitsgal, ⟨v⟩ was abolished in 1735.[51] The character was reintroduced in 1758 (cf. section 4.4.1). It would therefore have been expected that ⟨v⟩ would be absent from the 1744 edition, but this is not the case. The 1715 edition has евангелїе while both subsequent editions have a variant with *izhitsa*: Евангелїе. This means that the decisions of the Academy of Sciences were not unanimously obeyed.

The spelling of reflexive verbs changes between the different editions. Thus, in 1715, we find ⟨касаетца⟩ (third person, singular, present), and ⟨отлучатца⟩, ⟨протївїтца⟩ (infinitives). In 1744, these have all been changed to ⟨касается⟩, and ⟨отлучатися⟩, ⟨противитися⟩ respectively:

> въ караулахъ въ работахъ и въ протчїхъ случаяхъ, должное чїнїть послушанїе и весма повелѣнїю ихъ непротївїтца (1715).

> въ караулахъ, въ работахъ и въ протчихъ случаяхъ, должное чинить послушанїе, и весма повелѣнїю ихъ не противитися (1744).

An orthographical feature that clearly saw change between the editions was the use of capital letters. Whereas in 1715, capital letters are found at the beginning of sentences and in words denoting the tsar and God (the latter, however, not obligatory), by 1744 the use of capital letters has spread to include the word Евангелїе. When denoting human beings, the distribution of capital letters seems to be based on social hierarchy. Words denoting higher officers are written with a capital initial, while other ranks are not:

> Штабъ, Оберъ и ундеръ офицерамъ, и салдатамъ при полку или ротѣ …

The latter rule is not used consistently. Spellings contradicting the "hierarchy rule" are also encountered:

> … а ундеръ Офицерамъ и Салдатамъ все.

How does the orthography of the *Artikul* compare to other printed texts from the 1740s? For reasons of comparison, we compared it to two other printed texts

51 Shitsgal, *Russkii grazhdanskii shrift*, 82.

from the 1740s: the *Ustav o bankrutakh*, a legislative text regulating bankruptcy, printed at the beginning of the decade, and M. V. Lomonosov's textbook on rhetoric, the *Kratkoe rukovodstvo k krasnorechiiu* from the end of the 1740s.[52] These particular texts were chosen exclusively on the basis of their date of production.

They were printed in separate printing offices. The *Ustav* was produced at the Senate's printing office, which had been established at the Senate chancellery in 1727 and charged with the printing of edicts.[53] The *Kratkoe rukovodstvo* was printed at the Academy of Sciences, as was the *Artikul*.

Beginning with the issue of capital letters, we find that the *Ustav* uses them at the beginning of sentences, in proper names, and in words denoting origin:

> … и во ономъ числѣ кураторовъ, быть двумъ Иноземцамъ, двумъ же Россїйскимъ …

The hierarchical perspective is visible in words denoting the tsar, the state, institutions, and individuals in the imperial administration.

In the *Kratkoe rukovodstvo*, the hierarchical rule is applied in a way similar to the *Ustav*:

> Ибо Генералы, Сенаторы, и сами Консулы, какъ Ирцїй и Панса, будучи на высочайшемъ степени Римскїя власти …[54]

The *Kratkoe rukovodstvo*, however, also uses captitalization for emphasis:

> Первымъ образомъ сочиняются Проповѣди, Исторїи, учебныя книги; другимъ составляются Имны, Оды, Комедїи, Сатиры, и другихъ родовъ стихи.[55]

In both the *Ustav* and the *Kratkoe rukovodstvo*, the distribution of ⟨ï⟩ agrees with that found in the 1744 edition of the *Artikul*.

Spelling both in the *Ustav* and the *Kratkoe rukovodstvo* is relatively consistent. The character ⟨ѣ⟩ is employed in its etymologically correct places.

---

52 *Ustav o bankrutakh*; Lomonosov, *Kratkoe rukovodstvo k krasnorechiiu*.
53 "Peterburgskaia senatskaia tipografiia," Putevoditeli po rossiiskim arkhivam, accessed November 13, 2021, https://guides.rusarchives.ru/funds/peterburgskaya-senatskaya-tipografiya.
54 Lomonosov, *Kratkoe rukovodstvo*, 3.
55 Ibid., 5.

All three texts use stress markings in word forms that might cause ambiguity, such as ⟨слова̀⟩. In the examined portion of the *Artikul*, such a stress marking is encountered only once, in the word ⟨нижè⟩. It does, however, occur in other parts of the book. In the *Kratkoe rukovodstvo*, stress markings sometimes occur several times on a page and it is not always clear why. Thus, on page 287 we find ⟨пото́мъ, ча́сти, сво́йства, пра́вилахъ⟩, and also ⟨сво́йствъ⟩ where it is clearly redundant since the word only has a single syllable.

The rules for spelling reflexive verbs is unstable in the *Ustav*, which has ⟨лишаетца, почитаетца, называетца⟩ alongside ⟨име́ется, обрѣ́тается⟩ for the third person, singular, present. Infinitives are spelled with ⟨тьс⟩: ⟨оберегаться⟩. The *Kratkoe rukovodstvo* has no examples of ⟨-тца⟩.

In the field of morphology, earlier editions of the *Artikul* contain archaic forms, some of which have been changed, and some remain in the later editions. To the first of these belong the Dative plural of nouns, where the 1715 and 1735 editions have ⟨нашïмъ генераломъ⟩, and in 1744, this has been changed to ⟨нашимъ генераламъ⟩. On the other hand, all editions agree on another case: ⟨честнымъ воинскимъ людемъ благопристойно⟩.

When examining the linguistic characteristics of the text, the most striking change takes place between the editions of 1735 and 1744. In the latter, the dative plural генераломъ has been changed to генераламъ. This is an example of *a-expansion* and indicates the following changes: -омъ/-емъ → -амъ/-ямъ (Dative plural), -ы/-ьми → -ами (Instrumental plural) and -ехъ/-ѣхъ → -ахъ/-яхъ (Locative plural). The process whereby an older system of case forms in the plural was supplanted by forms characterized by -a- has been investigated by Zhivov, among others.[56] In his 2012 investigation of the instrumental case in sources from the eighteenth century, Nikita Mikhaylov reports that the whole process of *a-expansion* among nouns in the plural had been concluded by the beginning of the eighteenth century.[57] However, traces of the earlier system remain. Therefore, людемъ is encountered in all three editions of the *Articles of War*, rather than the *a-expansion* form людямъ.

In the Instrumental plural, the excerpt contains two examples of the old type: ⟨двѣмя большими персты⟩ and ⟨всякими образы⟩, but no examples of *a-expansion* forms. According to Mikhaylov, the old declension is encountered as a stylistic variant for masculine and neuter nouns in texts until the late 1760s.[58]

---

56 Zhivov, *Ocherki*, chapter 3.
57 Mikhaylov, "Tvoritel'nyi padezh," 24.
58 Ibid., 270.

In addition to the section of the text analyzed here, endings in -ами are found in many places throughout the *Article of War*. For example:

> Артикулъ 4. Кто пресвятую Матерь Божїю Дѣву Марїю, и святыхъ ругателными словами поноситъ, оный имѣетъ по состоянїю его особы и хуленїя, тѣлеснымъ наказанїемъ отсѣченїя сустава наказанъ, или живота лишенъ быть.[59]

In the Locative plural, only forms in -ахъ/-яхъ occur.

The endings of adjectives in Nominative/Accusative plural have been the object of detailed studies by Zhivov.[60] Of particular interest to the present investigation are the developments following the so-called Rule of 1733 (masculine -ые/-ие; feminine and neuter -ыя/-ия), which remained in force until the orthographic reform of 1917–1918.[61] As Zhivov points out, the so-called Rule of 1733 was not universally implemented during the 1740s: "в середине XVIII в. многие авторы, непосредственно не связанные с Академией наук, продолжали писать так, как они привыкли."[62] However, the *Articles of War* were, indeed, a product of the academy's printing shop. Does this mean that the spelling rules were consistently implemented?

In the excerpt from the *Articles of War*, the endings concerned appear three times, producing a mixed impression. The first example,

> … сїи послѣдствующїе пункты …

has the endings -їи and -їе referring to a masculine noun in the plural. A search performed in the Russian National Corpus reveals more than a hundred examples of сии from the 1740s. The demonstrative was gender-neutral.[63] In the second example,

> … въ протчихъ воинскихъ случаяхъ, какова оныя званїя нїесть …

---

59 *Artikul voinskii* (1744), 16 (Article 4. Whoever reviles the most holy Mother of God, the Virgin Mary, and the saints with bad language, he should, considering the position of his person and the abuse, be punished corporally by the severing of a limb, or lose his life).

60 Zhivov, *Ocherki*, 408–528.

61 Ibid., 488–489.

62 Ibid., 489–490 (in the middle of the eighteenth century, many authors who were not directly connected with the Academy of Sciences, continued writing as they were used to).

63 "Sii," Natsional'nyi korpus russkogo iazyka, accessed September 27, 2021, https://ruscorpora.ru/new/search-main.html.

-ыя refers to a masculine noun (случай). This ending could also be used as a gender-neutral variant. The third example

> ... что въ ... воинскихъ артикулахъ, что оные въ себѣ содержати будутъ, все исполнять исправно ...

has the ending -ые, which can be interpreted either as a masculine by the "Rule of 1733" or as a gender-neutral form.

Moving on to verbs, we see that the 1744 edition of the *Articles of War* preserves infinitives in -ти (five instances: вспомогати, жалѣти, знати, отвращати, содержати) alongside infinitives in -ть (twenty-five instances). This contrasts with Zhivov's findings, according to which infinitives in -ти gradually fell out of use, reduced to a variant found in the poetic language of individual authors, notably Sumarokov.[64]

In infinitives of reflexive verbs, the 1715 edition uses -тца exclusively (непротïвïтца, прïлучïтца, отлучатца), and the 1735 edition uses -тца and -итися (не противитися, отлучатца). The 1744 edition has abandoned -тца in favor of -итися and -атся for the infinitive (не противитися, отлучатся).

In the area of syntax, the *Articles of War* often place the verb at the end of sentences:

> и всѣ пункты сего артикула право исполнять, и всякому особо высокаго и низкаго чина, безъ всякаго изъятïя, Намъ яко Государю своему присягу чинить.

While there may exist other possible explanations, it is likely that verb placement was influenced by the German parallel text of the *Articles:* "und alle Puncta dieser Artickul getreulich zu erfüllen, und sollen alle und jede so wohl hohen als niedrigen Standes ohne einige Ausnahm, Uns als Ihrem Czaaren und Herren einen Eyd ablegen." Remember, the *Articles* were modeled on foreign examples.

The examined portion of the *Articles* has one example of a Locative plural where the editions diverge. In the 1715 and 1735 editions, the ending is ⟨-ѣхъ⟩:

> надлежïтъ сеи артïкулъ на смотрѣхъ, а особлïво про всякомъ полку по едïножды прочïтать въ недѣлю (1715).

---

64 Zhivov, *Ocherki*, 198–209.

In 1744, this has been changed to ⟨-ахъ⟩.

All editions agree in their use of an archaic ending in the Instrumental plural in the sentence

> а правую руку поднять вверхъ съ простертыми двѣмя большими персты.

In the *Kratkoe rukovodstvo* Instrumental plurals in –ами dominate, but there are occasional examples of –ы:

> §215. Отвѣтствованїе есть. когда сочинитель слóва самъ себѣ на свой вопросъ отвѣщаетъ, что бываетъ разными óбразы … [65]

Such examples are not surprising since the ending was used as a stylistic variant during the period.

7.4.3 Parallel Editions: Field-Marshal de Lacy's Reports from the Front

In rare cases, separate versions of a single text were printed twice within a short period. The rarity of this phenomenon makes existing parallel editions all the more interesting. Studying two versions of a single text, printed within a short time of each other by separate organizations, gives us an excellent understanding of the degree of variation at the time.

It is possible that other parallel editions exist, but during the preparation for this investigation only one example from the 1740s was encountered: Field-Marshal Peter de Lacy's reports from the front in the Russo-Swedish war of 1741–1743.[66] Twelve such reports, written during the summer and fall of 1742, have been available for the present investigation. The first version of these texts

---

65 Lomonosov, *Kratkoe rukovodstvo*, 198.

66 Peter de Lacy (1678–1751) was born in Ireland as Pierce Edmond de Lacy but is better known under his Germanized name Peter von Lacy, or sometimes Peter Lacy. In certain older sources, he is also known as Lascy: Friedrich Rühs, *Finland och dess invånare*, vol. 1 (Stockholm: Olof Grahn, 1811), 207. Beginning in 1700, de Lacy spent more than half a century in Russian service and is known in Russia as Pëtr Petrovich Lassi (Пётр Петрович Ласси) and various other spelling variants. De Lacy himself signed his name "P. Cte de Lacy": Swedish National Archives, Militaria 1588. Cf. Timothy C. Dowling, ed., *Russia at War: From the Mongol Conquest to Afghanistan, Chechnya, and Beyond* (Santa Barbara, CA: ABC-Clio, 2015), 463.

was printed in Moscow, at the Senate printing office ("Moscow version"). The second version was issued in St. Petersburg, in the *Primechaniia* ("St. Petersburg version").

Front reports such as these were not new. Similar reports were prepared during the Turkish war of the 1730s.[67] Some of these reports were probably also printed in the Senate printing office since they have ornaments that are identical to those found in de Lacy's Moscow editions of 1742.

De Lacy's reports contain very detailed information about operations, as well as weapons and material conquered from the enemy, translations of interrogation protocols and confiscated letters. The composite nature of the reports shows that they were assembled from a large number of individual sources and contained language from a variety of registers.[68]

Of the Moscow version, only the editions dated July 10, 14, 18, 21, 28, 31; August 9, 22, 24, 31; September 4 and 11 have been found, even though it is possible that other reports exist. These reports include lengthy and cumbersome descriptive titles, as the following example demonstrates:

> Послѣ публикованныхъ сего мѣсяца 5 и 10 чиселъ, о благополучныхъ отъ арміи Ея императорскаго величества надъ непріятелемъ в Финляндіи дѣйствіяхъ изъ репортовъ генерала фельдьмаршала Лессія экстрактовъ сего мѣсяца 10 числа, вновь еще отъ него жъ фельдмаршала изъ лагеря при рѣкѣ Кимисъ отъ 4 сего настоящаго мѣсяца полученъ репортъ слѣдующаго содержанія.[69]

---

67 For example, *Ekstrakt iz donosheniia generala feldmarshala fon Lessiia, iz lageria pri Berdnike ot 28 maiia 1738 godu: Poluchennogo v Sanktpeterburge 8 iiuniia* 1738, accessed May 6, 2021, http://primo.nlr.ru.

68 Although not relevant to a discussion of Russian in the 1740s, the texts contain examples of language from preceding centuries, as in the case of a church bell found by the Russian troops in the city of Borgå/Porvoo, on the Southern coast of Finland: "7053 году слитъ бысть колоколъ сій къ живоначальнѣй Троицѣ въ Александрову пустыню при великомъ Князѣ Иванѣ Васильевичѣ всеа Руссіи, и при Архїепискупѣ Ѳеодосїи Великаго Новагорода и Пскова, повелѣнїемъ Игумена Родїона Кочнева" (Moscow version, August 22, page 2). The year 7053 corresponds to 1544/1545 AD.

69 (Following the extracts published here on the fifth and tenth day of this month from reports by General Field-Marshal Lacy on the tenth of this month, concerning the successful actions against the Enemy in Finland by the Army of Her Imperial Highness, yet another report, from the fourth of this month, has been received from the said Field-Marshal from the camp at the river Kimis, of the following content.)

A few weeks later, in St. Petersburg, the same reports appeared in the *Primechaniia*. The reports are found in the 1742 issues of the *Primechaniia* from 61 and 62 (July 29) to 84 (September). Front reports had been printed prior to this as well, as evidenced by issues 30–32, but the parallel versions are not available for consultation. Also, it has not been possible to establish whether all reports were printed twice or if this happened only to parts of the material.

Due to the size of the parallel sources, reproducing all texts below is not feasible. We can, however, use the Moscow version of a report dated July 14, 1741 as an illustration.

Послѣ публикованныхъ сего мѣсяца 5 и 10 чиселъ, о благополучныхъ отъ арміи Ея императорскаго величества надъ непріятелемъ в Финляндіи дѣйствіяхъ изъ репортовъ генерала фельдьмаршала Лессія экстрактовъ сего мѣсяца 10 числа, вновь еще отъ него жъ фельдмаршала изъ лагеря при рѣкѣ Кимисъ отъ 4 сего настоящаго мѣсяца полученъ репортъ слѣдующаго содержанія.

Сего мѣсяца отъ 1 числа всеподданнѣйше отъ меня донесено, что я отъ урочища Сумъ съ высокославною Вашего ИМПЕРАТОРСКАГО ВЕЛИЧЕСТВА арміею маршировалъ налехкѣ въ слѣдъ за непріятелемъ до рѣки Кимисъ, и того числа до оной рѣки маршировали 15 верстъ, къ которой прибыли на вечеръ и непріятеля на нашей сторонѣ рѣки уже не застали, а ретировался на другую сторону, и мостъ, какъ видѣть можно, незадолго до нашего приходу зжегъ, и на той сторонѣ {непріятель} имѣлъ весьма крѣпкое мѣсто. Перьвое что рѣка неуская быстрая и глубокая. Второе съ той стороны по берегу горы, и по тѣмъ горамъ поставлены были въ разныхъ мѣстахъ пушки, изъ которыхъ по насъ производили жестокую пальбу, и за тѣмъ не можно было близъ рѣки лагеремъ стать; ибо мѣсто случилось открытое, и принуждены были къ ночѣ остановиться въ лѣсу, пока наша артилерія прибыла. И какъ поставлена наша артилерія въ пристойныхъ мѣстахъ и взаимно имъ отвѣтствовано, то и пушки ихъ съ преждепоставленныхъ мѣстъ збиты, которые они принуждены были съ мѣста на мѣсто перевозить, и тако со обѣихъ сторонъ изъ пушекъ произвождаема была чрезъ 12 часовъ прежестокая пальба, причемъ съ нашей стороны и изъ гоубицъ дробью по непріятелѣ дѣйствовано было. И какъ подъ обороною нашихъ пушекъ мы начатые работою чрезъ рѣку мосты ко окончанію приводить стали, и изъ нашихъ пушекъ у непріятеля съ немалою торопостію ретировался, и прошедъ съ три версты паки за рѣку {которая сей вдвое ширѣ будетъ} позади себя мостъ зжегъ, и хотя наши гусары за нимъ и гонялись; но дальняго поиску учинить не могли, понеже шелъ имѣя въ аріергардіи пушки; а что жъ непріятель съ торопостію ту свою ретираду производилъ, изъ того наиболѣе видно: ибо 12 ящиковъ съ пулями въ своемъ лагерѣ намъ въ добычю оставилъ, и во время мой бывшей у насъ съ непріятелемъ пушечной стрѣльбы съ нашей стороны побито и ранено съ 30 человѣкъ, а у непріятеля, какъ языки показываютъ, отъ нашихъ гоубицъ зѣло немалое число побитыхъ и раненыхъ считаютъ.

Упомянутая жъ впереди лежашая рѣка называется Кимисъ же, {ибо сего званія рѣка въ здѣшнемъ мѣстѣ натрое раздѣлилась,} и впереди непріятеля третья неуже жъ здѣшней находится, и /для/ // для того, ради осмотру ситуаціи я вчерашняго числа подъезжалъ къ непріятельскому лагерю, которой по усмотрѣнію стоитъ за второю отъ сей лежащею рѣкою полумѣсяцомъ и въ немаломъ числѣ; а по тракту къ намъ здѣланы батареи, и поставлены пушки; и хотя жъ и въ вышеупомянутомъ первомъ непріятельскомъ лагерѣ такіежъ батареи здѣланы, и на нихъ пушки поставлены были, однако они оной покинули.

Сего числа вверхъ по сей рѣкѣ отъ нашего лагеря близъ версты, за рѣкою на мысу оказалась немалая непріятельская партія, имѣя при себѣ 4 пушки; но посланную съ нашей стороны партіею съ 2 пушками съ помощію божіею съ немалымъ урономъ прогната, причемъ съ нашей стороны ранено изъ пушки кананеровъ два.

Отъ галерной эскадры Генерал-Лейтенанта де Брильи отъ 1 числа сего мѣсяца репортуетъ, что онъ обрѣтается при островѣ Мартинсарѣ, и уже и отъ карабельнаго флота два прама и три бомбандирскія карабля къ нему прибыли же; но въ дальней путь за противною погодою итти ему тогда было не возможно: непріятельскіе же де галеры стоятъ напротиву ихъ за островомъ не въ дальности, а какъ де погода поутихнетъ, то онъ Генералъ Лейтенантъ призвавъ Бога въ помощь имѣетъ слѣдовать къ поиску надъ непрїятельскими галеры.

брегадиръ Краснощокой съ Донскими и Чюгуевскими казаками, отправленъ отъ меня для диверсїи непрїятелю и учиненїя поиска до Тавастъ-Густа.

По непрїятельскимъ же всѣмъ робостнымъ поступкамъ видится, что когда онъ сей немало крѣпкой лагерь оставилъ, то и далѣе ретираду свою продолжать намѣренъ. И хотя въ поискѣ надъ онымъ намъ немало препятствуютъ частые переправы чрезъ рѣки; однако мы съ непрїятельской стороны ежедневно языковъ получаемъ, но по большей части попадаются фины, которые заподлинно о непрїятельскомъ состоянїи и преднамѣренїяхъ ево хотя и не знаютъ, но однако какъ тѣ въ полкахъ служащїе фины, такъ и изъ мужиковъ почти всѣ большею частїю показываютъ, что имѣютъ склонность къ подданству Вашего ИМПЕРАТОРСКАГО ВЕЛИЧЕСТВА, и для того отъ меня наижесточайше посылаемымъ въ партїи гусарамъ и казакамъ, также и во всей армїи подтверждается, отнюдь жителей, кои ружьемъ не противятся, не токмы не побивать и не грабить, но и жилищъ ихъ не жечь и не разорять.

Впрочемъ за благодать всемогущаго Бога состоитъ у насъ благополучно. А каковъ при самомъ сего отправленїи полученъ съ галерной эскадры отъ Генерала-Лейтенанта де Брильлїя, отъ 2 сего мѣсяца репортъ, съ онаго копїю всенижайше присемъ подношу. /копїя/ // Копїя съ репорта генерала-лейтенанта де Брильлїя.

Сего числа по полуночи въ 7 мъ часу отъ острова Мартинсара съ галернымъ флотомъ въ походъ благополучно я выступилъ, и дошедъ до острова Люмилота разстоянїемъ верстъ съ 8 остановился для ожиданїя идущихъ позади насъ бомбандрирскихъ караблей и прамовъ, понеже для буксированїя оныхъ командировано отъ флота 10 галеръ тако жъ и за противнымъ вѣтромъ. А поставленная отъ непрїятельскаго флота на брандъ-вахтѣ галера съ судами стоитъ на томъ же мѣстѣ разстоянїемъ отъ насъ верстахъ въ двухъ, и ежели завтрешняго дня будетъ благополучная погода, то призвавъ всемогущаго Бога въ помощь надъ оною галерою и съ имѣющимися при ней судами {чтобъ ихъ въ наши руки получить,} поискъ чинить буду, и что впредъ чиниться будетъ, покорнѣйше репортовать буду жъ.

Печатано въ Москвѣ при Сенатѣ Іюля 14 дня 1742 года.

Beginning with the differences between the two printed versions, the most eye-catching feature is the use of stress marks in the St. Petersburg version in words such as ⟨ужѐ⟩, ⟨сторонь́⟩, ⟨числа̀⟩, ⟨по́сты⟩, and so forth:

Вчерашнягожъ числа̀ по утру для поиску надъ тѣмъ непріятелемъ отправлены были драгунскіе полки и гранодерскіе роты тожъ гусары и казаки, которые пришедъ въ семъ мѣстѣ непріятеля ужѐ не застали, для того что оной на переправахъ чрезъ рѣки мосты всѣ пожегъ, и отъ того нашимъ въ погонѣ за нимъ немалое задержаніе происходило.[70]

The versions differ in the use of stress marks and a few obvious misprints, such as ⟨ьъ⟩ for intended ⟨въ⟩.[71] In both versions the soft sign occurs inconsistently: ⟨фельдмаршала⟩/⟨фелдмаршала⟩, ⟨больные⟩/⟨болные⟩, ⟨мѣльничной⟩/⟨мѣлничной⟩, and so forth. It appears that free variation in the use of the soft sign occurs in both versions of the texts.

A more stable example of variation, which clearly separates the Moscow and St. Petersburg versions, is offered by the spelling of prefixes. The Moscow version favors an unchanging form: ⟨разстояніемъ⟩, ⟨разсуждаетъ⟩, ⟨подтвердили⟩, ⟨изтекающаго⟩, while the St. Petersburg version has varying forms, depending on the voicing of the consonant following the prefix: ⟨расстояніемъ⟩, ⟨рассуждаетъ⟩, ⟨поттвердили⟩, ⟨истекающаго⟩.

For the most part, the Moscow and St. Petersburg versions show identical case endings, with a few minor differences. In the Nominative/Accusative plural of adjectives and pronouns, the texts contain 181 instances of -ые (119) and -іе (62). These may refer to masculine nouns like ⟨А драгунскіе швецкіе четыре полка⟩ (полк, m., "regiment"), neuter nouns such as ⟨бомбандирскіе суда⟩ (бомбандирское судно, n., "bomb vessel"), and feminine nouns like ⟨двѣ лежащіе по тому тракту рѣки⟩ (река, f., "river"). The endings -ыя/-ія are represented by a total of 71 cases (29 -ыя and 42 -ія) referring to masculine nouns

три бомбандирскія карабля (корабль, m., "ship"),

---

70 St. Petersburg version, *Primechaniia*, issue 61, 238.
71 Moscow version, July 10, 2.

feminine nouns

> пѣхотные гранодерскія роты и мушкатеръ 200 человѣкъ
> (рота, f., "company"),

> пули лѣтающія около головъ нашихъ побуждаютъ насъ къ
> бѣгу (пуля, f., "bullet"),

and neuter nouns:

> опредѣленныя свои мѣста (мѣсто, n., "place").

The ending -ïи is only represented in the St. Petersburg version:

> въ полкахъ служащïи фины.[72]

The Moscow version has ⟨служащïе⟩.

No differences in verbs can be found between the St. Petersburg and Moscow versions.

Among nouns in the Dative plural, only forms in -амъ/-ямъ are encountered: ⟨бастіонамъ⟩, ⟨обывателямъ⟩, and so forth. Similarly, in the locative, forms in -ах/-ях are pervasive with only two exceptions, both involving the noun люди:

> хотябъ онъ и въ половинѣ вышеписаннаго числа полковъ
> былъ, немалыебъ намъ препятствïи и убытокъ въ людехъ
> причинить могъ.[73]

The instrumental case in nouns is represented by the endings -ами/-ями, -'ми and -ы. As reported by Mikhaylov in his investigation of the Instrumental, -ами/-ями is the most frequent ending during the eighteenth century, while -'ми and -ы occur occasionally.[74] In de Lacy's reports, -'ми is encountered with a few nouns: ⟨вещьми, дверьми, дѣтьми, лошадьми, людьми, обывательми, перевезьми, принадлежностьми⟩. Of these, only принадлежность (belonging, accessory) also occurs with -ями: ⟨принадлежностями⟩. The ending -ы

72 St. Petersburg version, *Primechaniia*, issues 61 and 62, 244.
73 Moscow version, July 31, 7; St. Petersburg version, *Primechaniia*, issues 70–72, 286.
74 Mikhaylov, "Tvoritel'nyi padezh," 270.

occurs a total of thirteen times. The latter is sometimes encountered in cases of "hypercorrection" for feminine nouns.[75] Our selection of de Lacy's reports contains one such example:

Генералъ Лейтенантъ призвавъ бога въ помощь имѣетъ слѣдовать къ поиску надъ непрїятельскими галеры.[76]

The Soviet philologist and literary scholar G. O. Vinokur noted the importance of the administrative language (приказной язык) for the study of Russian historical syntax and exemplifies this by mentioning the widespread relative construction with a repeated antecedent:

А по отписям, *каковы отписи* положил в Володимерской чети перед дьяком перед Михаилом Огарковым.[77]

Zhivov observes that the construction with a repeated antecedent entered the "Petrine pool" from the non-literary registers and that it was adopted by the academy translators who prepared the *Primechaniia* during the 1730s. After the 1730s, however, "эта конструкция из текстов нового языкового стандарта навсегда устраняется."[78] As a basis for this claim, Zhivov presents Trediakovskii's 1737 translation of Marsigli's *L'état militaire de l'Empire Ottoman* and Hüttl-Folter's 1996 investigation of that text.[79] In de Lacy's reports the construction occurs in several cases:

Какъ то отъ 29 минувшаго Іюня всеподданнѣйше отъ меня донесено, коимъ образомъ непрїятель зажегши крѣпость Фридригсъ-Гамскую ретировался по Гелсинъ-Форской

---

75 Cf. ibid., 25.

76 St. Petersburg version, *Primechaniia*, issue 61, 243. Галера (galley) is a feminine noun attested in Russian since the seventeenth century: *Slovar' russkogo iazyka XI–XVII*, vol. 4 (Moscow: Nauka, 1977), 9.

77 G. O. Vinokur, "Russkii iazyk. Istoricheskii ocherk," in *Izbrannye trudy po russkomu iazyku*, ed. S. G. Barkhudarov (Moscow: Uchpedgiz, 1959), 112.

78 Zhivov, "Literaturnyi iazyk i iazyk literatury," 18 (this construction disappears forever from the texts of the new linguistic standard).

79 Pekarskii, *Istoriia Imperatorskoi Akademii nauk*, vol. 2, 66–67; *Voennoe sostoianie Ottomanskiia Imperii* (St. Petersburg: Imperatorskaia akademiia nauk, 1737); Luigi Ferdinando Marsigli and Richard F. Kreutel, *Stato militare dell' imperio ottomanno / L'état militaire de l'Empire Ottoman* (Graz: Akademische Druck- und Verlagsanstalt, 1972); Hüttl-Folter, *Syntaktische Studien*.

дорогѣ, … которую ретираду непрїятель съ такою робостїю производилъ, что довольно багажу по тракту металъ. …[80]

… двѣ впереди отъ насъ лежащїе рѣки мостовъ, которые рѣки текутъ по каменью порогами такъ быстро, что съ превеликимъ трудомъ чрезъ оные мосты утвердить могли. …[81]

… непрїятельскїя галеры и прочїе суда назадъ тому третей день пошли къ Боргову и Гельсинъ-Форсу, на которыхъ галерахъ для покупки табаку онъ и самъ былъ. …[82]

… но имъ дали волю во всей землѣ до Фридрихсъ-Гама жечь и палить, подъ которымъ городомъ они нынѣ стоятъ.[83]

… два депутата … которымъ даны на весь уѣздъ 11 Салвогвардїй, которые депутаты за весь вышеписанной уѣздъ въ подданствѣ Вашему Императорскому Величеству и присягали.[84]

While Zhivov's conclusion is right concerning the texts that he offers as evidence, additional facts show that this construction was common in other registers.

---

80 Moscow version, July 10; St. Petersburg version, issue 61, 238.
81 Moscow version, July 21.
82 Moscow version, July 28.
83 Ibid.
84 Moscow version, July 31.

CHAPTER 8

Functional Analysis

Following an investigation of the circumstances surrounding the creation of different documents in Russian during the 1740s, and after an analysis of the language found in texts representing different registers, this investigation has arrived at its third step: the functional analysis of registers. In the register analysis framework, the aim of a functional analysis is to explain why certain linguistic features are encountered in a particular context.[1]

The functional uses of linguistic elements during the seventeenth and eighteenth centuries are well-known and have been discussed by V. M. Zhivov, S. Mengel, and O. Siebert, among others.[2] However, as far known to this author, vernacular Russian of the 1740s has not been the subject of such discussions. Also, the decade had not seen the publication of Lomonosov's ideas about the three styles, which were published a decade later, in 1758.[3]

A comparison of the findings in the preceding subsections of this investigation enables us to identify a number of *functional factors*. In the individual registers, the relative proportions of these factors influence the characteristics of the language.

Before going on to a presentation of the functional factors, we must first briefly review some delimitations. In section 5.2.2 of this investigation, a hypothetical set of registers was suggested for Russian in the 1740s following an application of the uniformitarian principle. Three of the registers in this tentative set were not examined in this investigation: "traditional literature and religious language," "informal speech," and "non-native Russian speech." These registers were left out

---

1 Biber and Conrad, *Register, Genre and Style*, 69.
2 Zhivov, *Iazyk i kul'tura*, 20–30; S. Mengel and O. Siebert, "O 'prostote' iazyka 'russkikh knig' Simeona Todorskogo (Galle 1729–1735): perevodcheskie strategii i ikh analiz pri ispol'zovanii komp'iuternykh tekhnologii," Thesen MKS 18, accessed November 20, 2021, https://www.slavistik.uni-halle.de/16.slavistenkongress/mks18themblockmengel/thesenmks18mengelsiebert/.
3 M. V. Lomonosov, "Predislovie o pol'ze knig tserkovnykh v rossiiskom iazyke," in his *Izbrannye proizvedeniia* (Leningrad: Sovetskii pisatel', 1986), 473–478, accessed November 20, 2021, https://rvb.ru/18vek/lomonosov/01text/02addenda/11addenda/138.htm.

for specific reasons. The register "traditional literature and religious language" was not investigated because the language of its texts is predominantly hybrid Church Slavic and Church Slavic. Since vernacular Russian formed, at best, a minor linguistic component in this register, it should logically be excluded from an inventory of Russian linguistic registers. Nonetheless, it was kept in the list of registers since its texts—notably the Bible and the religious sphere—were important parts of Russian literate culture of the eighteenth century. By ignoring the existence of this register, we run the risk of creating a faulty image of eighteenth-century Russian language.

The registers "informal speech" and "non-native Russian speech" were not investigated due to lack of data. From the modern linguistic situation we can infer that these registers must have existed, but since they were inadequately recorded in writing, or not recorded at all, we cannot study them. Court documents, such as the witness statements discussed in section 6.3.2, contain fragments of informal speech, but have been edited. This fact casts doubt on their value as evidence. Our conclusions about factors influencing a register from a functional perspective are also most likely applicable to the registers that have not been investigated. But, for the reasons explained above, we cannot say that for sure.

8.1 Tradition

Tradition is an important factor in the employment of linguistic elements for functional purposes. In the material analyzed above, we encounter a few cases of such traditional uses. Thus, in Emperor Ioann Antonovich's manifesto (section 6.4), we see that the Genetive singular of feminine adjectives in -ыя is used, rather than the -ой/-ей, which was common in most texts of the period:

> … при предкахъ Нашихъ **Блаженныя** и **Вѣчнодостойныя** памяти Императорскихъ Величествъ …

In the same text, an aorist of the verb, rather than the usual past tense form in -ла is used in order to emphasize the gravity of the situation:

> … что помянутая корона Шведская **наруша** явно имѣющей съ Нами вѣчнаго мира трактатъ и союзъ.

In another context (see section 7.1.2), an example of the aorist is used to talk about death:

... а шхиперъ куртъ умре въ их швецком ѳлоте авг૪стá „22„
дня ...

It should be emphasized that these examples are in no way typical for Russian in the 1740s. Examples of the Genetive singular of feminine adjectives in -ыя are found in the imperial diplomatic correspondence, another high-status text. Forms of the aorist, however, have not been found outside of the contexts previously mentioned.

8.2 Education

The educational background of an author was arguably the most important factor determining the form of written language in the 1740s. The vast majority of Russian speakers had very basic education, and most were unable to compose a written text of any kind. On the other hand, their abilities to create oral texts may have been considerable, but this escapes our judgement due to lack of evidence.

In a semi-literate society like eighteenth-century Russia, people were aware of the power of the written word, and the value of being able to send information in writing. We should interpret the widespread use of formulaic language during the eighteenth century with this in mind.

Since most people did not know how to write or chose not to write for some other reason, such as social status, most writing was done by a corps of professional scribes who often did not know the intended recipient of the message they created. Resorting to a predetermined structure and formulaic expressions was a practical way of conforming to social expectations. At the same time, this structure provided a practical framework into which important pieces of information could be inserted.

8.3 Social Identity

In the Russian Empire, "[a]mong civil and military servicemen of all ranks there were enormous socioeconomic, cultural and political differences."[4] From 1722 and onwards, the entire state apparatus was divided according to the *Tabel' o*

---

4   Wirtschafter, *Social Identity in Imperial Russia*, 47.

rangakh (*Table of Ranks*).[5] In the registers of the language employed in the state administration and in maintaining relations with foreign powers, the idea of hierarchy is constantly present.

As seen in the examples of imperial correspondence discussed in the preceding chapters, titles and long marks of courtesy were characteristic. They often dominated the text, taking up more than half of the entire document. Since both addressor and addressee were well informed about each other's titles, the preoccupation with titles in letters was clearly not due to a desire to provide new information. Instead, the titles can be interpreted as verbal signals of power and prestige of monarchs. As we saw in section 3.4.1, the rules prescribed the full title of the emperor to be used in letters going abroad, while a considerably shorter one was intended for domestic use. Interestingly enough, flamboyant demonstrations of power and prestige were combined with courteous expressions according to the fashion of the period.

In Russian majority society, family hierarchy was also keenly felt, but its linguistic expressions were different. As evidenced by the private letters we examined, social identities were communicated in terms of expressions of submission that reduced the importance of the letter-writer, inquiries about the health of the addressee, and so forth.

In the highest levels of society, expressions of social identity and status—real or perceived—also formed a central part of written communication. This is a likely interpretation of the many *Vedomosti* texts that deal with events at court. They described—and were most likely also read by—the involved parties: courtiers, ladies-in-waiting, officers, and foreign ambassadors—people to whom rank and status at court were significant. Descriptions of festivities and ceremonies followed certain compositional patterns that remained similar for long periods. With their elaborately detailed composition, these texts communicated the prestige and importance of the court to the readers in Russia and abroad.

---

5   *Tabel' o rangakh vsekh chinov, voinskikh, statskikh, i pridvornykh* … (Moscow, January 30, 1722), accessed November 18, 2021, https://www.prlib.ru/item/454265.

8.4 Efficiency of Administration

Historian Simon Franklin writes about the role of the written word in the administration of the Russian Empire during the eighteenth century:[6]

> An oral message depends on the reliability of its bearer. Writing
> is an improvement, both because it is visible and verifiable, and
> because the handwritten text can be preserved and re-used. In
> production, however, each handwritten message depends on the
> reliability of its scribe.[7]

Franklin notes that the widespread use of printed texts facilitated distribution, standardization, and the "emblematic projection of authority." The term "emblematic projection of authority" refers to the perceived power in the printed text itself when displayed in public, even to illiterate persons. But from sources such as Ivan Pososhkov's *Book of Poverty and Wealth* (cf. section 3.2.2) we see that handwritten texts possessed the same power. The sources suggest that the authority of the written or printed word in eighteenth-century Russia was so great that it was enough to show a decree, or even to claim to possess one, for people to obey.

The use of formulaic expressions, either in print or in written form, was an important functional factor in the linguistic and administrative life of the Russian state. If the central authorities of the empire received information from the provinces written in similar or even identical wording, the interpretation of the information was made easier. It also minimized the risk of misunderstanding. Texts also moved in the opposite way. By distributing printed texts to provincial representatives, the central authorities could guarantee that all intended recipients got the same information. For the next step, however, the printed text would be copied by hand and distributed at the provincial level, as the following example from the archives of the Consistory of Hamina, Finland, demonstrates:

---

6   Simon Franklin, "Printing and Social Control in Russia 1: Passports," *Russian History* 37 (2010): 208–237; idem, "Printing and Social Control in Russia 2: Decrees," *Russian History* 38 (2011): 467–492; idem, "Printing and Social Control in Russia 3: Blank Forms," *Russian History* 42 (2015): 114–135.

7   Franklin, "Printing and Social Control in Russia 2," 481.

Printed decree[8]	Handwritten copy[9]
Указъ Ея Императорскаго Величества самодержицы Всероссїискои, изъ Правительствующаго Сената, объявляется во всенародное извѣстїе.	ꞌꞌУказ ея jмператорскаго величества/ самодержицы всероссїискои jз выборскои г҃убернскои/ канцелярїи в ѳридриꙁгамскꙋю консисторию сего июня „24„ дня/ в ꙋказе ея jмператорскаго величества/ jз правителствующаго сената в выборскꙋю г҃убернскꙋю/ канцелярию напечатанѡ
Въ вѣдѣнїи въ Правительствующїи Сенатъ, изъ Святѣишаго Правительствующаго Сунода написано: Ея Императорское Величество повелѣтъ соизволила, книги Ѳеатронъ гисторическїи всѣ у кого есть собрать отвсюды въ Святѣишїи Сунодъ, и о томъ куда надлежитъ послать съ наикрѣпчаишимъ подтвержденїемъ указы ...	в ведении де в правител/ствующїи сенатъ jз святеишагѡ правителствую/щаго синода написанѡ
	ея jмператорское величество повелеть соизволила кн҃ги Ѳеатрон/ гисторическии все ꙋ кого есть собрать отвсюды в святеи/шїи синод j о том кꙋда надлежит послать с наикре/пчаишим подтверждением ꙋказы ...

As the extract shows, the handwritten copy alters the text by adding words and by changing the orthography from the civil to the traditional. Further copying of handwritten texts could potentially lead to further alterations, influencing not only the language, but also the message.

8.5 Informativity

At the heart of administrative documents, such as supplications, is informational content often introduced by formulae such as "а о чем мое доношение, тому следуют пункты."[10] The private letter of naval cadet Mikhail Turchenikov also contains elements of administrative language:

> ... а кто изъ нашихъ ꙋчениковъ со мною обретаютъца о том явъствуетъ ниже сего.

---

8   *Ukaz eia imperatorskago velichestva … V vedenii v Pravitel'stvuiushchii Senat …* (Moscow: Senat, June 3, 1749).

9   Finnish National Archives, 1 Hamninan konsistorin arkisto, saapunet asiakirjat (1720–1784), June 26, 1749.

10   Mikhail Lomonosov, "Donoshenie v Akademiiu Nauk ob uderzhanii deneg, poluchennykh v shchët zhalovan'ia," April 23, 1743, in his *Polnoe sobranie sochinenii*, vol. 10 (Moscow and Leningrad: Izdatel'stvo Akademii nauk SSSR, 1952), 329–330, accessed November 18, 2021, http://feb-web.ru/feb/lomonos/texts/lo0/loa/loa-329-.htm?cmd=p.

Besides administrative texts, the informative function played an important role in the printed output of books from the Academy of Sciences and from the editorial office of *Vedomosti* and *Primechaniia*.[11] In printed books and newspapers, the reading public accustomed to texts in the civil typeface could keep abreast of world affairs, happenings at court, private advertisements, science, literature, and more. However, the portion of the public capable of—or interested in—reading these kinds of texts remained small throughout the 1740s. As we saw in section 3.2.2, although statistics pertaining to the mid-eighteenth-century are not available, it is likely that considerably less than 1.5 % of the population read these types of texts in the 1740s. Zhivov describes the situation around the middle of the eighteenth century:

> Новый языковой стандарт остается достоянием небольшой части образованной элиты, а возникшие за этот период образовательные институции (Академическая гимназия, Шляхетный корпус, Московский университет) существенной экспансии нового идиома пока еще не дают.[12]

8.6 Conclusion

Above, an attempt has been made to identify some functional factors that were relevant for text production in Russian during the 1740s. We must not exclude the possible existence of additional factors that have not been identified here.

If, during earlier periods, registers were distinguished with the help of morphological forms, this was not frequent during the 1740s. As far as can be seen from the material, during this period, the primary markers were lexical: specific collocations and formulae. A collocation in this context is a combination of words, a lexical bundle, that is, a recurrent sequence of words,[13] while formula is a longer unit of the same kind. For example, the following formula is found in imperial decrees:

---

11 *Union Catalogue of Russian Eighteenth-Century Secular Printed Book (1708–1800).*

12 Zhivov, "Literaturnyi iazyk i iazyk literatury," 20 (The new linguistic standard remains the property of a small portion of the educated elite, and the educational institutions appearing during this period [the Academy Grammar School, the Cadet Corps, Moscow University] do not yet result in any significant expansion of the new idiom).

13 Douglas Biber and Federica Barbieri, "Lexical Bundles in University Spoken and Written Registers," *English for Specific Purposes* 26, no. 3 (2007): 263–286.

Того ради Мы о томъ чрезъ сіе ко всенародному извѣстію публиковать повелѣли ...

The reliance on collocations and formulaic language at many levels of written Russian language during the 1740s is a lasting impression of this analysis. We find formulaic language in diplomatic correspondence, throughout the administration, in newspapers, and in private letters. The formulaic language did not fulfill identical purposes in all varieties of written Russian. Different collocations and formulae were employed in various functions depending on the needs, or social status of the writer. In a society like the Russian, where most people could not communicate independently in writing, formulae played an important role. They were used in countless documents during the 1740s for a range of purposes, and at all levels of society. In private letters, they were an expression of traditional Russian culture. When employed by the authorities, they helped to organize the administration of the world's biggest empire.

CHAPTER 9

General Conclusions

This investigation of written Russian during the 1740s reveals that the conditions in which the linguistic registers existed were quite diverse. While some registers were closely interconnected and displayed similarities in the use of formulaic expressions, others appear to have had a more independent existence. The linguistic situation of the 1740s is best understood when viewed against the background of concurrent societal developments.

9.1 Territorial Expansion and the Need for Trained Specialists

Events earlier in the eighteenth century led to the expansion of the Russian Empire's territory. New population groups had been incorporated, speaking languages not previously represented. These languages included Estonian, Livonian, Latvian, and the German of the Baltic Nobility. Russia's large population centers, notably Moscow and St. Petersburg, became increasingly multilingual, at least in their leading circles. Among foreign languages, the prestige of French as a language of the elite grew in importance.

Russia's newly acquired role as a great power in Europe demanded everexpanding cadres of educated administrators. Research on the development of education shows that, during the 1740s, the student recruitment problems were not satisfactorily solved. The number of students graduating from Russian schools and the Academy University remained low and failed to meet demands. Russia therefore continued to invite foreign specialists and to send Russians abroad for higher education. Perhaps the most important academic development that had great significance for the future was the coming of age of a first generation of Russian-born scholars who assumed leading positions during the 1740s.

9.2 Education and Literacy

Throughout the 1740s, most Russian speakers were serfs, who were restricted in terms of movement. They spoke the local dialect of their village and the immediate surrounding area. While the nobility doubled in size during the initial decades of the eighteenth century, and members of the nobility—almost exclusively men—received a far broader education than had previously been available, the access to education did not significantly improve for the majority of the population.

Literacy cannot be taken for granted even for those members of society who held respectable positions, such as mid-ranking military officers. For example, if they had come from a modest background and worked their way up through the ranks, their formal schooling did not result in high levels of literacy, ultimately barring them from further advancement.

Literacy levels feature prominently in the discussion of education. In Russia, basic literacy training during the first half of the eighteenth century was carried out according to traditional methods. Based on what is known today, we must deal with rudimentary literacy rates below ten percent for the majority of the population and intermediate literacy rates below five percent. For the production of texts, this had immediate consequences: only a fraction of the population received education that enabled them to produce texts independently. In the sources, texts written by professional and often anonymous scribes are the rule, while autographs are exceptions.

Research on literacy in eighteenth-century Russia stands out as a field where much work remains to be done. Such research should include both methodological refinement and introduction of new types of sources, but also where possible, studies of how people's attitudes towards the written word may have changed. Kravetskii's and Pletnëva's research on Church Slavic literacy as opposed to literacy in the vernacular deserves to be taken into account for the eighteenth century.

Low literacy levels explain the lack of Russian ego-documents during the 1740s. For the present investigation, this has significant consequences. The number of documents in which the voices of the peasant population or women of all classes can be heard is virtually non-existent. For these strata of the population, not a single primary source document has surfaced during the archival searches underlying the present investigation. Ego-documents are difficult to find in Russia, despite being a rich source of knowledge about the lives and languages of non-elite people in the eighteenth century in other European countries. In the absence of primary sources, we must rely on information offered in secondary sources. Continued work on "semi-ego-documents" such as petitions, court documents, and so forth is therefore a necessity.

9.3 Organized Language Management

Established in the 1720s, the Imperial Academy of Sciences had grown into an important hub for the production and dissemination of information by the 1740s and was the leading operator in organized language management activities. During the 1730s, its staff had launched important language management initiatives. Notable in this respect are the head of the academy, Baron Johann Albrecht von Korff, and its Russian translators and linguists such as V. K. Trediakovskii and V. E. Adodurov. Arguably most important was the formation of the Russian Conference in 1735, a terminology committee where translators discussed each other's work and suggested new items to be potentially added to the Russian vocabulary to represent concepts occurring in foreign texts. When compared to the 1730s, the 1740s stand out as a period of decline. Leading figures in language left the academy, the publication of the academy's journal, *Primechaniia*, was discontinued and the Russian Conference petered out towards the end of 1742. In fact, the academy itself lacked leadership for much of the decade, and it was only towards the end of the 1740s that language management once more became a priority. The middle of the decade appears uneventful in terms of linguistic matters, and it is only towards the end of the 1740s that language management activities were once again revived. The publication of Lomonosov's handbook on rhetoric and Trediakovskii's treatise on orthography provide evidence of ongoing debate on linguistic matters.

9.4 Functional Spheres of Russian in the 1740s

The analyses undertaken in this investigation were conducted in order to uncover the properties of the functional spheres, or registers, represented in the source material. Chapter 5 discussed and evaluated various existing methods. It was determined that an analysis should be based on a combination of methods, striving towards informational maximalism in order to find answers to the questions posed in the Introduction. The uniformitarian principle was implemented to identify a plausible set of registers in Russian of the 1740s. According to this principle, language in society is likely to function similarly today as it did in the past. Therefore, compared to the set of functional spheres for modern Russian suggested in the early 1990s by Iu. N. Karaulov, a revised set of hypothetical registers were suggested for the 1740s:

- traditional literature and religious language;
- the language of printed texts (imaginative literature, the press, state documentation, science, and technology);
- traditional administrative documentation;
- informal speech;
- professional language;
- non-native Russian speech.

The register analysis framework—a combination of methods involving situational analysis, linguistic analysis and functional analysis—inspired this investigation's analytical instruments for texts of the 1740s. The sources were subjected to three types of analysis. First, a situational analysis explored the circumstances surrounding the creation of the preserved source material. Second, a linguistic analysis mapped the characteristic features of the sources. Third, the functional analysis identified a number of factors determining the choice of linguistic features.

The results of these analyses highlighted the need for revision of the hypothetical set of registers proposed in chapter 5. First of all, vernacular printed texts should have a register of their own. In 1740s' Russia, the editing of printed texts in the vernacular was the responsibility of a small cadre of highly professional translators, editors and printers. The printed texts resulting from their work look modern since printed texts often use capitalization and punctuation in ways similar to that of today's printed material. However, since there was no codified spelling norm at the time, texts produced in different printing-shops show minor differences, such as in the use of ⟨ъ⟩.

According to the analyses, it seems relevant to combine state documentation, administrative documents and private papers under the heading "vernacular handwritten language." Sources ranging from imperial diplomatic correspondence to simple, every-day documents, such as receipts, are included in this category. Clearly, the handwritten vernacular register contains many subregisters. Nonetheless, all documents in this category share important features.

The first feature they share is that the graphic and orthographic principles of handwritten texts are the same in high-status documents and simple notes. All forms of handwriting make use of supralinear characters, diacritics and abbreviations. The use of capitalization in handwriting differs markedly from that found in printed texts, and the same is true for punctuation. When a printed text in the civil typeface was copied by hand, scribes did not simply imitate the printed text. Instead, they transliterated it into the traditional system, which contained a broader range of character variants as well as entirely different diacritics. Certain characters, notably ⟨ѣ⟩, are often absent or used inconsistently in handwritten documents. Even the elaborate handwritten texts written in ceremonial cursive, produced by the central imperial administration, under what we can assume were very closely supervised circumstances, employ sets of characters and orthographical conventions reminiscent of earlier periods.

A second shared feature found in handwritten high-status documents as well as simple notes is the important role of formulaic expressions. The vocabulary in these formulae varies depending on the subject of the document and its function. In administrative documents, the language and structure adhere to rules dictated by the central authorities. When applied correctly by the team of administrators behind writing an official report, such rules guaranteed that their document would meet their superiors' expectations.

Private letters continued to be written as they had been for most of the century. They were influenced by formulae from the administrative language. However, in private correspondence, the formulaic language was used less to achieve administrative accuracy, and rather to highlight the addressee's social status and express courtesy and respect for parents and older relatives.

In diplomatic correspondence dispatched from the imperial court, the use of formulaic language is ubiquitous. The informational part of such letters is often limited to half a page, while the titles of the author and the addressee, and intricate marks of courtesy and well-wishing, make up most of the letter. In addition to being carriers of messages, such letters can be interpreted as symbols of power and prestige.

It should be noted that printed texts are not entirely devoid of formulaic language. Among them, newspaper texts most closely resemble handwritten administrative texts. In particular, advertisements make use of formulae that remain consistent throughout the 1740s.

9.5 Perspectives

Libraries and archives in the Russian Federation and its neighboring countries preserve rich collections of handwritten texts in eighteenth-century Russian. The results of this investigation clearly indicate that these handwritten texts form a crucial key to a fuller understanding of how the written language functioned in Russian society.

Handwritten texts inform us about people's everyday lives, relationships, administration, and education. Until now the study of handwritten texts has not been particularly prioritized, and it deserves considerably more attention in the research endeavors of the eighteenth-century language.

This investigation has illustrated that the inventory of characters and the underlying orthographic systems in documents from the 1740s were not uniform. It remains to be seen how regionally based or register-based orthographic systems were distributed. Hopefully, this will be achieved through studies of other periods of the century and documents from a wider geographical area. While there exist investigations that discuss specific regions, a general synthesis of the various factors remains a thing of the future.

The work done on regional business language by researchers in the Russian Federation (E. N. Borisova, N. V. Chugaev, V. Ia. Deriagin, L. A. Glinkina, O. V. Nikitin, and many others) deserves special attention, as does work on historical dialectology. Hopefully, in this century, the research of Russian language history will continue and receive increased support.

The research of non-elite language of the eighteenth century would be greatly helped by the creation of a corpus on a large scale. The goal of creating such a corpus appears realistic given the potential of today's computer-driven resources, such as optical character recognition software. When combined with innovative research methods, a corpus of handwritten texts will yield important new insights into the linguistic life of the fascinating society that was eighteenth-century Russia.

Bibliography

Archival Sources

Danish National Archives (Rigsarkivet), Copenhagen. https://www.sa.dk/da/.

    301 Tyske Kancelli, Udenrigske Afdeling, 1516–1769, Rusland: Breve fra russiske kejser og kejserinder. Kejserinde Anna Ivanovna Romanov 1730–1740 m.m.

        Anna Ioannovna (1730–1740),

            August 13, 1740, to King Christian VI (1730–1746).

        Ioann Antonovich (1740–1741),

            October 18, 1740, to Christian VI;

            November 11, 1740, to Christian VI;

            July 17, 1741, to Christian VI;

            August 8, 1741, to Christian VI;

            October 13, 1741, to Christian VI.

        Anna Leopoldovna, regent (1740–1741),

            November 11, 1740, to Christian VI.

        Elizabeth (1741–1761),

            May 25, 1744, to Christian VI;

            July 22, 1745, to Christian VI;

            August 26, 1745, to Christian VI.

            September 29, to King Frederik V (1746–1766);

            August 31, 1747, to Frederik V;

            August 6, 1749, to Frederik V;

            December 14, 1749, to Frederik V.

National Archives of Finland (Kansallisarkisto), Helsinki. https://www.arkisto.fi/.

    Hamninan konsistorin arkisto, saapunet asiakirjat (1720–1784), Vanhan Suomen tilejä. 10034 Kamarikonttorin käsittelemiä ja ratkaisemia asioita, jotka koskevat Viipurin provinssia (1749).

Archives of the Russian Academy of Sciences, St. Petersburg branch (Sanktpeterburgskii filial Arkhiva Rossiiskoi akademii nauk, SPbFARAN), St. Petersburg. http://vek.roerich.info/node/350.

    F. 121, op. 2, no. 84, Letter from Johann Albrecht von Korff to Johann Daniel Schumacher.

Swedish National Archives, Stockholm, Sweden. http://www.riksarkivet.se.

    Extranea Ryssland 157.4,

        Witness statements by Russian soldiers.

    Kabinettet UD E1 A2,

        Letter from Russian Plenipotentiary, Count A. I. Rumiantsev to the Swedish Chancellery president, Count Carl Gyllenborg, November 29, 1742.

    Microfilm F035.31094, "Manifest. Bozhieiu milostiiu My Ioann tretii, imperator i samoderzhets vserossiiskii."

Militaria 1588,

> Letter of safe conduct for Swedish vessels, signed by Russian General-en-chef Count Peter de Lacy, in the camp at Helsinki, August 27, 1742;

> Report from Commissary of the Fleet, Prince Mikhail Ukhtomskii to the *Kollegiia* of the Admiralty, November 17, 1742;

> Letter by Prince Mikhail Ukhtomskii to one Ivan Ivanovich, November 17, 1742;

> Letter by Prince Mikhail Ukhtomskii to one Vasilii Pavlovich, November 17, 1742;

> Letter by Mikhail Gerasimovich Turchenikov to his father, November, 1742.

Muscovitica 623,

> Letters from Russian rulers to members of the Swedish Royal family:

>> Anna Ioannovna (1730–1740),

>>> February 1, 1740, to King Fredrik I (1720–1751);

>>> August 13, 1740, to Fredrik I.

>> Ioann Antonovich (1740–1741),

>>> October 18, 1740 (a), to Fredrik I;

>>> October 18, 1740 (b), to Queen Ulrika Eleonora (ruling Queen 1718–1720, Queen 1720–1741);

>>> November 11, 1740, to Ulrika Eleonora.

>> Ernst Johann von Bühren (Biron), regent (1740),

>>> October 18, 1740 (a), to Fredrik I;

>>> October 18, 1740 (b), to Ulrika Eleonora.

>> Anna Leopoldovna, regent (1740–1741),

>>> November 11, 1740, (a) to Fredrik I;

>>> November 11, 1740, (b) to Ulrika Eleonora.

>> Elizabeth (1741–1761),

>>> July 30, 1742, to Fredrik I;

>>> November 7, 1743, to Fredrik I;

>>> January 14, 1744, to Fredrik I;

>>> January 18, 1744, to Fredrik I;

>>> March 16, 1744, to Fredrik I;

>>> June, 15, 1744, to Fredrik I;

>>> November 10, 1744, to Fredrik I;

>>> February 12, 1745, to Adolf Fredrik, heir apparent;

>>> June 7, 1745, to Fredrik I;

>>> July 5, 1745, to Fredrik I;

>>> August 26, 1745 (a), to Fredrik I;

>>> August 26, 1745 (b), to Adolf Fredrik;

>>> January 22, 1746, to Fredrik I;

>>> February 22, 1746, to Fredrik I;

>>> September 16, 1746, to Fredrik I;

>>> March 14, 1747, to Fredrik I;

>>> May 20, 1747, to Fredrik I;

>>> June 30, 1747, to Fredrik I;

>>> September 7, 1747, to Fredrik I;

>>> October 16, 1747, to Fredrik I;

> February 1, 1748 (a), to Fredrik I;
>
> February 1, 1748 (b), to Fredrik I;
>
> February 1, 1748 (c), to Fredrik I;
>
> July 9, 1748, to Fredrik I;
>
> November 3, 1748, to Fredrik I;
>
> December 9, 1748, to Fredrik I

Muscovitica 628,

> Ryska beskickningar, memorial och noter 1744–58, Panin 1748–58,
>> Receipt by Filipp Lanikin, August 7, 1748.

Muscovitiva 664,

> January 13, 1743, Letter from Plenipotentiaries Andrei Rumiantsev and Ivan fon Liuberas (Johann Ludwig Pott von Luberas) to their Swedish counterparts, Barons Cedercreutz and von Nolcken.

Originaltraktater med främmande makter (traktater),

> 25 juni 1745, SE/RA/25.3/2/28/E (1745), Assurance of subsidies, June 22, 1745.

Military Archives, Stockholm.

> KrA, 1742-58 års krigsrustningshandlingar, vol. 10,
>> Receipt by Ensign K. Shakhovskii, February 6, 1744.

Swedish National Archives, Regional Archives, Uppsala.

> Södermanland, Landskontoret, D VI, 17.
>> Letter from the Russian General Patrick Stuart to the Swedish provincial governor, Count Nils Bonde. Nyköping, January 12, 1744.
>
> Södermanlands län, Nyköpings rådhusrätt och magistrat, Inneliggande handlingar, F VIa, 47, Stuart.
>> Copy of letter by Patrick Stuart, dated June 24, 1744.

Central State Historical Archives of Ukraine (TsDIAK Ukraïny), Kyiv. https://cdiak.archives.gov.ua/.

> F. 1812, op. 1, no. 3, "1740 god genvaria 1 dnia Pavlovskago garnizonnogo pekhotnogo polku Imennoi spisok" shtap" i ober" afitserom". ..."

Archival Sources on the Internet

Arkhivnyi fond Vologodskoi oblasti. Accessed November 16, 2021. https://uniqdoc.gov35.ru/docs/.

War Manifestos Database. Accessed May 28, 2021. https://documents.law.yale.edu/manifestos.

Printed Sources

Artikul voinskii kupno s protsesom nadlezhashchii sudiashchim. Napechatasia poveleniem tsarskago velichestva. St. Petersburg, April 26, 1715. Accessed May 3, 2021. https://kp.rusneb.ru/item/material/artikul-voinskii-1.

Artikul voinskii s kratkim tolkovaniniem. Napechatasia poveleniem tsarskago velichestva. St. Petersburg, November 16, 1715. Accessed November 12, 2021. https://kp.rusneb.ru/item/reader/artikul-voinskii-2.

Artikul voinskii s kratkim tolkovaniem. 2nd ed. St. Petersburg: Imperatorskaia akademiia nauk, 1735.

Artikul voinskii s kratkim tolkovaniem. 3rd ed. St. Petersburg: Imperatorskaia akademiia nauk, 1744.

Belegard, Abat [Jean-Baptiste Morvan de Bellegarde]. *Sovershennoe vospitanie detei.* ... Translated by Sergei Volchkov. St. Petersburg: Imperatorskaia akademiia nauk, 1747.

Bonekki, I. *Selevk opera.* ... Moscow: Imperatorskaia akademiia nauk, April 25, 1744.

Ego Tsarskogo Velichestva general'nyi reglament ili ustav. St. Petersburg, February 27, 1720. Accessed November 5, 2021. https://raritety.rusarchives.ru/dokumenty/generalnyy-reglament.

Ekstrakt iz donosheniia generala feldmarshala fon Lessiia, iz lageria pri Berdnike ot 28 maiia 1738 godu: Poluchennogo v Sanktpeterburge 8 iiuniia 1738. Accessed May 6, 2021. http://primo.nlr.ru.

Forma o titulakh Ego Imperatorskago Velichestva. St. Petersburg: Senat, October 19, 1740. Accessed November 1, 2021. https://rusneb.ru/catalog/000200_000018_RU_NLR_UK_2094/.

Formuliar. Protiv kotorogo spetsial'noe. ... Moscow: n. p., 1744.

Gazeta "Sanktpeterburgskie vedomosti" XVIII veka: ukazatel' k soderzhaniu. Accessed May 28, 2021. https://www.vedomosti1728.ru/. Issues for the years 1740–1741, 1748, and 1771. For the years 1743–1747 and 1749, microfilms have been available. The investigation has not had access to *Sanktpeterburgskie vedomosti* from the year 1742.

"Iavlenie, vidennoe v Karfagene 6 ianvaria 1744 goda." NĖB Knizhnye pamiatniki. Accessed October 14, 2021. https://kp.rusneb.ru/item/reader/yavlenie-vidennoe-v-karfagene-6-yanvarya-1744-goda.

Lacy, Peter de. *Posle publikovannogo zdes' sego mesiatsa v 5 den' iz relatsei generala feldmarshala i kavalera grafa Lessia o blagopoluchnykh deistviiakh armieiu Ee imperatorskogo velichestva nad nepriiatelem v Finliandii, i o vziat'e nepriiatelskoi kreposti Fridrikhs-gama ekstrakta, 6 chisla v nochi chrez narochno prislannogo ot nego generala feldmarshala ofitsera ot 1 sego mesiatsa iz lageria pri Sumakh, poluchena vnov' reliatsiia sleduiushchego soderzhaniia* (varying titles),

 July 10, 1742,

 July 14, 1742;

 July 18, 1742;

 July 21, 1742;

 July 28, 1742;

 July 31, 1742;

 August 9, 1742;

 August 22, 1742;

 August 24, 1742;

 August 31, 1742;

 September 4, 1742;

 September 11, 1742;

 October, 17, 1742.

Lomonosov, Mikhailo. *Kratkoe rukovodstvo k krasnorechiiu.* St. Petersburg: Imperatorskaia akademiia nauk, 1748.

Opisanie oboikh triumfal'nykh vorot. ... St. Petersburg: n. p., 1742.

Ponezhe My s pomoshchiiu i blagosloveniem bozhiim. ... St. Petersburg: Senat, March 17, 1745.

Primechaniia k Vedomostiam, 1742. Microfilm, issues 30–32 and issues 61–62 (July 29, 1742) to issue 84 (September 1742).

Selevk opera. . . . Translated by Iozef Bonekki. Moscow: Imperatorskaia Akademiia nauk, April 25, 1744.

Trediakovskii, Vasilii. *Razgovor mezhdu chuzhestrannym chelovekom i rossiiskim ob orfografii starinnoi i novoi i o vsëm chto prinadlezhit k sei materii. . . .* St. Petersburg: Imperatorskaia akademiia nauk, 1748.

Ukaz eia imperatorskago velichestva . . . V vedenii v Pravitel'stvuiushchii Senat. Moscow: Senat, June 3, 1749.

Ustav o bankrutakh. St. Petersburg: Senat, December 17, 1740.

Literature

Académie française. *Statuts et règlements*, 1995. Accessed February 15, 2021. http://www.academie-francaise.fr/sites/academie-francaise.fr/files/statuts_af_0.pdf.

Accademia della Crusca. Accessed May 17, 2021. https://accademiadellacrusca.it/it/contenuti/storia/6981.

Afanas'eva, T. A. "Izdaniia zakonodatel'nogo kharaktera kirillicheskoi pechati XVIII v." In *Istochniki po istorii otechestvennoi kul'tury v sobraniiakh i arkhivakh Otdela rukopisei i redkikh knig. Sbornik nauchnykh trudov*, edited by G. P. Enin and N. A. Efimova, 96–114. Leningrad: Gosudarstvennaia publichnaia biblioteka im. Saltykova-Shchedrina, 1983.

———. "Izdaniia kirillicheskoi pechati XVIII veka svetskogo soderzhaniia." In *Problemy istochnikovedcheskogo izucheniia rukopisnykh i staropechatnykh fondov. Sbornik nauchnykh trudov*, edited by I. N. Kurbatova, 183–199. Leningrad: Gosudarstvennaia publichnaia biblioteka im. Saltykova-Shchedrina, 1979.

Agha, Asif. "Register." *Journal of Linguistic Anthropology* 9, nos. 1–2 (2000): 216–219.

Akhmetshina, Zarina. "'Selevk' F. Araii: opera i ee rukopisi v biblioteke Peterburgskoi konservatorii." *Opera musicologica* 3 (2014): 38–62.

Alpatov, V. M., A. N. Baskakov, and G. K. Venediktov. *Diakhronicheskaia sotsiolingvistika.* Moscow: Nauka, 1993.

Alston, Patrick L. *Education and the State in Tsarist Russia.* Stanford: Stanford University Press, 1969.

Amburger, Erik. *Geschichte der Behördenorganisation Russlands von Peter dem Grossen bis 1917.* Leiden: Brill, 1966.

Anipa, K. "The Use of Literary Sources in Historical Sociolinguistic Research." In *The Handbook of Historical Sociolinguistics*, edited by Juan Manuel Hernández-Campoy and Juan Camilo Conde-Silvestre, 170–190. Oxford: Wiley-Blackwell, 2012.

Anisimov, Evgenii. *Derzhava i topor: tsarskaia vlast', politicheskii sysk i russkoe obshchestvo v XVIII veke.* Moscow: Novoe literaturnoe obozrenie, 2019.

Argent, Gesine, Derek Offord, and Vladislav Rjéoutski. "The Functions and Value of Foreign Languages in Eighteenth-Century Russia." *The Russian Review* 1 (2015): 1–19.

Ariskina, O. L. "Izlozhenie ucheniia o morfemike i slovoobrazovanii v 'grammatike …' V. E. Adodurova." *Vestnik Mordovskogo universiteta* 1 (2011): 1–16.

Ashby, William J. Review of *Sociolinguistic Variation in Seventeenth-Century France* by Wendy Ayres-Bennett. *The French Review* 6 (2006): 1403–1404.

Aston, Nigel. "The Established Church." In *The Oxford Handbook of the Ancien Régime*, edited by William Doyle, 285–301. Oxford: Oxford University Press, 2012.

Babich, M. V. *Gosudarstvennye uchrezhdeniia Rossii XVIII v. Spravochnoe posobie.* Moscow: URSS, 1999.

"Baron Iogann Albert Korf, 1697–1766." In *Recueil des actes de la séance publique de l'Académie Impériale des sciences de Saint-Pétersbourg*, 73–101. St. Petersburg: Eggers, 1847.

Belikov, V. I., and L. P. Krysin. *Sotsiolingvistika: Uchebnik dlia vuzov.* Moscow: RGGU, 2001.

Belova, L. A. *Kniga sekretnykh del Glavnogo zavodov pravleniia 1738–1740: Pamiatniki delovoi pis'mennosti I poloviny XVIII veka.* Perm': Permskii gosudarstvennyi pedagogicheskii universitet, 2011.

Berkov, P. N. *Istoriia russkoi zhurnalistiki XVIII veka.* Moscow: Izdatel'stvo Akademii nauk SSSR, 1952.

Berkov, P. N. "Neizvestnye stikhotvoreniia Lomonosova v 'Sanktpeterburgskikh vedomostiakh' 1743 i 1748 godov." *Russkaia literatura* 4 (1961):128–130.

———. "O perekhode skoropisi XVIII v. v sovremennoe russkoe pis'mo." In *Issledovaniia po otechestvennomu ostochnikovedeniiu: Sbornik statei posviashchennykh 75-letiiu professora S. N. Valka*, 36–50. Moscow and Leningrad: Nauka, 1964.

Biber, Douglas, and Federica Barbieri, "Lexical Bundles in University Spoken and Written Registers." *English for Specific Purposes* 26, no. 3 (2007): 263–286.

Biber, Douglas, and Susan Conrad. *Register, Genre, and Style.* 2nd ed. Cambridge: Cambridge University Press, 2019.

Birgegård, Ulla. "En ständig huvudvärk i relationerna mellan Sverige och Ryssland: Tsarens och kungens titlar." *Slovo* 55 (2014): 34–46.

Birnbaum, Henrik. "Fact and Fiction Concerning the Genesis of Literary Russian." Review of *Mythen und Tatsachen über die Entstehung der russischen Literatursprache* by Alexander Issatschenko. *Russian Linguistics* 2 (1976): 167–180.

Blum, Alain, and Irina Troitskaya. "Mortality in Russia during the 18th and 19th Centuries: Local Assessments Based on the Revizii." *Population: An English Selection* 9 (1997): 123–146.

Bogdanov, I. M. *Gramotnost' i obrazovanie v dorevoliutsionnoi Rossii i v SSSR (istoriko-statisticheskie ocherki).* Moscow: Statistika, 1964.

Brickman, William T., and John T. Zepper. *Russian and Soviet Education 1731–1989: A Multilingual Annotated Bibliography.* New York and London: Garland Publishing, Inc., 1992.

Britannica Academic. "Chapbook." Accessed May 17, 2021. https://academic-eb-com.ezproxy. ub.gu.se/levels/collegiate/article/chapbook/22474.

Britannica Academic. "Peter I." Accessed May 8, 2021, https://academic-eb-com.ezproxy.ub.gu. se/levels/collegiate/article/Peter-I/108537.

Britannica Academic. "Ship." Accessed May 28, 2021, https://academic-eb-com.ezproxy.ub.gu. se/levels/collegiate/article/ship/110744#259195.toc.

Buck, Christopher D. "The Russian Language Question in the Imperial Academy of Sciences, 1724–1770." In *Aspects of the Slavic Language Question*, edited by Riccardo Picchio and Harvey Goldblatt, vol. 2, 187–233. New Haven: Yale Concilium on International and Area Studies, 1984.

Bunčić, Daniel. "Diachronic Observations." In *Biscriptality: A Sociolinguistic Typology*, edited by D. Bunčić, S. L. Lippert, and A. Rabus, 321–333. Heidelberg: Winter, 2016.

Caruso, Marcelo, and Daniel Töpper. "Schooling and the Administrative State: Explaining the Lack of School Acts in Nineteenth-Century Prussia." In *School Acts and the Rise of Mass*

Schooling: Education Policy in the Long Nineteenth Century, edited by Johannes Westberg, Lukas Boser, and Ingrid Brühwiler, 41–66. Cham: Palgrave Macmillan, 2019.

"Charles Rollin (1661–1741)." Bibliothèque Nationale de France. Accessed May 17, 2021, https://data.bnf.fr/en/12731899/charles_rollin/.

Cherepnin, L. V. *Russkaia paleografiia*. Moscow: Gosudarstvennoe izdatel'stvo politicheskoi literatury, 1956.

Cherubim, Dieter, and Ariane Walsdorf. "Die Tradition der Sprachgesellschaften: Leibniz—Schottelius—Gottsched." In *Sprachkritik als Aufklärung: Die Deutsche Gesellschaft in Göttingen im 18. Jahrhundert*, edited by Elmar Mittler, 53–92. 2nd rev. and ext. ed. Göttingen: Niedersächsische Staats- und Universitätsbibliothek, 2005. Accessed May 19, 2021. https://www.yumpu.com/de/document/read/5068142/sprachgesellschaften-im-18-jahrhundert.

Chugaev, N. V. "Paleografiia dvukh dokumentov Pyskorskogo medeplavil'nogo zavoda 1741 g." In *Zhivaia rech' Permskogo kraia v sinkhronii i diakhronii: materialy i issledovania*, edited by I. I. Rusinova, 257–269. Perm': Permskii gosudarstvennyi universitet, 2009.

———, ed. *Stolp prikhodnoi denezhnoi kazny pyskorskoi zavodskoi kantory 1741 godu*. Perm': PGNIU, 2016.

———. "O nekotorykh osobennostiakh chislitel'nykh v prikamskom pis'mennom pamiatnike XVIII veka." *Acta linguistica petropolitana. Trudy Instituta lingvisticheskikh issledovanii* 13, no. 2 (2017): 630–659.

———. "Stolp prikhodnoi denezhnoi kazny pyskorskoi zavodskoi kantory 1741 godu kak istochnik izucheniia russkogo iazyka XVIII v." Kand. nauk diss., Permskii universitet, Perm', 2019.

Consett, Tho. *The Present State and Regulations of the Church of Russia Establish'd by the Late Tsar's Royal Edict*. London: S. Holt, 1729.

Cracraft, J. *The Petrine Revolution in Russian Culture*. Cambridge, MA, and London: The Belknap Press of Harvard University Press, 2004.

Christy, T. Craig. *Uniformitarianism in Linguistics*. Amsterdam and Philadelphia: John Benjamins Publishing Company, 1983.

"Content and Structure of the Corpus." Russian National Corpus. Accessed April 13, 2021. http://www.ruscorpora.ru/en/corpora-structure.html.

Crystal, David. *A Dictionary of Linguistics and Phonetics*. 4th ed. Oxford: Blackwell, 1997.

Daniels, Michael, Ruprecht von Waldenfels, Aleksandra Ter-Avanesova, et al. "Dialect Loss in the Russian North: Modeling Change across Variables." *Language Variation and Change* 31 (2019): 353–376.

Dekker, Rudolf. "Jacques Presser's Heritage: Ego Documents in the Study of History." *Memoria y Civilización* 5 (2002): 13–37.

Demidov, D. G. "Dve tocki nad glasnoi bukvoi v XVII–XVIII vv. (iz istorii russkoi diakritiki)." In *Pis'mennaia kul'tura narodov Rossii. Materialy Vserossiiskoi nauchnoi konferentsii 19–20 noiabria 2008 g.*, 32–36. Omsk: Omskii gosudarstvennyi universitet, 2008.

Derschau, E. G. von. "Nekrolog: Johann Albrecht Freyherr von Korff." *Beylage zur Allgemeinen deutschen Zeitung für Rußland* 8 (1826). http://dspace.ut.ee/handle/10062/44439.

Dixon, Simon. *The Modernisation of Russia 1676–1825*. Cambridge: Cambridge University Press, 1999.

Dowler, Wayne. *A History of Education in Modern Russia: Aims, Ways, Outcomes*. London: Bloomsbury, 2021.

Dowling, Timothy C., ed. *Russia at War: From the Mongol Conquest to Afghanistan, Chechnya, and Beyond*. Santa Barbara, CA: ABC-Clio, 2015.

Egorov, S. F., ed. *Khrestomatiia po istorii shkoly i pedagogiki v Rossii (do Velikoi Oktiabr'skoi Sotsialisticheskoi Revoliutsii)*. 2nd rev. ed. Moscow: Prosveshchenie, 1986.

Egorov, S. F., ed. *Rossiiskoe obrazovanie: istoriia i sovremennost'*. Moscow: ITPIMIO, 1994.

Eichhorn, C. *Die Geschichte der „St. Petersburger Zeitung" 1727–1902. Zum Tage der Feier des 175-jährigen Bestehens der Zeitung, dem 3. Januar 1902*. St. Petersburg: Buchdruckerei der St. Petersburger Zeitung, 1902.

Elspaß, Stephan. "A Twofold View 'from Below': New Perspectives on Language Histories and Language Historiographies." In *Germanic Language Histories 'from Below' (1700–2000)*, edited by Stephan Elspaß, Nils Langer, Joachim Scharloth, and Wim Vandenbussche, 3–10. Berlin and New York: De Gruyter, 2011.

Épshtein, Éduard. "Opyt XVIII veka nel'zia vziat' i perenesti v XXI vek." *Gazeta.ru*, July 08, 2016. Accessed April 22, 2021. https://www.gazeta.ru/science/2016/07/08_a_8372981.shtml.

Evtiukhin, V. B. "'Rossiiskaia grammatika' M.V. Lomonosova." Accessed March 19, 2021. http://www.ruthenia.ru/apr/textes/lomonos/add02.htm.

Filippov, K. A., N. V. Kareva, and S. S. Volkov, eds. *Vasilii Evdokimovich Adodurov: "Anfangs-Gründe der Rußischen Sprache" ili "Pervye osnovaniia rossiiskogo iazyka". Formirovanie russkoi akademicheskoi grammaticheskoi traditsii*. St. Petersburg: Nauka and Nestor-Istoriia, 2014.

"Fingerprinting History." Accessed May 26, 2021. https://tri-statefingerprinting.com/fingerprinting-history/.

Fonkich, B. L. *Greko-slavianskie shkoly v Moskve v XVII veke*. Moscow: Iazyki slavianskikh kul'tur, 2009.

Franklin, Simon. "Printing and Social Control in Russia 1: Passports." *Russian History* 37 (2010): 208–237.

———. "Printing and Social Control in Russia 2: Decrees." *Russian History* 38 (2011): 467–492.

———. "Printing and Social Control in Russia 3: Blank Forms." *Russian History* 42 (2015): 114–135.

Freeze, Gregory L. *From Supplication to Revolution: A Documentary Social History of Imperial Russia*. New York and Oxford: Oxford University Press, 1988.

Gazeta "Sanktpeterburgskie vedomosti" XVIII veka: ukazatel' k soderzhaniu. Accessed May 28, 2021. https://www.vedomosti1728.ru/.

Germanova, N. N. *Teoriia i istoriia literaturnogo iazyka v otechestvennom i angloiazychnom iazykoznanii*. Moscow: URSS, 2011.

Glinkina, L. A., and E. A. Sivkova, eds. *Delovoi iazyk XVIII–nachala XIX vekov na Iuzhnom Urale i v Zaural'e*. Cheliabinsk: Poligraf-Master, 2006.

Gorecki, Danuta M. "The Commission of National Education and Civic Revival through Books in Eighteenth-Century Poland." *The Journal of Library History* 2 (1980): 138–166.

Goriacheva, Iuliia. "Vitalii Kostomarov: 'Sekret prost: dlia togo, chtoby poliubit' russkii iazyk, nado poliubit' Rossiiu.'" *Novyi russkii mir*, January 14, 2020. Accessed February 17, 2021. https://russkiymir.ru/publications/267504/.

Gorshkov, Boris B. *Peasants in Russia from Serfdom to Stalin: Accomodation, Survival, Resistance*. London: Bloomsbury Academic, 2018.

Gorshkova, K. V. *Istoricheskaia dialektologiia russkogo iazyka*. Moscow: Prosveshchenie, 1972.

Grachëv, M. A. "Sovremennaia klassifikatsiia sotsial'nykh dialektov." In *Prepodavanie i izuchenie russkogo iazyka i literatury v kontektste sovremennoi iazykovoi politiki Rossii*, edited by L. I. Ruchina, 72–74. Nizhnii Novgorod: Natsional'nyi issledovatel'skii Nizhegorodskii gosudarstvennyi universitet im. N. I. Lobachevskogo, 2002.

Graff, Harvey J. "Introduction to historical Studies of Literacy." In *Understanding Literacy in Its Historical Contexts: Socio-cultural History and the Legacy of Egil Johansson*, edited by Harvey J. Graff, Alison Mackinnon, Bengt Sandin, and Ian Winchester, 14–22. Lund: Nordic Academic Press, 2009.

Grannes, Alf. *Vsjakaja vsjatjina: Om folk og språk i "Sovjetunionen", Russland og Bulgaria.* Bergen: Universitetet i Bergen, Russisk institutt, 1992.

Groening, Michael. *Rossiiskaia grammatika Thet är Grammatica Russica, Eller Grundelig Handledning till Ryska Språket.* Introduction by B. O. Unbegaun. Munich: Fink, 1969. Original edition Stockholm: Hos Directeuren Pet. Momma, 1750.

Guseva, A. A. *Svod russkikh knig kirillovskoi pechati XVIII veka tipografii Moskvy i Sankt-Peterburga i universal'naia metodika ikh identifikatsii.* Moscow: Indrik, 2010.

Gutschmidt, Karl. "Die ostslawische Region / The East-Slavic Area." In *Sociolinguistics: An International Handbook of the Science of Language and Society*, edited by Ulrich Ammon, Norbert Dittmar, Klaus J. Mattheier, and Peter Trudgill, vol. 3, 1851–1863. 2nd rev. and ext. ed. Berlin and New York: Walter de Gruyter, 2006.

Hans, N. "Russian Students at Leyden in the 18th Century." *The Slavonic and East European Review* 35 (85) (1957): 551–562.

Helder, Bodil. *Textual Analysis.* Frederiksberg: Samfundslitteratur, 2011.

Hennings, Jan. "The Semiotics of Diplomatic Dialogue: Pomp and Circumstance in Tsar Peter I's Visit to Vienna in 1698." *The International History Review* 3 (2008): 515–544.

Henry, Louis, and Yves Blayo, "La Population de la France de 1740 à 1860," *Population* 30, no. 1 (1975): 71–122.

Hernández-Campoy, Juan M., and J. Camilo Conde-Silvestre, eds. *The Handbook of Historical Sociolinguistics.* Oxford: Wiley-Blackwell, 2012.

Hoffmann, Peter, and V. I. Osipov, eds. *Geographie, Geschichte und Bildsungswesen in Russland und Deutschland im 18. Jahrhundert: Briefwechsel Anton Friedrich Büsching—Gerhard Friedrich Müller 1751 bis 1783.* Berlin: Akademie, 1995.

Hosking, Geoffrey. *Russia and the Russians. A History.* 2nd ed. Cambridge, MA: The Belknap Press of Harvard University Press, 2011.

Hudson, R. A. *Sociolinguistics.* 2nd ed. Cambridge: Cambridge University Press, 1996.

Hughes, Lindsey. *Russia in the Age of Peter the Great.* New Haven, CT: Yale University Press, 1998.

———. "Russian Culture in the Eighteenth Century." In *The Cambridge History of Russia*, edited by Dominic Lieven, vol. 2: *Imperial Russia, 1689–1917*, 67–91. Cambridge: Cambridge University Press, 2006.

Hüttl-Folter, Gerta. "Russkii literaturnyi iazyk novogo tipa. Innovatsii v sintaksise 30-ykh godov XVIII v." *Wiener Slavistisches Jahrbuch* 38 (1992): 21–36.

———. *Syntaktische Studien zur neueren russischen Literatursprache: die frühen Übersetzungen aus dem Französischen.* Vienna: Böhlau, 1996.

Issatschenko, A. [A. V. Isachenko]. "Vopros № 3: Kakova spetsifika literaturnogo dvuiazychiia v istorii slavianskikh narodov?" *Voprosy iazykoznaniia* 7, no. 3 (May–June 1958): 42–45.

———. "Vorgeschichte und Entstehung der modernen russischen Literatursprache." *Zeitschrift für slavische Philologie* 37, no. 2 (1974): 235–274.

———. "Russian." In *The Slavic Literary Languages*, edited by Alexander M. Schenker and Edward Stankiewicz, 119–142. New Haven: Yale Concilium on International and Area Studies, 1980.

———. *Geschichte der russischen Sprache*, vol. 2: *Das 17. und 18. Jahrhundert*, edited by Henrik Birnbaum, L'ubomir Ďurovič, and Eva Salnikow-Ritter. Heidelberg: Winter, 1983.

Istrin, V. A. *1100 let slavianskoi azbuki.* 3rd ed. Edited by L. P. Zhukovskaia. Moscow: LKI, 2010.

Ivanova, N. A., and Zheltova, V. P. *Soslovnoe obshchestvo Rossiiskoi imperii (XVIII–nachalo XX veka)*. 2nd ext. ed. Moscow: Novyi khronograf, 2019.

Janda, Richard D., and Brian D. Joseph. "On Language, Change, and Language Change—Or, Of History, Linguistics, and Historical Linguistics." In *The Handbook of Historical Linguistics*, edited by Brian D. Joseph and Richard D. Janda, 3–180. Malden, MA and Oxford: Blackwell Publishing, 2003.

Johnson, W. H. Eckart. "Russia's Educational Heritage: Teacher Education in the Russian Empire, 1600–1917." PhD. diss., Columbia University, New York, 1950.

Jonçich Clifford, Geraldine. "Buch und Lesen: Historical Perspectives on Literacy and Schooling." *Review of Educational Research* 4 (1984): 472–500.

Kabuzan, V. M. *Narodonaselenie Rossii v XVIII–pervoi polovine XIX v. (po materialam revizii)*. Moscow: Izdatel'stvo Akademii nauk SSSR, 1963.

———. *Narody Rossii v XVIII veke: chislennost' i ėtnicheskii sostav*. Moscow: Nauka, 1990.

Kachalkin, A. N. "Iz istorii kul'tury i pis'mennosti. Nazvaniia delovykh bumag v XVIII veke." *Russkaia rech'* 2 (2003): 79–84.

Kahan, A. *The Plow, the Hammer and the Knout: An Economic History of Eighteenth-Century Russia*. Chicago and London: University of Chicago Press, 1985.

Kahn, Andrew, Mark Lipovetsky, Irina Reyfman, and Stephanie Sandler. *A History of Russian Literature*. Oxford: Oxford University Press, 2018.

Kamchatnov, A. M. *Istoriia russkogo literaturnogo iazyka XI–pervaia polovina XIX veka*. 2nd ed. Moscow: Academia, 2013.

Kamenskii, Aleksandr B. *Ot Petra I do Pavla I. Reformy v Rossii XVIII veka. Opyt tselostnogo analiza*. Moscow: RGGU, 2001.

Kamusella, Tomasz. *The Politics of Language and Nationalism in Modern Central Europe*. Basingstoke: Palgrave MacMillan, 2009.

Kappeler, Andreas. *Rußland als Vielvölkerreich: Entstehung, Geschichte, Zerfall*. 2nd ed. Munich: C. H. Beck, 2008.

Karaulov, Iu. N. *O sostoianii russkogo iazyka sovremennosti: doklad na konferentsii "Russkii iazyk i sovremennost'. Problemy i perspektivy razvitiia rusistiki."* Moscow: AN SSSR. Institut russkogo iazyka, 1991.

"Karl fon Brevern." Prezidenty Akademii Nauk. Accessed September 25, 2021. http://www.ras.ru/presidents/9a3d4acd-5c39-4fc9-a5b2-a9e8f57ecf96.aspx.

Kasatkin, L. L. "Ekan'e." In *Russkii iazyk: Ėntsiklopediia*, edited by F. P. Filin, 81. Moscow: Sovetskaia ėntsiklopediia, 1979.

———. *Sovremennaia russkaia dialektnaia i literaturnaia fonetika kak isthochnik dlia istorii russkogo iazyka*. Moscow: Nauka and Iazyki russkoi kul'tury, 1999.

Keipert, Helmut, and Andrea Huterer, eds. *Compendium Grammaticae Russicae (1731). Die erste Akademie-Grammatik der russischen Sprache*. Munich: Verlag der Bayerischen Akademie der Wissenschaften, 2002.

Keipert, Helmut. Review of *Teoreticheskie osnovy istorii russkogo literaturnogo iazyka* by A. I. Gorshkov. *Russian Linguistics* 8 (1984): 159–166.

———. "Geschichte der russischen Literatursprache." In *Handbuch des Russisten*, edited by Helmuth Jachnow, 444–481. Wiesbaden: Harrassowitz, 1984.

———. "Die Christianisierung Rußlands als Gegenstand der russischen Sprachgeschichte." In *Tausend Jahre Christentum in Rußland: Zum Millenium der Taufe der Kiever Rus'*, edited by Karl

Christian Felmy, Georg Kretschmar, Fairy von Lilienfeld, and Claus-Jürgen Roepke, 313–346. Göttingen: Vandenhoeck & Ruprecht, 1988.

———— [Kaipert, G.]. "Kreshchenie Rusi i istoriia russkogo literaturnogo iazyka." *Voprosy iazykoznaniia* 5 (1991): 85–112.

————. "Geschichte der russischen Literatursprache." In *Handbuch der sprachwissenschaftlichen Russistik und ihrer Grenzdisziplinen,* edited by Helmut Jachnow, 726–779. Wiesbaden: Harrassowitz, 1999.

Keuten, Alla. "K istorii russkikh i nemetskikh 'Primechanii k Vedomostiam' (1728–1742)." *Russian Literature* 75 (2014): 265–304.

Khoteev, P. I. "Biblioteka Sukhoputnogo shliakhetskogo kadetskogo korpusa v seredine XVIII v. (kolichestvennye dannye)." In *Kniga v Rossii XVI–serediny XIX v. Materialy i issledovaniia. Sbornik nauchnykh trudov,* edited by A. A. Zaitseva, 119–126. Leningrad: BAN, 1990.

Kislova, E. I., and E. M. Matveev. *Khronologicheskii katalog slov i rechei XVIII veka.* St. Petersburg: Filologicheskii fakul'tet SPbGU, 2011.

Kislova, E. I. "Grammaticheskaia norma iazyka propovedi elizavetinskogo perioda (1740-e gg.). Kand. nauk diss., Moskovskii gosudarstvennyi universitet, Moscow, 2007.

————. "Propoved' 1740-x godov v istorii russkogo iazyka." In *Okkazional'naia literatura v kontekste prazdnichnoi kul'tury Rossii XVIII veka,* edited by P. E Bukharkin, U. Ekuch, and N. D. Kochetkova, 33–52. St. Petersburg: Filologicheskii fakul'tet SPbGU, 2010.

————. "'Grazhdanskoe' i 'tserkovnoslavianskoe' izdanie propovedei v XVIII v.: K voprosu o statuse dvukh tipov orfografii." In *Problemy izucheniia russkoi literatury XVIII veka* 15, 78–89. St. Petersburg and Samara: As Gard, 2011.

————. "Sermons and Sermonizing in 18th-Century Russia: At Court and Beyond." *Slověne* 2 (2014): 175–193.

Kliuchevskii, V. O. *Kurs russkoi istorii.* Part 5. Moscow: Mysl', 1989.

Kobrin, Vladimir B. "Istoricheskaia sotsiolingvistika kak spetsial'naia istoricheskaia distsiplina." In *Oprichnina, genealogiia, antroponimika: izbrannye trudy,* edited by E. G. Astvatsaturian, A. G. Makarov, and Iu. M. Eskin, 246–254. Moscow: RGGU, 2008.

Kopanev, N. A. "Knigi imperatritsy Elizavety Petrovny." In *Kniga v Rossii XVI–serediny XIX v.,* edited by A. A. Zaitseva, 109–118. Leningrad: BAN, 1990.

Kopelevich, Iu. Kh. *Osnovanie Peterburgskoi akademii nauk.* Leningrad: Nauka, 1977.

Kopotev, Mikhail, Olga Lyashevskaya, and Arto Mustajoki, eds. *Quantitative Approaches to the Russian Language.* Abingdon, Oxon: Routledge, 2018.

Kornilaeva, I. A. "Iz istorii russkoi aktsentuatsii XVIII veka." In *Slavianskoe i balkanskoe iazykoznanie: prosodiia,* edited by A. A. Zalizniak, V. A. Dybo, and R. V. Bulatova, 192–200. Moscow: Nauka, 1989.

Korpus M.V. Lomonosova. Accessed April 13, 2021. http://lomonosov.pro/.

Kostin, A. A. "Akribiia i ameleiia, ili Gde byt' dobroi zemle? (grammatika V. E. Adodurova v kontekste i bez)." *Slověne* 1 (2016): 263–299.

Kostomarov, V. G. *Iazyk tekushchego momenta: poniatie pravil'nosti.* S. l.: Zlatoust, 2014.

————. *Stilistika, liubov' moei zhizni.* St. Petersburg: Zlatoust, Moscow: IRIa, 2019.

Kotkov, S. I. "Russkaia chastnaia perepiska XVII–XVIII vv. kak lingvisticheskii istochnik." *Voprosy iazykoznania* 6 (1963): 107–116.

Kravetskii, A. G., and A. A. Pletnëva. *Istoriia tserkovnoslavianskogo iazyka v Rossii: konets XIX–XX v.* Moscow: Iazyki russkoi kul'tury, 2001.

Kretschmer, Anna. Review of *V. K. Trediakovskijs 'Gespräch zwischen einem Fremden und einem Russen über die alte und neue Orthographie und alles, was zu dieser Materie gehört': eine philologisch-kritische Darstellung* by Marianne Müller. *Russian Linguistics* 21, no. 3 (1997): 327–330.

———. *Zur Geschichte des Schriftrussischen. Privatkorrespondenz des 17. und frühen 18. Jahrhunderts.* Munich: Otto Sagner, 1998.

———. "Chelovek za pis'mom (russkii chelovek Petrovskogo vremeni v chastnoi perepiske)." In *Die russiche Sprache und Literatur im 18. Jahrhundert: Tradition und Innovation. Gedenkschrift für Gerta Hüttl-Folter,* edited by Juliane Besters-Dilger and Fedor B. Poljakov, 267–287. Frankfurt am Main and New York: Peter Lang, 2009.

Kruglov, V. M. "O kharaktere normy v russkom iazyke pervoi chetverti XVIII veka." *Petra philologica, Literaturnaia kul'tura Rossii XVIII veka,* vol. 6, edited by N. A. Gus'kov, E. M. Matveev, and M. V. Ponomarëva, 167–180. St. Petersburg: Nestor-Istoriia, 2015.

Krysin, L. P. "Sotsial'naia markirovannost' iazykovykh edinits." In *Sovremennyi russkii iazyk: sotsial'naia i funktsional'naia differentsiatsiia,* edited by L. P. Krysin, 79–100. Moscow: Iazyki slavianskoi kul'tury, 2003.

———. "Evgenii Dmitrievich Polivanov." In *Stat'i o russkom iazyke i russkikh iazykovedakh,* 495–504. 2nd ed. Moscow: Flinta, 2016.

Kuliabko, E. S. "Pervye prezidenty." *Vestnik AN SSSR* 2 (1974): 144–151.

Kunik, A. A. *Sbornik materialov dlia istorii Imperatorskoi akademii nauk v XVIII veke.* Vol. 1. St. Petersburg: Imperatorskaia akademiia nauk, 1865.

Labov, William. *Principles of Linguistic Change.* Vol. 1: *Internal Factors.* Oxford: Blackwell, 1994.

"Language Management Theory." Accessed June 26, 2019. http://languagemanagement.ff.cuni.cz/en/LMT.

Larionov, A. A. "Studenchestvo v Slaviano-greko-latinskoi akademii v pervoi polovine XVIII veka." *Rossiiskaia istoriia* 6 (2010): 30–40.

Leitner, Barbara. "Die ‚Sanktpeterburgskie Vedomosti': die Entstehung der modernen russischen Standardsprache im Spiegel der frühen Presse." Mag. phil. diss., Universität Wien, Vienna, 2010.

Leitsch, Walter. "The Russian Nobility in the Eighteenth Century," *East European Quarterly* 3 (1977): 317–340.

Liechtenhan, Francine-Dominique. *La Russie entre en Europe: Elisabeth Ire et la Succession de l'Autriche (1740–1750).* Paris: CNRS, 1997.

Lieven, Dominic. "The Elites." In *The Cambridge History of Russia,* edited by Dominic Lieven, vol. 2: *Imperial Russia, 1689–1917,* 225–244. Cambridge: Cambridge University Press, 2006.

Likhachëv, D. S. *Tekstologiia.* 2nd rev. and ext. ed. Leningrad: Nauka, 1983.

Liubzhin, A. I. *Istoriia russkoi shkoly imperatorskoi ėpokhi.* Vol. 1: *Russkaia shkola XVIII stoletiia.* Moscow: Nikeia, 2014.

Lomonosov, Mikhailo. *Rossiiskaia grammatika.* St. Petersburg: Imperatorskaia akademiia nauk, 1755. Rpt. Leipzig: Zentralantiquariat der Deutschen Demokratischen Republik, 1972.

——— [Lomonosov, M. V.]. "Donoshenie v Akademiiu Nauk ob uderzhanii deneg, poluchennykh v shchët zhalovan'ia." April 23, 1743. In his *Polnoe sobranie sochinenii,* vol. 10, 329–330. Moscow and Leningrad: Izdatel'stvo Akademii nauk SSSR, 1952. Accessed November 18, 2021. http://feb-web.ru/feb/lomonos/texts/lo0/loa/loa-329-.htm?cmd=p.

——— [Lomonosov, M. V.]. "Predislovie o pol'ze knig tserkovnykh v rossiiskom iazyke." In his *Izbrannye proizvedeniia,* 473–478. Leningrad: Sovetskii pisatel', 1986. https://rvb.ru/18vek/lomonosov/01text/02addenda/11addenda/138.htm.

Luppov, Sergei P. *Kniga v Rossii v poslepetrovskoe vremia 1725–1740*. Leningrad: Nauka, 1976.

Maier, Ingrid. Review of *Zur Geschichte des Schriftrussischen. Privatkorrespondenz des 17. und frühen 18. Jahrhunderts* by Anna Kretschmer. *Zeitschrift für Slavische Philologie* 1 (2000): 186–193.

Maiorov, A. P. *Ocherki leksiki regional'noi delovoi pis'mennosti XVIII veka*. Moscow: Azbukovnik, 2006.

———. "Sverkhtekst v Zabaikal'skoi delovoi pis'mennosti XVIII v. kak istochnik rekonstruktsii regiolekta togo vremeni." *Izvestiia Iuzhnogo federal'nogo universiteta* (series: Filologicheskie nauki) 3 (2019): 34–45.

Malitikov, A. S., ed. *Kratkii slovar' vidov i raznovidnostei dokumentov*. Moscow: VNIIDAD, 1974.

Marker, Gary. *Publishing, Printing, and the Origins of Intellectual Life in Russia, 1700–1800*. Princeton, NJ: Princeton University Press, 1985.

———. "Literacy and Literacy Texts in Muscovy: A Reconsideration." *Slavic Review* 49, no. 1 (1990): 74–89.

———. "The Westernization of the Elite, 1725–1800." In *A Companion to Russian History*, edited by A. Gleason, 180–195. Malden, MA: Wiley Blackwell, 2014.

Marrese, M. L. *A Woman's Kingdom: Noblewomen and the Control of Property in Russia, 1700–1861*. Ithaca: Cornell University Press, 2002.

Marsigli, Luigi Ferdinando, and Richard F. Kreutel. *Stato militare dell' imperio ottomanno / L'état militaire de l'Empire Ottoman*. Graz: Akademische Druck- und Verlagsanstalt, 1972.

——— [Marsil'i, Graf de]. *Voennoe sostoianie Ottomanskiia Imperii*. St. Petersburg: Imperatorskaia akademiia nauk, 1737.

Matthews, W. K. *Russian Historical Grammar*. London: The Athlone Press, 1960.

Mengel, S., and O. Siebert. "O 'prostote' iazyka 'russkikh knig' Simeona Todorskogo (Galle 1729–1735): perevodcheskie strategii i ikh analiz pri ispol'zovanii komp'iuternykh tekhnologii." Thesen MKS 18. Accessed November 20, 2021. https://www.slavistik.uni-halle.de/16.slavistenkongress/mks18themblockmengel/thesenmks18mengelsiebert/.

Mengel', S., S. Arshembo [Archaimbault], M. K. Bragone, S. V. Vlasov, D. Grbich, L. V. Moskovkin, and T. Chelbaeva, eds. *Al'ternativnye puti formirovaniia russkogo literaturnogo iazyka v kontse XVII–pervoi treti XVIII veka: Vklad inostrannykh uchënykh i perevodchikov*. Moscow: Iazyki slavianskikh kul'tur, 2021.

Mezhenina, T. N., and A. P. Maiorov, eds. *Delovaia pis'mennost' Troitskogo Selenginskogo monastyria pervoi poloviny XVIII v.* St. Petersburg: Nestor-Istoriia, 2015.

Mikhaylov, Nikita. "Tvoritel'nyi padezh v russkom iazyke XVIII veka." PhD diss. Uppsala University, Uppsala, 2012.

Mironov, B. N. "Gramotnost' v Rossii 1797–1917 gg.: Poluchenie novoi istoricheskoi informatsii s pomoshch'iu metodov retrospektivnogo prognozirovaniia." *Istoriia SSSR* 4 (1985): 137–153.

———. "The Development of Literacy in Russia and the USSR from the Tenth to the Twentieth Centuries." *History of Education Quarterly* 2 (1991): 229–252.

———. *Sotsial'naia istoriia Rossii perioda imperii (XVIII–nachalo XX v.)*. 3rd rev. and ext. ed. St. Petersburg: Dmitrii Bulanin, 2003.

———. "Uchënost'—vot chuma, uchënost'—vot prichina. …" *Rodina* 6 (2006): 2–8. Accessed June 14, 2011. http://www.istrodina.com/rodina_articul.php3?id =190 5&n=99.

——— [Mironov, Boris N.]. *The Standard of Living and Revolutions in Russia, 1700–1917*. London: Routledge, 2012.

———. *Rossiiskaia imperiia: Ot traditsii k modernu*, 3 vols. St. Petersburg: Dmitrii Bulanin, 2014–2015.

Modzalevskii, B. L. *Spisok chlenov Imperatorskoi akademii nauk 1725–1907*. St. Petersburg: Imperatorskaia akademiia nauk, 1908.

Morozova, T. Iu., "Organizatsiia sbora i obrabotki original'noi informatsii v russkikh gazetakh XVIII v. (na primere izdaniia 'Sanktpeterburgskikh vedomostei')." In *Rossiia v XVIII stoletii*, vol. 1, edited by E. E. Rychalovskii, 24–37. Moscow: Iazyki slavianskikh kul'tur, 2002.

Moser, Michael. „*Iunosti chestnoe zertsalo" 1717 g.: U istokov russkogo literaturnogo iazyka*. Vienna: LIT, 2020.

Moskovkin, L. V. *Iazykovoe obrazovanie v Akademicheskom universitete i gimnazii v XVIII veke*. St. Petersburg: Izdatel'stvo Sankt-Peterburgskogo universiteta, 2019.

Mühlpfordt, Günther. "Rußlands Aufklärer und die Mitteldeutsche Aufklärung: Begegnungen, Zusammenwirken, Partnerschaft." In *Deutsch-Russische Beziehungen im 18. Jahrhundert: Kultur, Wissenschaft, Diplomatie*, edited by Conrad Grau, Sergueï Karp, and Jürgen Voss, 83–171. Wiesbaden: Harrassowitz, 1997.

Mustajoki, Arto. "Raznovidnosti russkogo iazyka: analiz i klassifikatsiia." *Voprosy iazykoznaniia* 5 (2013): 3–27.

Nagy, Pál. "Roma in semi-ego documents in 18th century Hungary." *Frühneuzeit-Info* (2019): 91–105.

Natsional'naia élektronnaia biblioteka. Accessed May 24, 2021. https://kp.rusneb.ru.

Natsional'nyi korpus russkogo iazyka. Accessed September 27, 2021. https://ruscorpora.ru/new/search-main.html.

Nekvapil, Jiří. "From Language Planning to Language Management." *Sociolinguistica* 20 (2006): 92–104.

———. "Prologue: The Integrative Potential of Language Management Theory." In *Language Management in Contact Situations: Perspectives from Three Contintents*, edited by Jiří Nekvapil, Tamah Sherman, and Petr Kaderka, 1–11. Frankfurt am Main: Peter Lang, 2009.

Neustupný, Jiří V. "Sociolinguistic Aspects of Social Modernization." In *Sociolinguistics: An International Handbook of the Science of Language and Society*, edited by Ulrich Ammon, Norbert Dittmar, Klaus J. Mattheier, and Peter Trudgill, vol. 3, 2209–2223. 2nd rev. and ext. ed. Berlin and New York: Walter de Gruyter, 2006.

Nevalainen, Terttu, and Helena Raumolin-Brunberg. "Historical Sociolinguistics: Origins, Motivations, and Paradigms." In *The Handbook of Historical Sociolinguistics*, edited by J. M. Hernández-Campoy and J. C. Conde-Silvestre, 22–40. Oxford: Wiley-Blackwell, 2012.

Nikitin, O. V. "Vasilii Evdokimovich Adodurov i ego rol' v istorii russkoi lingvisticheskoi traditsii XVIII veka: K 300-letiiu so dnia rozhdeniia." Slovo. Accessed September 12, 2021. https://www.portal-slovo.ru/philology/41666.php.

———. *Delovaia pis'mennost' v istorii russkogo iazyka (XI–XVIII vv.): lingvisticheskie ocherki*. 3rd ed. Moscow: Flinta, 2017.

———. *Problemy étnolingvisticheskogo izucheniia pamiatnikov delovoi pis'mennosti*. 3rd ed. Moscow: Flinta, 2017.

Offord, Derek. "Sociolinguistics and History: An Interdisciplinary View of Bilingualism in Imperial Russia." *Journal of Historical Sociolinguistics* 1 (2020): 1–33.

Offord, Derek, Vladislav Rjéoutski, and Gesine Argent. *The French Language in Russia: A Social, Political, Cultural, and Literary History*. Amsterdam: Amsterdam University Press, 2018.

"O gazete." *Gazeta "Sanktpeterburgskie vedomosti" XVIII veka: ukazateli k soderzhaniiu (1728-1781 gg.)*. Biblioteka Akademii nauk. Accessed April 26, 2021. https://www.vedomosti1728.ru/?r=12

Okenfuss, Max J. *The Discovery of Childhood in Russia: the Evidence of the Slavic Primer*. Newtonville, MA: Oriental Research Partners, 1980.

———. *The Rise and Fall of Latin Humanism in Early-Modern Russia*. Leiden: Brill, 1995.

Orrman, Eljas, and Jyrki Paaskoski, eds. *Vanhan Suomen arkistot. Arkiven från Gamla Finland*. Helsinki: Suomalaisen Kirjallisuuden Seura, 2012.

Papmehl, K. A. *Freedom of Expression in Eighteenth-Century Russia*. The Hague: Martinus Nijhoff, 1971.

Pekarskii, P. P. *Istoriia Imperatorskoi akademii nauk*, 2 vols. St. Petersburg: Imperatorskaia akademiia nauk, 1870–1873.

Pekarskii, P. P. "Adodurov, Vasilii Evdokimovich, ad"iunkt matematicheskikh nauk." In *Vasilii Evdokimovich Adodurov: "Anfangs-Gründe der Rußischen Sprache" ili "Pervye osnovaniia rossiiskogo iazyka". Formirovanie russkoi akademicheskoi grammaticheskoi traditsii*, edited by K. A. Filippov, N. V. Kareva, and S. S. Volkov, 209–218. St. Petersburg: Nauka and Nestor-Istoriia, 2014.

"Peterburgskaia senatskaia tipografiia." Putevoditeli po rossiiskim arkhivam. Accessed November 13, 2021. https://guides.rusarchives.ru/funds/peterburgskaya-senatskaya-tipografiya.

Pivovarov, E. G. "Perevodchiki Akademii nauk v period ee stanovleniia." *Sotsiologiia nauki i tekhnologii* 4 (2015): 40–51.

———. "K istorii sozdaniia Rossiiskogo sobraniia Akademii nauk." *Sotsiologiia nauki i tekhnologii* 4 (2018): 7–20.

Pletnëva, A. A. "Sotsiolingvistika i problemy istorii russkogo iazyka XVIII–XIX vekov." In *Zhizn' iazyka: Sbornik statei k 80-letiiu Mikhaila Viktorovicha Panova*, edited by S. M. Kuz'mina, 269–279. Moscow: Iazyki slavianskoi kul'tury, 2001.

———. "K kharakteristike iazykovoi situatsii v Rossii XVIII–XIX vv." *Russkii iazyk v nauchnom osveshchenii* 2 (12) (2006): 213–229.

———. "Russkii lubok: mezhdu Srednevekov'em i Novym vremenem." *Russkaia rech'* 6 (2014): 77–84.

Podtergera, I. A. "Chto takoe istoriia iazyka? / What is Language History?" *Slověne* 1 (2015): 394–455.

Polivanov, E. D. "Fonetika intelligentskogo iazyka." In his *Izbrannye raboty: Stat'i po obshchemu iazykoznaniiu*, edited by A. A. Leont'ev, 225–235. Moscow: Nauka, 1968.

Polnoe sobranie zakonov Rossiiskoi imperii. Accessed October 31, 2021. http://nlr.ru.

Porter, Eugene O. "The Articles of War." *The Historian* 2 (1946): 77–102.

Pososhkov, I. T. *Kniga o skudosti i bogatstve i drugie sochineniia*. Edited by B. B. Kafengauz. Moscow: Izdatel'stvo Akademii nauk SSSR, 1951.

——— [Pososhkov, Ivan]. *The Book of Poverty and Wealth*. Edited and translated by A. P. Vlasto and L. R. Lewitter. London: The Athlone Press, 1987.

Press, Ian. *A History of the Russian Language and Its Speakers*. Munich: Lincom, 2007.

"Prezidenty Rossiiskoi akademii nauk za vsiu istoriiu." Rossiiskaia akademiia nauk. Accessed April 9, 2021. http://www.ras.ru/about/president/allpresidents.aspx.

Račkauskas, John A. "The First National System of Education in Europe: The Commission for National Education of the Kingdom of Poland and the Grand Duchy of Lithuania (1773–1794)." *Lituanus—Lithuanian Quarterly Journal of Arts and Sciences* 4 (1968).

Ragazzoli, Chloé, Ömür Harmanşah, Chiara Salvador, and Elizabeth Frood, eds. *Scribbling through History: Graffiti, Places and People from Antiquity to Modernity*. London: Bloomsbury Academic, 2018.

Reyfman, Irina. *Vasilii Trediakovsky: The Fool of the "New" Russian Literature*. Stanford: Stanford University Press, 1990.

Rissanen, Matti. "Corpus Linguistics and Historical Linguistics." In *Corpus Linguistics: An International Handbook,* edited by Anke Lüdeling and Merja Kytö, 53–68. Berlin and New York: Walter de Gruyter, 2008.

Rjéoutski, Vladislav. "Les écoles étrangères dans la sociéte russe à l'epoque des Lumières." *Cahiers du Monde russe* 46, no. 3 (July–September 2005): 473–528.

———— [Rzheutskii, V. S.]. "Frantsuzskie guvernëry v Rossii XVIII v. Rezul'taty mezhdunarodnogo issledovatel'skogo proekta 'Frantsuzy v Rossii.'" In *Frantsuzskii ezhegodnik 2011: Frankoiazychnye guvernëry v Evrope XVII–XIX vv.,* edited by A. V. Chudinov, 58–80. Moscow: IVI RAN, 2011.

———— [Rjeoutski, Vladislav]. "Migrants and Language Learning in Russia (Late Seventeenth–First Part of Eighteenth Century)." *Paedagogica historica* 6 (2018): 691–703.

Rogozhnikova, T. P., ed. *Istoriia russkogo literaturnogo iazyka: regional'nyi aspekt.* Moscow: Flinta, 2016.

Rosén, Thomas. "Fragmenty odnoi voiny. Russkoiazychnye materialy russko-shvedskoi voiny 1741–1743 godov v arkhivakh Shvetsii." *Slovo* 51 (2010): 53–67.

"Rossiia—XVIII vek." Vostlit. Accessed April 13, 2021. http://www.vostlit.info/Texts/Dokumenty/Russ/xviii.htm.

Rovinskii, D. A. *Russkie narodnye kartinki,* 5 vols. St. Petersburg: Imperatorskaia akademiia nauk, 1881.

Rühs, Friedrich. *Finland och dess invånare.* Vol. 1. Stockholm: Olof Grahn, 1811.

Russi, Cinzia, ed. *Current Trends in Historical Sociolinguistics.* Warsaw and Berlin: DeGruyter Open, 2016.

Russkie memuary. Accessed April 13, 2021. http://mikv1.narod.ru.

"Russkaia literatura XVIII veka." Fundamental'naia élektronnaia biblioteka. Accessed April 13, 2021. http://feb-web.ru/feb/feb/c18.htm.

"Russkaia literatura XVIII veka." Russkaia virtual'naia biblioteka. Accessed April 13, 2021. https://rvb.ru/18vek/.

"Russkaia literatura, Vek XVIII." Institut russkoi literatury (Pushkinskii dom) RAN. Accessed April 13, 2021. http://lib.pushkinskijdom.ru/.

Rutten, Gijsbert, Rik Voster, and Wim Vandenbussche. "The Interplay of Language Norms and Usage Patterns: Comparing the History of Dutch, English, French and German." In *Norms and Usage in Language History, 1600–1900: A Sociolinguistic and Comparative Perspective,* edited by Gijsbert Rutten, Rik Vosters, and Wim Vandenbussche, 1–17. Amsterdam and Philadelphia: John Benjamins Publishing Company, 2014.

Savchuk, S. O., and Sichinava, D. V. "Korpus russkikh tekstov XVIII veka v sostave Natsional'nogo korpusa russkogo iazyka: problemy i perspektivy." In *Natsional'nyi korpus russkogo iazyka: 2006–2008. Novye rezul'taty i perspektivy,* 52–70. Accessed January 19, 2019. http://ruscorpora.ru/sbornik2008/04.pdf.

Schneider, Edgar W. "Investigating Historical Variation and Change in Written Documents: New Perspectives." In *The Handbook of Language Variation and Change,* edited by J. K. Chambers and Natalie Schilling, 57–81. 2nd ed. Malden, MA: Wiley-Blackwell, 2013.

Schoenenberger, Margarita. "Une sociolinguistique prescriptive: la théorie des langues 'littéraires' dans la linguistique soviétique des années 60–90." *Langage et société* 4 (2004): 25–51.

Schofield, R. S. "The Measurement of Literacy in Pre-Industrial England." In *Literacy in Traditional Societies,* edited by Jack Goody, 311–325. Cambridge: Cambridge University Press, 1968.

Schulze, Ludmilla. "The Russification of the St. Petersburg Academy of Sciences and Arts in the Eighteenth Century." *The British Journal for the History of Science* 3 (1985): 305–335.

The Scots Magazine 6 (1744): 61. Accessed November 17, 2021. https://babel.hathitrust.org/cgi/pt?id=nyp.33433076839087&view=1up&seq=61.

Sdvizhkov, D. A. *Pis'ma s prusskoi voiny: liudi rossiisko-imperatorskoi armii v 1758 godu.* Moscow: Novoe literaturnoe obozrenie, 2019.

Serman, I. Z. "Trediakovskii i prosvetitel'stvo (1730-e gody)." In *XVIII vek*, vol. 5, edited by P. N. Berkov, 205–222. Moscow and Leningrad: AN USSSR, 1962.

——— [Serman, Ilya]. "The Eighteenth Century: Neoclassicism and the Enlightenment, 1730–90." In *The Cambridge History of Russian Literature*, edited by Charles A. Moser, 45–91. Rev. ed. Cambridge: Cambridge University Press, 1992.

Shitsgal, A. G. *Russkii grazhdanskii shrift 1708–1958.* Moscow: Iskusstvo, 1959.

———. *Russkii tipografskii shrift: voprosy istorii i praktika primeneniia.* Moscow: Kniga, 1985.

Sjöberg, Anders, Ľubomir Ďurovič, and Ulla Birgegård, eds. *Dolomonosovskii period russkogo literaturnogo iazyka / The Pre-Lomonosov Period of the Russian Literary Language.* Stockholm: Kungl. Vitterhets-, historie- och antikvitetsakademien, 1992.

Slovar' russkogo iazyka XVIII veka. Edited by Iu. S. Sorokin. Leningrad: Nauka, 1984.

Slovar' russkogo iazyka XI–XVII. Vol. 4. Edited by R. I. Avanesov, S. G. Barkhudarov, G. A. Bogatova. Moscow: Nauka, 1977.

Smirnov, S. K. *Istoriia Moskovskoi slaviano-greko-latinskoi akademii.* Moscow: V. Got'e, 1855.

Smith, Alison K. *For the Common Good and Their Own Well-Being: Social Estates in Imperial Russia.* Oxford and New York: Oxford University Press, 2014.

———. "Information and Efficiency: Russian Newspapers, ca. 1700–1850." In *Information and Empire: Mechanisms of Communication in Russia, 1600–1854*, edited by Simon Franklin and Katherine Bowers, 185–211. Cambridge: Open Book Publishers, 2017.

Smith, May. *The Influence of French on Eighteenth-Century Literary Russian: Semantic and Phraseological Calques.* Oxford: Peter Lang, 2006.

Sobko, E. M. "Uchastie Rossii v voine za avstriiskoe nasledstvo." *Voprosy istorii* 1 (2012): 166–172.

———. "Rossiisko-frantsuzskie otnosheniia v period voiny za avstriiskoe nasledstvo." *Vestnik Moskovskogo gosudarstvennogo oblastnogo universiteta* (series: Istoriia i politicheskie nauki) 3 (2017): 56–66.

Sorokin, Iu. S., ed. *Protsessy formirovaniia leksiki russkogo iazyka (ot Kantemira do Karamzina).* Moscow and Leningrad: Nauka, 1966.

"Sostav i struktura." Russian National Corpus. Accessed September 16, 2021. https://ruscorpora.ru/new/corpora-structure.html.

Shpilëvskaia, N. *Opisanie voiny mezhdu Rossieiu i Shvetsieiu v Finliandii v 1741, 1742 i 1743 godakh.* St. Petersburg: Iakov Trei, 1859.

Spolsky, Bernard. *Language Policy.* Cambridge: Cambridge University Press, 2004.

———. *Language Management.* Cambridge: Cambridge University Press, 2009.

Sukhomlinov, M. I., ed. *Materialy dlia istorii Imperatorskoi akademii nauk*, 10 vols. St. Petersburg: Imperatorskaia akademiia nauk, 1885–1900.

Sumkina, A. I., and S. I. Kotkov, eds. *Pamiatniki moskovskoi delovoi pis'mennosti XVIII veka.* Moscow: Nauka, 1981.

Sumkina, A. I. *Sintaksis moskovskikh aktovykh i èpistoliarnykh tekstov XVIII v.* Edited by S. I. Kotkov. Moscow: Nauka, 1987.

Sysoeva, E. K. *Shkola v Rossii XVIII–nachalo XX vv.: vlast' i obshchestvo.* Moscow: Novyi khrono-graf, 2015.

Tabel' o rangakh vsekh chinov, voinskikh, statskikh, i pridvornykh. ... Moscow, January 30, 1722. Accessed November 18, 2021. https://www.prlib.ru/item/454265.

Tarkhov, Boris. "Izmenenie administrativno-territorial'nogo deleniia Rossii XIII–XIX vv." *Logos* 1 (2005): 65–101.

Thomson, Francis J. "The Three Slavonic Translations of the Greek Catena in Job. With an Appendix on the Author of the First Prologue to the First Translation: Polychronius or Photius?" In *The Bible in Slavic Tradition,* edited by Alexander Kulik, Catherine Mary MacRobert, Svetlina Nikolova, Moshe Taube, and Cynthia M. Vakareliyska, 143–178. Leiden: Brill, 2016.

Tikhomirov, M. N., and A. V. Murav'ëv. *Russkaia paleografiia.* 2nd ext. ed. Moscow: Vysshaia shkola, 1982.

Tolstoi, D. A. "Vzgliad na uchebnuiu chast' v Rossii v XVIII stoletii do 1782 goda." *Sbornik otdele-niia russkogo iazyka i slovesnosti Imperatorskoi akademii nauk* 38, no. 4 (1885): 1–100.

———. "Akademicheskii universitet v XVIII stoletii, po rukopisnym dokumentam arkhiva Akademii nauk." *Sbornik otdeleniia russkogo iazyka i slovesnosti Imperatorskoi akademii nauk* 38, no. 6 (1885): 1–67.

Trediakovskii, V. K. *Razgovor mezhdu chuzhestrannym chelovekom i rossiiskim ob orfografii starinnoi i novoi.* St. Petersburg: Imperatorskaia akademiia nauk, 1748.

——— [Tred'iakovskii, V. K.]. "Ezda v ostrov liubvi." In *Sochineniia Tred'iakovskogo,* edited by A. Smirdin, vol. 3. St. Petersburg: Imperatorskaia akademiia nauk, 1849.

Trofimova, Ol'ga. "Russkii dokument XVIII veka: punktuatsiia rukopisnogo originala i trans-literirovannoi ego publikatsii." *Annales Universitatis Paedagogicae Cracoviensis. Studia Russologica* 7 (2014): 57–71.

"Ukhtomskie kniaz'ia." Istoriia russkikh rodov. Accessed February 5, 2021. https://russianfamily.ru/uhtom.

Unbegaun, Boris O., ed. *Henrici Wilhelmi Ludolfi Grammatica Russica, Oxonii A. D. MDCXCVI.* Oxford: Oxford University Press, 1959.

Unbegaun, Boris O., ed. *Drei russische Grammatiken: Nachdruck der Ausgaben von 1706, 1731 und 1750.* Munich: Fink, 1969.

Union Catalogue of Russian Eighteenth-Century Secular Printed Book (1708–1800). Primo. Accessed November 18, 2021. https://primo.nlr.ru/primo-explore/search?query=lsr07,exact,1749,AND&tab=default_tab&search_scope=A1XVIII_07NLR&sortby=rank&vid=07NLR_VU2&lang=en_US&mode=advanced&offset=0.

"Using the Corpus." Russian National Corpus. Accessed May 30, 2019. http://www.ruscorpora.ru/en/corpora-usage.html.

Usitalo, Steven A. *The Invention of Mikhail Lomonosov: A Russian National Myth.* Boston: Academic Studies Press, 2013.

Uspenskii, B. A. "Dolomonosovskie grammatiki russkogo iazyka (itogi i perspektivy)." In *Dolomonosovskii period russkogo literaturnogo iazyka / The Pre-Lomonosov Period of the Russian Literary Language,* edited by Anders Sjöberg, Ľubomir Ďurovič, and Ulla Birgegård, 63–169. Stockholm: Kungl. vitterhets-, historie- och antikvitetsakademien, 1992.

———. *Kratkii ocherk istorii russkogo literaturnogo iazyka (XI–XIX vv.).* Moscow: Gnozis, 1994.

———. "Starinnaia sistema chteniia po skladam (glava iz istorii russkoi gramoty)." In his *Izbrannye trudy,* vol. 3: *Obshchee i slavianskoe iazykoznanie,* 246–288. Moscow: Iazyki russkoi kul'tury, 1997.

———. *Vokrug Trediakovskogo: Trudy po istorii russkogo iazyka i russkoi kul'tury.* Moscow: Indrik, 2008.

"Vasilii Evdokimovich Adodurov (Ododurov)." Khronos. Accessed June 29, 2019. http://hrono. ru/biograf/bio_a/adadurov_ve.php.

Vasil'chikov, A. A. *Semeistvo Razumovskikh.* Vol. 1. St. Petersburg: M. M. Stasiulevich, 1880.

Vinokur, Grigorii O. "Russkii iazyk. Istoricheskii ocherk." In *Izbrannye trudy po russkomu iazyku,* edited by S. G. Barkhudarov, 11–110. Moscow: Uchpedgiz, 1959.

———. *Russkii iazyk: istoricheskii ocherk.* 3rd ed. Moscow: KomKniga, 2006.

Vlasto, A. P. *A Linguistic History of Russia to the End of the Eighteenth Century.* Oxford: Clarendon Press, 1986.

Vodarskii, Ia. E. *Naselenie Rossii v kontse XVII–nachale XVIII veka (chislennost', soslovno-klassovyi sostav, razmeshchenie).* Moscow: Nauka, 1977.

Volkov, S. S. "V. E. Adodurov: Neskol'ko dopolnitel'nykh zamechanii k traditsionnoi biografii." In *Vasilii Evdokimovich Adodurov: "Anfangs-Gründe de rußischen Sprache" ili "Pervye osnovaniia rossiiskogo iazyka". Formirovanie russkoi akademicheskoi grammaticheskoi traditsii,* edited by K. A. Filippov, N. V. Kareva, and S. S. Volkov, 17–29. St. Petersburg: Nauka and Nestor-Istoriia, 2014.

Wallén, Per-Edvin. Review of *Den karolinska militärstraffrätten och Peter den stores krigsartiklar* by Erik Anners. *Svensk juristtidning* 573 (1962). Accessed May 5, 2021. https://svjt.se/svjt/1962/573.

Watts, Richard J. *Language Myths and the History of English.* Oxford: Oxford University Press, 2011.

Weissmann, E. *Teutsch-lateinisch- und russisches Lexicon, samt denen Anfangs-Gründen der russischen Sprache / Nemetsko-latinskii i russkii leksikon kupno s pervymi nachalami ruskago iazyka.* St. Petersburg: Imperatorskaia akademiia nauk, 1731.

Werrett, Simon. "The Schumacher Affair: Reconfiguring Academic Expertise across Dynasties in Eighteenth-Century Russia." *Osiris* 25 (2010): 104–125.

West, M. L. *Textual Criticism and Editorial Technique Applicable to Greek and Latin Texts.* Stuttgart: Teubner, 1973.

Wirtschafter, Elise K. *Social Identity in Imperial Russia.* DeKalb, IL: Northern Illinois University Press, 1997.

———. "The Groups Between: *Raznochintsy,* Intelligentsia, Professionals." In *The Cambridge History of Russia,* edited by Dominic Lieven, vol. 2: *Imperial Russia, 1689–1917,* 245–263. Cambridge: Cambridge University Press, 2006.

———. "A State in Search of a People: The Problem of Civil Society in Imperial Russia." In: *Eighteenth-Century Russia: Society, Culture, Economy,* edited by Roger Bartlett and Gabriela Lehmann-Carli, 373–381. Berlin: LIT, 2007.

———. "Social Categories in Russian Imperial History." *Cahiers du monde russe* 50, no. 1 (2009): 231–250.

Wright, Sue. *Language Policy and Language Planning: From Nationalism to Globalisation.* Houndmills, Basingstoke: Palgrave Macmillan, 2004.

Zalizniak, A. A. *Ot praslavianskoi aktsentuatsii k russkoi.* Moscow: Nauka, 1985.

Zapadov, A. V., ed. *Istoriia russkoi zhurnalistiki XVIII–XIX vekov.* 3rd rev. ed. Moscow: Vysshaia shkola, 1973.

Zemskaia, E. A., and D. N. Shmelëv. *Gorodskoe prostorechie: problemy izucheniia.* Moscow: Nauka, 1984.

Zhivov, V. M., E. A. Zemskaia, and L. P. Krysin. Review of *Geschichte der russischen Literatursprache* by Helmut Keipert. *Voprosy iazykoznaniia* 5 (2000): 122–137.

Zhivov, V. M. *Kul'turnye konflikty v istorii russkogo literaturnogo iazyka XVIII–nachala XIX veka.* Moscow: IRIa, 1990.

———. *Iazyk i kul'tura v Rossii XVIII veka.* Moscow: Iazyki russkoi kul'tury, 1996.

———. "Literaturnyi iazyk i iazyk literatury v Rossii XVIII stoletiia." *Russian Literature* 52 (2002): 1–53.

———. *Ocherki istoricheskoi morfologii russkogo iazyka XVII–XVIII vekov.* Moscow: Iazyki slavianskoi kul'tury, 2004.

——— [Zhivov, Victor]. *Language and Culture in Eighteenth-Century Russia.* Boston: Academic Studies Press, 2009.

———. "Problemy formirovaniia russkogo literaturnogo iazyka." In *Trudy Otdeleniia istoriko-filologicheskikh nauk Rossiiskoi akademii nauk 2007*, edited by A. P. Derevianko, 53–63. Moscow: Nauka, 2009.

———. *Istoriia iazyka russkoi pis'mennosti*, 2 vols. Moscow: Universitet Dmitriia Pozharskogo, 2017.

Index

CPSIA information can be obtained
at www.ICGtesting.com
Printed in the USA
JSHW060019140323
38882JS00003B/21